WEIGHT WATCHERS®
PARTY & HOLIDAY COOKBOOK

Whether you're planning an intimate repast for two or a gala party for twelve, creating gourmet meals the slender way is simple and easy with these new Weight Watchers menus that can add spice and variety to your entire cooking year. From New Year's Day breakfast to Christmas dinner, from graduation day to a wedding celebration, you'll find this your complete guide to month-by-month, occasion-by-occasion dining pleasure:

BIRTHDAY FARE FOR EIGHT
Eggplant Puree
Minted Yogurt with Vegetable Dippers
Shoulder Steak Forestière
Carrot and Potato Velvet
Green Peas with Water Chestnuts
Apple Jelly Bars with Pineapple Tidbits

ERIN GO BRAGH FOR FOUR
Galway Bay Oyster Stew
Rolled Stuffed Fish Fillets
Colcannon
Steamed Spinach
"Irish Coffee"

A CHRISTMAS EVE BUFFET FOR TWELVE
Mushrooms in Soy Sauce Vinaigrette
Roasted Fresh Ham
Artichoke Hearts and Wild Rice Casserole
Puree of Carrots in Orange Cups
Apple "Crème"

WEIGHT WATCHERS® COOKBOOKS
from PLUME

WEIGHT WATCHERS®
PARTY & HOLIDAY COOKBOOK

With a Note from Jean Nidetch

A SIGNET BOOK

NEW AMERICAN LIBRARY

*WEIGHT WATCHERS is a registered trademark
of Weight Watchers International, Inc.*

Acknowledgments

The unselfish devotion of many people who gave of their time unstintingly has been essential in preparing this book for publication. We are grateful for those many dedicated hours spent in creating the themes, menus, and recipes, in testing and editing, and for the careful eye that led to the enticing food photography. We offer our wholehearted thanks to Patty Barnett, Bianca Brown, John Dietrich, Anne Hosansky, Ellen Loft-Shurgan, Eileen Pregosin, and Isabel Sobol for their efforts in this behalf.

We also wish to thank Nedda C. Anders for her ideas, and New American Library, our publishers, for editing this book.

WEIGHT WATCHERS INTERNATIONAL, INC.

Previously published in NAL BOOKS and PLUME editions by New American Library and simultaneously in Canada by The New American Library of Canada Limited.

SIGNET TRADEMARK REG. U.S. PAT. OFF. AND FOREIGN COUNTRIES
REGISTERED TRADEMARK—MARCA REGISTRADA
HECHO EN CHICAGO, U.S.A.

SIGNET, SIGNET CLASSIC, MENTOR, PLUME, MERIDIAN and NAL BOOKS are published by New American Library, 1633 Broadway, New York, New York 10019

Weight Watchers and 🟢 are registered trademarks of Weight Watchers International, Inc.

First Signet Printing, October, 1984

3 4 5 6 7 8 9

PRINTED IN THE UNITED STATES OF AMERICA

A Note from Jean Nidetch

Dear Reader,

A weight-control cookbook for parties and holidays?

If that seems incredible, it just points up what the Weight Watchers philosophy is all about, for our members have made the delightful discovery that weight control can actually mix with fun.

Once upon seventy-two pounds ago, I wouldn't have believed that possible. In the days before I lost those pounds, I shared, with most overweight people, the definition of a party or holiday as something-to-frantically-starve-for-so-you-could-gain-at!

These weight-conscious—and nutrition-conscious—days, savvy party-givers don't buy that self-destructive pattern. They want appetizing party feasts that won't strain the seams of party fashions.

To meet that basic requirement, our *Party and Holiday Cookbook* serves up more than 400 mouth-watering recipes—all keyed into expertly balanced menus that save you the hassle of meal planning. They range from our version of an elegant White House state dinner to a "Poolside Splash," from special-occasion parties to casual picnics. The dishes aren't just American: you can travel around the world at your own table via a Chinese Fire Pot, a Scandinavian Wedding Breakfast, an Indian Thali, a British High Tea, an Indonesian Rijsttafel. There are entertaining tips for every occasion, as well as plain (and-not-so-plain) techniques for turning everyday meals into holiday repasts.

Our menus fit every need, from an intimate dinner for two (even a tray for *one*) to lavish open-house buffets. You'll feast on a variety of textures and colors, with inexpensive ingredients that won't weigh down your budget and do-it-ahead recipes that let *you* join the party, too.

At Weight Watchers, we know a lot about the "slim world" and how important it is to learn the ways to live in it. Since the day the Weight Watchers Organization was born, back in 1963, more than 13 million people have come through our doors to gain entry to that world. Let me share with you a few of our "ingredients."

First, there are our nutritionally balanced, scientifically developed weight reduction and maintenance food plans. The weight-loss plan now comes in three "choices" to fit nearly every life-style and individual preference. There's so much freedom and variety that it's hard to think of it as a "diet." Actually, our Program is much more: it's a total learning experience, for it includes a Personal Action Plan of eating-management techniques to help members learn how to cope in productive ways with problem situations (like parties and holidays) and problem moods. We also include an optional Personal Exercise Plan, known as "Pepstep," geared toward helping members shape up while they slim down. And all of this is served up in an atmosphere of group support.

The Weight Watchers name appears on an ever-expanding array of convenient and popular food products, magazines, and, of course, on our best-selling cookbooks, among them this *Party and Holiday Cookbook*, now available in a paperback edition. As you scan its pages, you'll find some desserts from our exciting world to help you slim. Chances are you'll find your favorite party dish between these covers, translated into a "safer" version that's every bit as good. You'll also find decorating suggestions and ideas for ways to keep a party mood high.

You and your guests will welcome this cookbook that blends feasting and fellowship in such deliciously slimming style.

Jean Nidetch
FOUNDER
WEIGHT WATCHERS INTERNATIONAL, INC.

Contents

In January 1981, certain changes were made in the Weight Watchers Food Plan to make it more flexible and adaptable to today's life-styles. These changes opened kitchen doors to a host of new foods and cooking methods. For example, a limited amount of wine is now permitted, which means that wine may be used in recipes calling for it. Sugar, fructose, honey, peanut butter, popcorn, crispbreads, yams, raisins, olives and olive oil, barbecue sauce, dried apricots, fruit-flavored gelatin, low-calorie syrups and toppings all received "legal permits"—in carefully restricted amounts.

In addition, it is now permissible to sauté and stir-fry foods and to interchange lunch and dinner on the Food Plan.

Weight Watchers members are familiar with these revisions and may adjust the menus and recipes in this book accordingly.

Introduction

People are entertaining at home more than they have for many years, and most parties involve a meal.

There are several reasons for this increase in dining at home. One is the growing interest in food—specifically, food that is well-prepared and nutritious. Another is that a meal prepared at home is invariably less expensive—and often far better—than a comparable meal served in a restaurant. Then, too, home entertaining has become simplified in recent years. Modern appliances and utensils have made food preparation easier, and many of the formal rules for dining have fallen by the wayside. People now feel free to entertain in the style that suits them best. For some, this means casual one-dish suppers. For others, it means elaborate multi-course dinner parties or meals that show off an international culinary skill.

Still another trend is to entertain year-round, thus lessening some of the rush that always occurs during the holiday season. People have discovered the pleasure and ease of having friends over whenever the mood strikes.

The Party and Holiday Cookbook offers a multitude of recipes organized into individual menus appropriate for each of the twelve months of the year. There are suggestions for morning, midday, and evening meals, and international cuisines are highlighted throughout.

We felt it was especially important to present menus rather than individual dishes. While most cooks have a few special dishes that they prepare extremely well, the prospect of planning and preparing an entire menu can often be mind-boggling. Inspiration flies out the window the minute menus are mentioned, yet menus are really just meals.

Admittedly, menus can be tricky. Planning a successful one is a bit like juggling three different kinds of fruit with one hand, since a good menu balances a variety of aromas, tastes, textures, and colors. Weight Watchers professional chefs are the first to admit that it takes years of experience to master menu planning and meal preparation, and that is just what a successful dinner party is all about.

In *The Party and Holiday Cookbook,* Weight Watchers chefs and home economists have provided an abundance of ideas for successful entertaining. Preparing a meal for family and friends can be a most satisfying activity. It combines the challenge of cooking and the creative efforts of setting the scene for a party with the pleasure of spending several hours with friends. A good meal is a gift to all those present.

We hope you will enjoy this cookbook and discover within its pages the key to successful entertaining.

Setting the Scene

Many hosts and hostesses feel that setting the scene for a dinner party is the most exciting part of entertaining. It certainly is one of the more creative aspects. The many decisions you have to make—which linens and dishes to use, whether to have candles, what kind of table decorations will work best—all require ingenuity. This is one area of entertaining where there are few hard-and-fast rules. You can let your imagination run wild. And make no mistake about it, table setting is a creative activity. Here are a few suggestions to help you get started.

It helps to plan your table setting around the menu, especially if you are serving an ethnic meal or one in which a foreign dish is highlighted. For example, pottery would be appropriate for a Mexican meal, as would chopsticks for a Chinese banquet.

If the food does not suggest a particular theme, then you can create any kind of mood you want. Are you a romantic? Then think in terms of flowers, candlelight, and delicate china. Does your taste run to streamlined contemporary arrangements? Consider brightly colored place mats and napkins in a geometric print, low candles, and use a green plant or one simple flower as your centerpiece.

Sometimes the mood for a dinner party comes from the guests or the event. Are you entertaining your bridge group? Then how about bright red and black napkins and place mats, with playing cards used as place cards. Is the whole gang coming over to watch a big football game and eat supper? Autumn leaves and maybe even a football could be used in your table decorations.

If you have invited one or two friends to join a family dinner at the last minute, choose your prettiest dishes and set the table attractively, but that's really all you need worry about. There's something comfortable about being invited to a casual family-style dinner where little fuss is made. On the other hand, if you have invited several people over for a special dinner, take the time and effort to go all-out to create a party atmosphere.

The kind of table you set also depends on the dishes, flatware, and glasses that you choose to use. Gone, fortunately, are the days when entertaining meant you had to own fine china, crystal, and sterling flatware. The most savvy hostesses now choose to use unmatched pottery dishes, stainless-steel flatware, and inexpensive glasses. Nor is it necessary to own a great quantity of dishes. For example, if you don't have enough small plates to provide both butter plates and salad plates, you can simply do without butter plates—or your guests can use their dinner plates for the salad. If you are serving a buffet dinner for twelve and you have six white dinner plates and six plates from a different set, mix both kinds. That's how flexible today's rules are.

The trend is toward fine, well-prepared food and casual table settings. Even at formal dinners where three or more courses may be served, the table may still have an informal appearance.

Planning the Table Setting

For a sit-down dinner, each guest should have his or her own place setting. Allow enough space for comfortable seating. This usually means twenty-four inches per place setting, depending on the size of the table, the width of the chairs, and the number of people to be served.

If you have a large table and are entertaining only a few guests, seat them close enough to one another so they can talk and pass dishes comfortably.

Seating Arrangements

As a host or hostess, you are responsible for where guests sit at the table. If the meal is very casual or consists of one guest and your family, then each person may simply take a place without any prompting from you. Usually, though, your guests will expect you to tell them where to sit.

At a formal dinner, you can use plain white place cards with each guest's name written on one. For an informal party, you can use more casual and colorful place cards that you may either make or buy. You may also want to write in just the first names, whereas at a formal dinner you use "Miss," "Mrs.," "Ms.," or "Mr." and the last name only. Place cards go either above the plate or on it, on top of the napkin. If you are using place cards, you may also want to use menu cards, which you can either buy or make. They list the foods you are serving as well as the date of the dinner, and are a nice memento for your guests. One menu card is needed for every two guests and is placed between two place settings.

At informal dinners you can simply say, "John, why don't you sit next to Penny?" It is not only acceptable but expected that you will separate husbands and wives, since the point at a party is to mix. Most hostesses also try to alternate men and women, but if you have an uneven number this may not be possible.

Seat people together who you think will get along well or who have something in common, such as a job or an outside interest. Although you may be tempted to put a shy person next to an outgoing one, you may have better luck seating two slightly shy people side by side.

The Guest of Honor

A male guest of honor sits on the hostess's right, and a female guest of honor sits on the host's right. Most people are flattered to be so honored, so you needn't wait for someone "official" to visit. Anyone can become your guest of honor for the occasion. It helps to make the entire meal more festive.

Planning the Table Decorations

After you have made the seating arrangements and decided how much space to allow for each place setting, it is time to think about the table decorations. When choosing these decorations it is important to remember that they should not interfere with the diners. For example, as lovely as candlelight may be, no one is comfortable staring at a candle all night, so be sure to place candles so that they are either higher or lower than your guests' line of vision. Candles should only be used at night and should be lit before your guests are seated. Candles can blend with the table linens or decorations, or they can be plain white. For a formal dinner, white is best. You can use any kind of candle holder, from a sterling silver candelabra to a glass bottle, depending on how formal or informal your dinner is.

The centerpiece should be low enough so that everyone can see over it. Although flowers are traditional, there is no reason to limit yourself. You might want to make an interesting arrangement of fresh vegetables in a basket. Fall provides opportunities to use leaves and gourds in shades of gold and brown. During the holiday season a clear glass bowl filled with tiny Christmas tree balls will look beautiful by candlelight. Citrus fruit and evergreens in a crystal bowl also make a good winter decoration. Perhaps you have a favorite figurine that you might like to use as part of your table decor. Sometimes a piece of unusual fabric can be used to great effect. There are no limits—look around your home, outdoors, in stores, anywhere you go, for possible decorations to make your table interesting.

Nor does the centerpiece have to be in the middle of the table. A single flower in a small white vase set at each place is attractive and unusual. You might also use two or three small bouquets, or even place a bouquet at each corner of the table.

Setting the Table

The basic equipment for a dinner party—or for most family dinners—consists of table linens, dishes, flatware, and glasses.

Choosing Your Linens

At a formal dinner, the linens are usually white or off-white. Either a tablecloth or formal place mats and cloth napkins are the rule. For informal meals you have a wider variety of choices.

Today table linens come in many styles, patterns, and colors. Napkins can be either matching or contrasting. Be daring and try interesting color and texture combinations to add a note of excitement to the dinner table.

The napkins and place mats, or tablecloth, should be similar in style. Formal linen place mats would be incongruous with brightly colored cloth or paper napkins. It is acceptable, though, to use paper napkins with an informal tablecloth or place mats.

When choosing table linens, keep in mind the color and style of the dishes. If you have plain dishes in a solid color, you can use linens with bright geometric or flowered prints. If you have patterned dishes, be careful about mixing them with other patterns. It can be done, but have a "dress rehearsal." In fact, one good way to come up with unusual table settings is to try all the possibilities before deciding on the final arrangements; those flowered napkins may look surprisingly good with the checked place mats. Remember to coordinate linens with any table decorations you have planned.

The Table

While the number of dishes and utensils depends on how formal the dinner is and what foods you are serving, there are a few rules that guide their placement.

A dinner plate should be placed approximately two inches from the edge of the table (see Drawing 1). It should be centered on a place mat, if one is used (see Drawing 2). The plate is the center of the place setting. Except for the dessert flatware, knives, forks, and spoons go at either side of the place setting (see Drawing 3). In some parts of the country, the dessert fork and spoon are placed above the plate. In other areas, they go at the side with the other flatware. At a very formal dinner, the dessert flatware is brought in with the dessert plate, and is sometimes accompanied by a finger bowl. Remove the flatware from the plate and place the fork to the left and the spoon to the right. Put the finger bowl slightly to the left above the fork.

The handles of flatware are placed approximately one inch from the edge of the table (see Drawing 4). Forks go to the left of the plate. Knives

DRAWING 1

DRAWING 2

DRAWING 3

DRAWING 4

are on the right, with spoons next to them. The napkin is placed beside the outermost fork or, occasionally, on the dinner plate.

Anyone who has visions of being overwhelmed by flatware can relax. Flatware is arranged according to its order of use, with the first piece to be used on the outside and the last one on the inside (see Drawings 5, 6, and 7). It is never proper to place more than three of any one utensil on the table at one time.

DRAWING 5: BREAKFAST

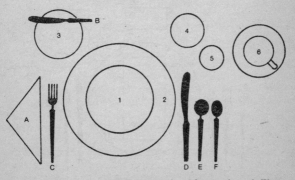

1. Cereal bowl or fruit dish. 2. Plate. 3. Bread-and-butter plate. 4. Water tumbler. 5. Juice glass. 6. Cup and saucer. A. Napkin. B. Spreader. C. Fork. D. Knife. E. Cereal spoon (a soup spoon is used). F. Coffee or tea spoon (if this spoon is used for fruit, another spoon may be placed on the saucer).

DRAWING 6: LUNCHEON/INFORMAL DINNER

1 & 2. Soup bowl or appetizer plate with liner. 3. Service plate. 4. Bread-and-butter plate. 5. Water glass. A. Napkin. B. Spreader. C. Appetizer fork. D. Fork. E. Salad fork (if salad is served after main course). F. Knife. G. Soup spoon. H. Dessert fork or spoon (coffee or tea spoon is brought at time of service).

DRAWING 7: FORMAL DINNER

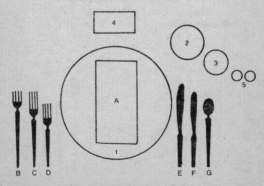

1. Service plate. 2. Water goblet. 3. Other beverage goblet. 4. Place card. 5. Salt and pepper shakers. A. Napkin. B. First-course fork. C. Main-course fork. D. Salad fork (if salad is served after main course). E. Main-course knife. F. First-course knife. G. Soup spoon.

The dinner plate is usually at the place setting when each diner sits down. Another smaller service plate may be on top of it, along with the soup bowl or appetizer dish. After everyone has eaten the first course, those dishes and the small service plates are cleared. The dinner plate always remains because a guest is never supposed to be without a plate, except just before dessert is served. However, since many hostesses today don't have enough dishes, or prefer not to use so many, these rules are optional.

Once you have arranged the plates and flatware, it's time to think about glassware. The water glass or goblet goes at the tip of the knife being used for the main course. Other beverage glasses go nearby, to the right (see Drawings 5 and 7). Glasses remain on the table until the meal has been completed, even though dishes and flatware are cleared as guests finish each course.

A Word About Service

Since few of us have servants these days, the average host and hostess do their own serving at a dinner party. Guests of honor are served first. Then go around the table, counterclockwise, serving guests in order. Good service means getting the dishes to the guests while hot foods are piping hot and cold foods are still chilled. Serve foods from the left, if possible. When clearing plates, try to remove them from the diner's right.

As an alternate serving method, the host or hostess may serve the food while seated at the head of the table. The plates are then passed around, usually beginning with the guest sitting farthest away.

Except at a very formal dinner, you can also serve family style—that is, by passing platters and bowls of food and letting guests help themselves.

Types of Dinner Parties

Dinner parties fall into one of three categories: formal, informal, or buffet. Of these, formal dinner parties are the rarest. Informal and buffet parties are by far the most popular. Here are a few hints about entertaining at each kind of dinner party.

The Formal Dinner

A formal dinner party is the time to use your finest china, silver, and crystal. There should be soft background music, candlelight, elegant flowers, and wonderful food. If possible, hire people to serve, so you can relax and enjoy the meal. You should have one server for every eight persons.

A formal dinner is served in courses. As noted earlier, the first course—either an appetizer or a soup—is on the table, on a service plate, when everyone sits down. When this course is finished, the dishes are cleared, leaving the service plate in front of each diner. Then comes the main course. At a formal dinner, salad is often served as a separate course following the main course. Dessert is served after the salad.

Coffee can be served as a separate course, following dessert. Drawing 7 shows how a table is properly set for a formal dinner.

The Informal Dinner

Informal dinners can be multi-course meals or casual soup-and-salad suppers. The table setting for an informal dinner is shown in Drawing 6.

You have much greater freedom in planning the table settings for an informal meal than for a formal dinner. Your choice of themes, colors, and dishes is larger, since you aren't expected to adhere to the guidelines for a formal dinner. At informal dinners you can experiment with different kinds of table decorations or flower arrangements and brightly colored table linens.

The Buffet Dinner

At buffet dinners, guests are expected to serve themselves. A buffet is also the perfect solution if your dining area is too small to accommodate many people.

Guests select foods from the buffet table, and then sit down at another table or small tables. It is helpful if the foods served are either in bite-sized pieces or can easily be cut with a fork.

The buffet is often situated in the center of the room, although you can put the table anywhere that space permits. You might also have one table for foods and another, often smaller one, for beverages. Experiment to see which arrangement works best for your home. Drawings 8 and 9 show suggested buffet arrangements.

Arrange the buffet table in a way that makes it convenient for guests to help themselves. Usually, this means putting dinner plates at the beginning of the serving line. Then comes the main dish, with any accompanying sauces nearby. Side dishes and salads are usually next, and flatware and napkins are placed at the end of the table. If there isn't room on the buffet table for flatware and napkins, you can place them on the other tables, so that guests have less to carry to their seats.

Although meals are not usually served in courses, you may find it more convenient to serve the salad and dessert separately.

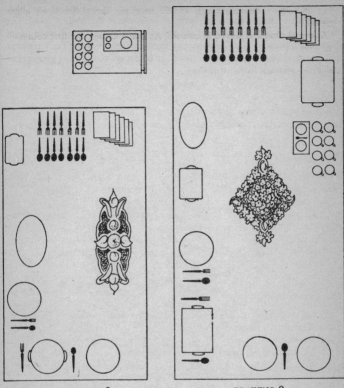

DRAWING 8   DRAWING 9

Since there are many items on a buffet table, a traditional centerpiece is often all you need to highlight the setting. More complicated decorations tend to make the table look too busy.

Your Personal Trademark

The way you choose to set your table is highly personal. In fact, it is the most personal thing about any dinner party you give. It is your trademark as a hostess.

[11]

Remember, though, that you may do as much or as little as you like. Sometimes a simple flower or sprig of greenery is the perfect touch. At other times, it is fun to spend time and energy tracking down more novel table decorations. No matter how you decide to set the scene for your next party, keep in mind that this is one of the best ways to tell your guests how delighted you are to be with them.

Garnishing and Special Techniques

"First feed the eyes, then the palate" is a good rule for serving food with a flair, for no matter how superbly cooked a meal may be, it's seen before it's tasted. How attractively a dish is "dressed" says volumes about the skill of the host, and fortunately it's easier to score high hosting grades than you may think. For instance, the art of garnishing doesn't call for a sculptor's skill. All it takes are a few basic ingredients, plus a careful blend of imagination and patience, as our easy-to-follow directions illustrate. Nor do garnishes have to be elaborate in order to be effective. In fact, since they're the accessories, they should be *simple* in order to accentuate the dish. Garnishes should always harmonize not only with each other but with the food they are decorating, as well as with the platter used for serving. Think in terms of contrasting colors and interesting arrangements. Artful presentations do take more time, but they help create a festive atmosphere, for they tell your guests that you went to extra effort to make the occasion special.

Carving is an art in itself, one well worth learning, for even the most elegant-looking entrée can be "undercut" by a poor carving job. First of all, invest in a good set of knives. Then follow our easy directions for cutting, dicing, and boning. Our step-by-step illustrated instructions for carving various cuts of meat will enable you to give an applause-worthy performance in your dining arena.

Carrot Curls

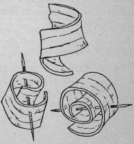

Prepare several hours beforehand. Using a vegetable peeler, slice carrot lengthwise so that strips are paper-thin. Loosely roll strips and secure each with a toothpick. Place in bowl of ice water for several hours. Remove toothpicks. The carrot strips will remain curled.

Celery Frills

Prepare several hours beforehand. Using a vegetable peeler, pare celery rib to remove stringy fibers. Cut rib into 2-inch lengths. Using a paring knife, cut deep slits, as close together as possible, into both ends of each piece, cutting up to center but not through it. Place in bowl of ice water for several hours. Ends will open and curl.

Cucumber Cartwheels

Wash cucumber but do not pare; cut off ends. Run the prongs of a fork lengthwise all around cucumber to score skin. Cut into ¼-inch-thick slices.

Fluted Mushrooms

Use medium-size mushrooms. With the tip of a sharp knife, mark the center of each mushroom cap. Then, holding the knife at a slight angle, make a curved cut from center to edge, approximately ⅛ inch deep. Repeat all around cap, making about 10 evenly spaced cuts. Make a second curved cut just behind each line, slanting the knife to create a narrow strip that can be lifted out. If desired, cut off stems close to caps.

Julienne Vegetables

Pare vegetable with vegetable peeler if necessary. With a sharp knife, cut vegetable into long, thin strips. Cut strips into 2- to 3-inch lengths.

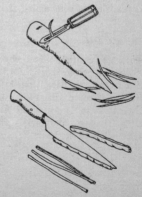

Leek Fuji Mums

Cut root and green tops off each leek.
Use white portion only. Insert toothpick
into root end, about ½ inch deep. Holding leek by toothpick, cut thin slices
through top of leek, about ⅛ inch apart,
just to tip of toothpick. Turn leeks and
cut thin slices, perpendicular to the other
slices, again just to tip of toothpick. Place
in bowl of ice water for several hours. The
slices will open like a flower in bloom.

Lemon or Lime Cups

Method 1:
Cut lemon in half. Using a grapefruit
knife, scoop out pulp and membranes
from rind.
Method 2:
Using a sharp knife make a crosswise cut
around fruit through rind, about ⅛ inch
deep. Do not cut through pulp. Insert
curved handle of teaspoon between rind
and pulp. Run spoon handle around in-
terior of rind. With a twist, pull rind
away from pulp.

Lilies

Pare and thinly slice a medium white
turnip. Cut a carrot into 2-inch-long
julienne strips. Roll a turnip slice around
a julienne strip to form a cone shape with
carrot extending through top of "cone."
Secure with small pins. Insert a wooden
skewer or florist wire through bottom of
"cone." Thread stem end of a scallion
over skewer to create "stem of flower."

Orange Bowls

Insert point of paring knife in center of orange at an angle (see Figure 1). Pull out knife; insert again, angling knife in opposite direction. Repeat all around fruit, alternating angle of knife, creating a zigzag cut (see Figure 2). Twisting slightly, pull orange halves apart to create Orange Bowls (see Figure 3).

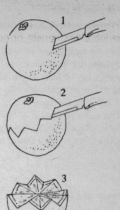

Parsley

Rinse parsley in cold water. Shake well to remove excess moisture. For *parsley sprig garnish*, use a sprig that has bright green leaves. Do not use if leaves are yellowish or wilting. Sprigs may be used individually or grouped in decorative clusters. For *chopped fresh parsley*, dry with paper towels. Remove as much stem as possible from the leaves. Bunch leaves together, place on cutting board, and chop. Watercress, mint, dill, and other fresh greens and herbs may be prepared in the same manner.

Pickle Fans

Make several lengthwise, evenly spaced slices through pickle to about ¼ inch from end. Spread slices to form a fan. More slices will create a wider fan. This technique also works well with pieces of zucchini and yellow squash.

Radish Accordions

Prepare several hours beforehand. Hold radish either upright or on its side. Cut thin slices in radish, being careful not to cut through bottom. Place in bowl of ice water for several hours. The slices will spread like an accordion.

Radish Mums

Follow directions for slicing Radish Accordions. Turn radishes and cut thin slices, perpendicular to the other slices, again being careful not to cut through bottom. Place in bowl of ice water for several hours. The slices will open like a flower in bloom.

Radish Roses

Prepare several hours beforehand. Choose round radishes. Cut a thin slice from both ends of each radish. Beginning at the top and cutting downward, cut thin slices around radish, as if paring, but leave "petals" attached at the bottom. Place in bowl of ice water for several hours. The "petals" will open like a flower in bloom. Radish roses can also be made by using a gadget that is available in many stores especially for this purpose.

Scallion Brushes

Prepare several hours beforehand. Trim off roots and top of each scallion, leaving a piece about 3 inches long, half white and half green. Beginning at either end and using a sharp paring knife, cut 4 or 5 slits halfway through each piece. Place in bowl of ice water for several hours. Cut ends will open and curl.

Tomato Roses

Use a vegetable peeler or sharp paring knife. Starting at one end, cut around the tomato, removing skin in a spiral and making one continuous strip. Roll one end of peel tightly to form center; loosely roll remaining peel around center to create a full-blown rose. This technique also works well with apples.

Turnip or Squash Daisies

Pare a medium white turnip or butternut squash and cut into ⅛-inch-thick slices. Using a flower-shaped cookie cutter, cut out "flowers" from vegetable slices. Pare a medium carrot and cut into ⅛-inch-thick slices. Using a smaller flower-shaped cutter, cut out "flowers" from carrot slices. Place small "flower" on top of large one. Insert tip of wooden skewer or florist wire through center of "flowers" to hold them together. Allow tip of skewer to extend ⅛ inch beyond small "flower." Secure a pea or ¼-inch square of green pepper to tip of skewer. Thread stem end of a scallion over exposed end of skewer to create "stem of flower."

White Onion Flowers

Prepare several hours beforehand. Peel onion. Cut thin slices through top of onion about ⅛ inch apart, just to but not through bottom. Turn onion and cut thin slices perpendicular to the other slices, being careful not to cut through bottom. Place in bowl of ice water for several hours. The slices will open like a flower in bloom.

Vegetable Basket

Here's how to create a vegetable basket (see photo insert) to use as a centerpiece. If you don't have a basket, a large bowl can be used to hold the "bouquet."

In order to hold the "flowers" in place, fill the bottom of the basket with polystyrene foam. Use green leafy vegetables such as chicory, red leaf lettuce, Boston lettuce, and spinach to cover the foam, allowing the green to extend beyond the edges of the basket.

Prepare the "flowers" by following the directions given in this chapter for Leek Fuji Mums, Lilies, Radish Accordions, Radish Mums, Radish Roses, and White Onion Flowers.

Arrange the "flowers" attractively in the basket, pushing those with stems into polystyrene foam to secure in place. Arrange crinkle-cut carrot and zucchini strips, green pepper strips, cauliflower florets, thick mushroom slices, cherry tomatoes, and peas in the shell around the "flowers" for additional color.

How to Use a Knife Correctly

Cutting skills are developed through practice. Follow these easy steps and start slowly. Speed will come in time.

1. Place your left* hand palm down on a cutting board. Tuck your thumb under, then wrap your other fingers around your thumb, as if to form a loose fist. Keep the "heel" of your hand flat on the cutting board (see Figure 1).

1

* If left-handed, use opposite hand.

2. Hold the knife in your right* hand with the flat side of the blade touching the upper portion of your fingers. This helps you to control the size of your cut, as well as to avoid cutting yourself (see Figure 2).

2

3. Place food to be cut under your left* hand with the portion to be cut exposed just beyond your fingers. With the tip of the knife on the cutting board, push blade downward to cut food. Move left hand backward and, keeping the knife against your fingers, cut downward again. Repeat until all food is cut. For safety, don't raise blade higher than the level of your first knuckle (see Figure 3).

3

* If left-handed, use opposite hand.

How to Dice an Onion

Use a very sharp knife and work as quickly as possible. This not only makes the job easier, it helps to control symptoms of "crying" while cutting.

1. Peel outer layer of onion, leaving root end intact.

2. Cut peeled onion in half, from top through root end. Place on cutting board, cut side down.

3. Make a few horizontal, evenly spaced slices through onion, just to, but not through, root end. You will need more slices for a small dice than for a large dice.

4. Make vertical slices the same distance apart as the horizontal slices, just to, but not through, root end. The root end will now hold the onion together.

5. Make crosswise slices, the same distance apart as the other slices. Discard slice containing root end. The onion should now be uniformly diced.

How to Bone Chicken Breasts

Use a sharp knife with a thin blade. A boning knife makes the job easier but is not essential.

1. Place chicken breast on cutting board, skin side down. With tip of knife, cut through gristle at neck end. Bend chicken breast backward until keel bone (dark bone in center) "pops" up. Loosen bone with index fingers and pull out (see Figure 1).

2. Work on each side of breast separately. Insert tip of knife under long rib bone. Work knife beneath bone, separating it from meat (see Figure 2). Lift bone and cut meat from rib cage. Remove bones. Repeat on other side of breast.

3. Scrape meat away from ends of wishbone. Cut out bone (see Figure 3). Slip knife beneath tendons (long white fibers) on both sides of breast. Loosen and pull out tendons. Remove skin.

When stuffing chicken breasts, to make rolling easier, flatten breasts to about ¼-inch thickness by pounding with a wet mallet. Wetting the mallet helps to prevent particles of meat from sticking to it. (This procedure may also be used with veal.)

The Art of Carving

Carving meats, fish, and poultry correctly is a valuable skill. It calls for both knowledge and the proper tools.

Three tools are necessary for proper carving.

1. A sturdy carving knife.

2. A sharpening steel with which to keep knife razor-sharp. (This should have a guard, in case the knife slips.)

3. A two-pronged fork to hold meat firmly in place. (This should also have a guard.)

It is important to understand the structure of the bones in the meat, fish, or poultry you carve. Knowledge of where they lie and are joined will keep you from striking an unexpected bone as you carve.

Check the grain of the meat before carving. Proper cutting will determine the texture of the finished dish.

1. Carve tender cuts of meat *with the grain*.
2. Carve large and less tender cuts of meat *across the grain*.
3. Carve thin cuts of meat (e.g., flank steak) *across the grain, with knife at a slight angle to the cutting board*.

Practice makes perfect carving, but practice out of sight! While learning, try to do your carving in the kitchen, out of the view of others. After you've gained skill and confidence, you can carve at the dinner table.

How to Sharpen a Knife

Although there are various implements available with which to sharpen a knife, a sharpening stone gives the best edge. When treated properly, your knives should last a lifetime. Use the stone whenever your blade becomes too dull to carve properly. Use the steel prior to each time you carve to keep your knife as sharp as possible.

Sharpening stone—The stone should be moistened with water or oil before use. Place stone on damp cloth to hold it in place. Hold the knife so that the blade is at a 15- to 20-degree angle. Run the blade against the stone in a curved motion, starting at the "heel" and ending at the tip, from one end of the stone to the other, applying slight pressure. Repeat on the other side of the blade. Repeat this procedure about 10 times. Clean blade to remove accumulated grit.

Sharpening steel—Hold sharpening steel in your left* hand, horizontally and at a slight angle upward, with tip away from you. With your right* hand, hold knife with the "heel" of the blade lightly touching the side of the steel at the tip. Holding the knife at a 15- to 20-degree angle, run the blade against the steel in a curved motion, ending with the tip of the knife near the guard. The blade of the knife should pass lightly over the steel. Repeat on other side of steel for the other side of the blade. Repeat this procedure about 12 times.

* If left-handed, use opposite hand.

Turkey

Position turkey so legs point to your right. Remove legs, including thighs, by pulling leg away from body, twisting to loosen joint, and cutting through skin, severing joint with tip of knife. Cut between wing and body in the same manner. Starting halfway up the breast, slice downward at a slight angle. Slice higher with each succeeding slice. After front of bird is carved, cut back portion of the breast, slicing it at an angle. Repeat entire carving procedure on other side of bird. To separate leg from thigh, sever at joint. To slice meat from legs, thighs, and wings, cut parallel to bone. These parts can also be served whole, if desired.

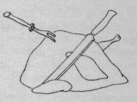

Roast Chicken

Position chicken on its back, neck toward you. Cut the legs away, including the thighs.

Turn chicken neck away from you. Using poultry shears, cut carefully along breastbone toward the neck. Spread chicken open. Cut along both sides of backbone, removing breasts. Cut diagonally through each breast, leaving some meat attached to the wing. With a knife, cut drumsticks from thighs. (*Note:* These directions are for chickens of 4 pounds or less. For larger chickens, see directions for carving turkey.)

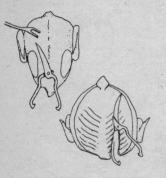
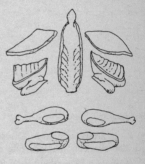

Roast Loin of Pork

Hold meat steady with fork, ribs facing up. Cut off backbone. (Remove as little meat as possible.) Position roast with ribs facing you. Steady roast with fork. Slice close to ribs, removing the slices one by one. (One slice will contain a bone; the next will be boneless.)

[25]

Whole Ham

Position ham, fat side up, with shank at your right. Hold firmly with fork. Slice lengthwise from thin side, forming a base. Stand ham on this base. Cut a wedge at start of leg bone. Slice vertically down to bone. Keep slices thin. Cut horizontally under slices, to release them. Stand leg up and hold it steady with fork as you slice rest of meat.

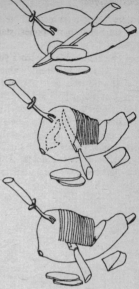

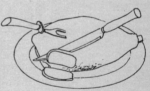

Roast Leg of Lamb

Hold meat firmly with fork. Cut several lengthwise slices in the thin side of the roast, forming a base. Stand roast on this base. Slice vertically down to leg bone. Cut horizontally under slices to release them. Turn leg up on large end. Hold it steady with a fork. Resume cutting on the thin side.

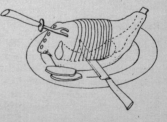

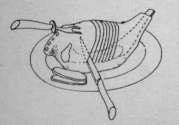

Rack of Lamb

Hold meat firmly with fork. To separate slices, cut between rib bones, starting at rib tips.

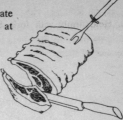

Flank Steak

Starting at the narrow end, cut thin slices across the grain, holding knife at a slight angle from the cutting board.

Porterhouse Steak

Hold steak steady with fork. With tip of knife, cut carefully around the bone. Discard the bone. Slice steak across entire width, cutting through top loin and tenderloin. Slice tail into small, even pieces.

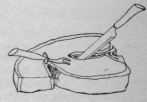

Crown Roast

Steady roast by placing fork in the side of the meat. Slice down from top to bottom, between each rib. Remove ribs as you cut.

Standing Rib Roast

Place meat on its wider end. Hold it steady with a fork. Slice until knife touches a rib. Using tip of knife, cut along the rib to release slice of meat.

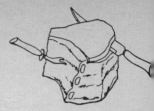

Rolled Roast

Place roast on end. Hold it steady with a fork. Slice straight across from the right. As you reach strings, remove them from roast.

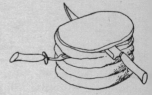

Whole Poached Fish

Cut through skin in back of head. Carefully peel the skin back to the tail, either in one piece or in strips. Turn fish over and repeat. Cut through flesh to the backbone, dividing fish into serving portions. Remove by slipping spatula between flesh and backbone. Grasp the tail, easing backbone from the fish. Cut the flesh underneath into portions.

General Information

1. Each of the Menus has been developed to fulfill the requirements of a complete meal, in accordance with the Weight Watchers Food Plan. To assist you in planning your food intake for the rest of the day, total menu equivalents for each serving appear in the Appendix at the end of the book.

2. Make certain you have every item on hand *ahead of time*. To aid your planning, each menu is prefaced by a suggested shopping list. It is divided into "staples and miscellaneous" items that can be kept on hand, and "additional items" that you may need to purchase. For your convenience, we have also included equipment lists.

3. For optimal results in any recipe, always take the time to measure and weigh—don't try to judge portions by eye. We recommend the use of the following items to help you with portion control: a food scale to weigh and measure your food, a set of measuring cups for liquid and dry measures, and measuring spoons. All dry measurements are level. Recipe directions may sometimes look as if they're taking the long way around, but remember, they're all shortcuts to weight control.

4. In any recipe for more than one serving it is important to mix ingredients well and, when serving, *to divide evenly*, so that each portion is the same size.

5. Nonstick cookware makes it possible for you to cook without fat. Use cookware manufactured with a nonstick surface, or spray an ordinary pan with a nonstick cooking spray.

6. When whipping chilled evaporated skimmed milk, to obtain the best results, mixing bowl and beaters should also be well chilled. This can be aocomplished rapidly by placing the bowl and beaters into the freezer for at least five minutes before using.

7. It is recommended that chilled foods be served on chilled plates and hot foods on warmed plates. Plates and glassware should be chilled in the refrigerator for approximately five minutes before serving. Plates and platters can be heated by placing them in a warm oven (no more than 200°F.) for five to ten minutes before serving, or in a warmer.

8. The fruit we use is fresh, or frozen or canned with no sugar added. Canned fruit may be packed in its own or another juice, in a juice blend, in water, or packed with artificial sweetener.

9. Meat should be well trimmed with all visible fat removed.

10. The vegetables used in these recipes are fresh unless otherwise indicated. If frozen or canned vegetables are substituted, it may be necessary to adjust cooking times accordingly.

11. The herbs used in these recipes are dried unless otherwise indicated. If substituting fresh herbs, use approximately four times the amount of dried (e.g., 1 teaspoon fresh rosemary instead of ¼ teaspoon dried). If substituting ground (powdered) herbs, use approximately half the amount of dried (e.g., ¼ teaspoon ground thyme instead of ½ teaspoon dried).

12. The spices used in these recipes are ground unless otherwise indicated. If substituting fresh, use approximately eight times the amount of ground (e.g., 1 teaspoon minced fresh ginger root instead of ⅛ teaspoon ground).

The following recipes are used in various menus throughout this book and are included here for ease of reference.

WHIPPED TOPPING

¾ teaspoon unflavored gelatin
2 tablespoons water
Artificial sweetener to equal 3
   teaspoons sugar

⅛ teaspoon vanilla extract
2 tablespoons evaporated
   skimmed milk, chilled

In small saucepan sprinkle gelatin over water; cook over low heat, stirring constantly, until gelatin is dissolved. Transfer to mixing bowl; add artificial sweetener and vanilla; cool. Add milk; beat at high speed until very thick. Cover and refrigerate. Makes 4 servings.

VINAIGRETTE DRESSING

¼ cup vegetable oil
¼ cup wine or tarragon vinegar

¼ teaspoon salt
Dash white pepper

Combine all ingredients in a jar with tight-fitting cover. Cover and shake vigorously before using. Makes 8 servings.

HOMEMADE STOCK

In any recipe calling for bouillon, you may substitute homemade stock. (To make bouillon, you may use instant broth and seasoning mixes, instant bouillon, or bouillon cubes.)

Chicken Stock

2 chicken carcasses
2 quarts water
1 celery rib with leaves, sliced
1 medium carrot, sliced
6 parsley sprigs

6 peppercorns
1 bay leaf
¼ teaspoon thyme
Salt to taste

Combine all ingredients in large saucepan. Bring to a boil; reduce heat and simmer for 1½ hours. Strain and discard solids. Refrigerate liquid until fat congeals on top. Remove and discard congealed fat. Makes about 1 quart.

Beef Stock

3 pounds beef bones
1 cup chopped celery
1 cup sliced carrots
1 cup chopped onion
¼ cup sliced turnip
1 garlic clove, crushed
4 quarts water

½ cup canned crushed tomatoes
½ bunch parsley stems
10 peppercorns, crushed
2 bay leaves
½ teaspoon thyme
2 cloves

Place bones on rack in roasting pan. Combine celery, carrots, onion, turnip, and garlic in another roasting pan. Roast at 425°F. until bones and vegetables are browned. Combine bones, vegetables, water, tomatoes, and seasonings in large pot. Bring to a boil; reduce heat and simmer 3 hours. Strain and discard solids. Refrigerate liquid until fat congeals on top. Remove and discard fat. Makes about 2 quarts.

Lamb, Ham, or Veal Stock

1½ pounds lamb, ham, or veal
   bones
2 quarts water
1 celery rib with leaves, sliced
1 medium carrot, sliced
1 tablespoon dehydrated onion
   flakes

6 parsley sprigs
6 peppercorns
1 bay leaf
1 garlic clove, crushed

Place bones on rack in roasting pan. Roast at 425°F. until bones are browned. Combine bones with remaining ingredients in large saucepan. Bring to a boil; reduce heat and simmer for 1½ hours. Strain and discard solids. Refrigerate liquid until fat congeals on top. Remove and discard congealed fat. Makes about 1 quart.

RICE

In any recipe calling for cooked enriched or brown rice, you may use the following basic recipes, or cook rice according to package directions.

White Rice

> 1½ cups uncooked enriched rice   1½ teaspoons salt (optional)
> 3 cups water (3¾ cups for
>   parboiled rice)

Place rice in 3-quart saucepan; add water, and salt if desired. Bring to a boil, then stir once or twice. Reduce heat; cover saucepan and simmer about 14 minutes without removing lid or stirring (20 to 25 minutes for parboiled rice). If rice is not tender enough, cook, covered, 2 to 3 minutes longer. Makes about 4 cups. Refrigerate or freeze any remaining rice for future use.

Fluffy White Rice

> 1 cup uncooked enriched rice   ½ teaspoon salt (optional)
> 1¾ cups cold water

Place rice in 2-quart saucepan; add cold water, and salt if desired. Cover and bring to a boil; reduce heat and cook over low heat for 20 minutes. Remove from heat and let rice "relax," covered, for 20 or more minutes. Stir to separate grains. Makes about 3 cups. Refrigerate or freeze any remaining rice for future use.

Brown Rice

> 1 cup uncooked brown rice   1 teaspoon salt (optional)
> 2½ cups water

Combine all ingredients in large saucepan. Bring to a boil; then stir once or twice. Reduce heat; cover saucepan and simmer for about 45 minutes or until all water is absorbed. Makes about 3 cups. Refrigerate or freeze any remaining rice for future use.

Reheating Rice:
Rice can be prepared in advance and reheated. To reheat, use any of the following methods:

1. Place 1 cup cooked rice in strainer. In medium saucepan bring ½ cup water to a boil. Place strainer in saucepan, over boiling water. Cover and steam over medium heat about 5 minutes or until thoroughly heated. Be sure that water does not boil out; add more if necessary.

2. Combine 1 cup cooked rice and 2 tablespoons water in saucepan. Cover and cook over low heat for about 4 minutes or until thoroughly heated.
3. Place 1 cup cooked rice in top half of double boiler, over boiling water. Cover and cook about 10 minutes or until thoroughly heated.

Note: The methods for reheating rice also work well with cooked enriched pasta.

BARLEY

In any recipe calling for cooked barley you may use the following basic recipe or cook according to package directions.

Use 1 teaspoon salt, 1½ quarts water, and 8 ounces uncooked barley. In saucepan bring salted water to a boil. Stir in barley; reduce heat, cover, and simmer for one hour or until tender. Drain. Makes 8 servings, about 4 cups. Any barley that is not used may be refrigerated or frozen for future use. To reheat, follow procedure for reheating rice (see page 32).

Tips on Gelatin

1. For easier unmolding, rinse mold in cold water or spray with non-stick cooking spray.
2. One tablespoon of unflavored gelatin will mold 2 cups of liquid or liquid and solids combined. Do not add fresh or frozen pineapple, papaya, or kiwi fruit to gelatin.
3. If gelatin mixture becomes too firm to fold in solid ingredients, place bowl containing mixture in bath of hot water; water should be 2 inches below rim of bowl. Stir until desired consistency; add solid ingredients and transfer mixture to mold. Chill.
4. Allow 2 to 3 hours for chilling of gelatin. A gelatin mixture that contains solids will take longer to chill than one that is totally liquid.
5. To unmold, gently run a knife along the inside edges of mold. Dip base of mold in bath of hot water. Place serving plate upside down over mold and invert both mold and plate. Shake mold and plate and, if necessary, cover inverted mold with a warm towel until gelatin loosens. Carefully remove mold.

Oven Heats

Oven thermostats should be checked at least once a year. If your oven does not have a thermostat or regulator, the following chart will give you an idea of the equivalent amount of heat required for each temperature range.

250° to 275°F.   Very slow oven
300° to 325°F.   Slow oven
350° to 375°F.   Moderate oven
400° to 425°F.   Hot oven
450° to 475°F.   Very hot oven
500° to 525°F.   Extremely hot oven

An oven thermometer can be purchased and placed in the oven to help determine the degree of heat.

Since foods bake faster in heat-resistant glass than in shiny metal pans, when baking in glass, lowering the temperature 25°F. is generally recommended.

Your Microwave Oven

Many of our recipes can be done in your microwave oven. Since there is no one standard that applies to all ovens, you will have to experiment with your unit and follow the manufacturer's advice for timing. Generally, you should allow about ¼ of the cooking time. That is, if our recipe suggests 20 minutes, allow 5 minutes in your microwave oven (or slightly less, since it's wiser to undercook than overcook). Please also note that our roasting procedures for beef, ham, lamb, and pork require the use of a rack so that fat can drain off into the pan. A plastic rack is available for use in the microwave oven.

Slow Cookers

If you enjoy using this appliance, there's no reason why you can't adapt many of our recipes to its use. We're giving you a headstart on Chicken Stock: combine all ingredients; cook covered, on low, for 12 hours. Strain and proceed as in the basic recipe.

Artificial Sweeteners

The use of artificial sweeteners on the Weight Watchers Food Program has always been optional. Natural sweetness is available in the form of fruits, which we do permit on our eating plan. Your use of artificial sweeteners is completely optional; and we believe that the decision about using them should be made by you and your physician. If you decide against these products, we hope you'll enjoy the more than 300 sweetener-free recipes included in this book.

January

As the temperature takes a downward plunge, our hot soups, drinks, desserts, and hearty meals will keep you warm on the inside and help keep you slim on the outside . . . and if weight control was one of your resolutions, these menus will give your New Year a happy start.

NEW YEAR'S DAY BREAKFAST FOR FOUR

Clam Shot
Sardines with Dill Sauce
Lettuce and Tomato Salad
Hot Spiced Pears
Beverage

New Year's Day has many traditions, among them, various foods, such as herrings, that are believed to bring good luck. Why not launch your year with a "Lucky Breakfast"? Feature a delectable sardine dish (sardines belong to the herring family) accompanied by a tangy Dill Sauce. Hearty pumpernickel is a good accompaniment to strong-flavored foods like these, and the dark bread adds eye appeal by underscoring the snowy whiteness of the sauce. The salad lends a special touch to this holiday breakfast. To cast a bright glow on the year, add bright tomatoes and *red* onions! Pears are a popular winter fruit, and we've blended in a trio of seasonings that harmonize especially well with them. Add to the spirit of the occasion with a warming "Clam Shot"—our zesty version of the traditional morning-after "Bull Shot." What a lucky way to begin the New Year—with a party-style breakfast that steers a straight course toward your slimming resolutions!

SUGGESTED SHOPPING LIST

Staples and Miscellaneous

Artificial sweetener
Cinnamon sticks
Cloves
Instant beef broth and seasoning mix
Nutmeg
Salt
White pepper

Dijon mustard
Red wine vinegar or tarragon vinegar

Cornstarch

Imitation mayonnaise
Vegetable oil

Pumpernickel bread

Additional Items

Plain unflavored yogurt, 1 8-ounce
  container

Dill, 1 bunch
Garlic clove, 1 small
Lettuce, 1 head
Red onion, 1 small
Tomatoes, 2 medium

Clam juice, 1 8-fluid-ounce bottle

Canned pear halves, no sugar added,
  2 16-ounce cans

Canned sardines, 3 3¾-ounce cans

SUGGESTED EQUIPMENT LIST

Blender
Bowls
Can opener
Chef's knife
Cutting board
Jar with cover
Measuring cups

Measuring spoons
Pot holder
Saucepan (medium)
Scale
Soup tureen (1-quart)
Toaster
Wooden spoon

CLAM SHOT

*4 packets instant beef broth and
  seasoning mix*

*3 cups boiling water
½ cup clam juice*

In 1-quart soup tureen dissolve broth mix in boiling water. Add clam juice; stir to combine. Divide evenly into 4 mugs. Makes 4 servings.

SARDINES WITH DILL SAUCE

*¼ cup plain unflavored yogurt
1 garlic clove, minced
½ teaspoon chopped fresh dill
½ teaspoon Dijon mustard
1 tablespoon plus 1 teaspoon
  imitation mayonnaise*

*8 ounces drained canned sardines
4 slices pumpernickel bread,
  toasted*

In blender container combine yogurt, garlic, dill, and mustard. Process for 10 seconds. Transfer to small bowl. Add mayonnaise and stir until smooth. Place 2 ounces of sardines on each slice of toast. Spoon ¼ of the sauce over each slice. Makes 4 servings.

LETTUCE AND TOMATO SALAD

*1 cup lettuce leaves
2 medium tomatoes, sliced
1 cup diced red onion*

*½ recipe Vinaigrette Dressing
  (see page 30)*

Line a serving plate with lettuce. Arrange tomato slices and diced onion over lettuce; add dressing. Makes 4 servings.

HOT SPICED PEARS

8 canned pear halves with ½ cup
    juice, no sugar added
½ cup water
1 cinnamon stick
4 cloves
⅛ teaspoon nutmeg

1 tablespoon plus 1 teaspoon
    cornstarch, dissolved in 1
    tablespoon water
Artificial sweetener to equal 2
    teaspoons sugar

In medium saucepan combine first 5 ingredients. Simmer for 5 minutes. Stirring constantly, add cornstarch and cook until slightly thickened. Remove and discard cinnamon stick and cloves. Stir in sweetener. Divide evenly into 4 dessert dishes. Makes 4 servings.

SCANDINAVIAN KOLDT BORD FOR EIGHT

Pickled Beets □ Marinated Cucumbers
Fluted Mushrooms
Tomato Aspic in a Sea of Crudités
Red Russian Dressing □ Dill Dressing
Tangy Bean Salad □ Elbow Macaroni Salad
Julienne Zucchini with Anchovy Dressing
Smoked Salmon Canapés □ Dill-Flavored Creamy Herring
Turkey Rolls with Pineapple-Bean Sprout Salad
Tuna-Stuffed Peppers □ Sardines in Aspic
Potato Salad with White Garlic Dressing
Hot Blueberry Dessert
Sparkling Mineral Water with Twist of Lemon

Enhance your buffet table with a Decorative Ice Mold

Brighten your mid-winter hosting by serving in hospitable Scandinavian style. A *koldt bord* (cold board)—the Danish equivalent of Sweden's famed *smorgasbord*—traditionally features cold foods at one end and hot dishes at the other. To keep cold foods at the right temperature, chill the platters ahead of time.

Fish is an ever-present *koldt bord* item—understandably, since ocean-rimmed Scandinavia abounds in lakes and fjords. The versatile herring appears in a multitude of dishes, as does that great favorite, salmon, which is customarily accompanied by dill. The Scandinavians like to use this feathery herb as a reminder that spring will come again after the long Nordic winter. Sharp-flavored beets, marinated cucumbers, and the mushrooms that grow in profusion in the Danish forests are buffet staples. And, of course, Danish desserts are widely famed—and feared! We've translated Scandinavia's abundant berry crop into a luscious Blueberry Dessert that does justice to Denmark's "sweet" reputation—but in figure-saving style. As a contrast to the chilled dishes, serve the dessert hot.

A prime ingredient of Danish menus is visual appeal, so take time to follow our simple directions for garnishing and for arranging foods and flowers in eye-catching sculptured ice molds. Set an exquisite table with a woven linen cloth and finely designed serving pieces, illuminated by glowing candles. Then enjoy the gleam in your guests' eyes!

SUGGESTED SHOPPING LIST

Staples and Miscellaneous

Almond extract
Artificial sweetener
Bay leaves
Celery seed
Cinnamon
Cinnamon sticks
Cloves
Dehydrated onion flakes
Dry mustard
Garlic powder
Onion powder
Paprika
Peppercorns
Pickling spice
Salt
Vanilla extract
White pepper

Capers
Chili sauce
Cider vinegar
Dijon mustard
Hot sauce
Ketchup
Prepared horseradish
Prepared mustard
Red wine vinegar or tarragon vinegar
White vinegar
Worchestershire sauce

Cornstarch
Unflavored gelatin

Imitation mayonnaise
Vegetable oil

Additional Items

Cooked sliced turkey, ½ pound
Skinned herring fillets, ½ pound
Smoked salmon, 3 ounces

Plain unflavored yogurt, 3 16-ounce
  containers

Lemons, 3 medium

Carrots, 3 medium
Celery, 1 stalk
Cucumbers, 6 medium
Dill, 1 bunch, or dill weed
Garlic clove, 1
Green peppers, 5 medium
Mushrooms, 1 pound
Onion, 1 large
Parsley, 1 bunch

Potatoes, 1 pound
Shallots, 4
Spinach, 1 pound
White asparagus stalks, medium,
  1 bunch or 8 stalks
Zucchini, 4 medium (approximately
  5 ounces each)

Choice of any combination (for
  crudités and garnishes)
    Broccoli, 1 bunch
    Celery, 1 stalk
    Chinese cabbage, 1 head
    Cucumbers, 2 medium
    Green peppers, 2 medium
    Mushrooms, 1 pound
    Radishes, 1 bag
    White turnips, 2
    Zucchini, 2 medium

(continued)

Frozen blueberries, no sugar added,
1 16-ounce package

Canned pineapple chunks, no sugar
added, 1 8-ounce can

Canned bean sprouts, 2 16-ounce cans
Canned cut green beans, 1 16-ounce
can
Canned cut wax beans, 1 16-ounce
can
Canned hearts of palm, 2 14-ounce
cans

Canned sliced beets, 2 16-ounce cans
Dill pickles, 1 16-ounce jar

Anchovies, 1 4-ounce can
Sardines, 2 3¾-ounce cans
Tuna, 1 13-ounce can

Tomato juice, 1 18-fluid-ounce can

Evaporated skimmed milk, 1 13-fluid-
ounce can

Enriched elbow macaroni, 1 16-ounce
box
Prunes, medium, 1 16-ounce box

SUGGESTED EQUIPMENT LIST

Bowls (small, medium, large)
Can opener
Chef's knife
Cutting board
Fork
Measuring cups
Measuring spoons
2-cup mold
2-cup ring-shaped mold

Paring knife
Pepper mill
Pot holder
Saucepans (with covers)
Scale
Strainer
Vegetable peeler
Wire whisk
Wooden spoons

PICKLED BEETS

⅔ cup cider vinegar
Artificial sweetener to equal 4
teaspoons sugar
4 cloves

1 small garlic clove, crushed
1 small cinnamon stick
3 cups drained canned sliced
beets

Combine all ingredients except beets in saucepan. Simmer for 10 minutes.
Remove and discard cloves, garlic, and cinnamon stick. Combine remaining vinegar and beets in large bowl; chill. Makes 8 servings.

MARINATED CUCUMBERS

4 medium cucumbers, pared,
scored, and sliced
¼ cup white vinegar
2 teaspoons chopped fresh
parsley

Artificial sweetener to equal
1 teaspoon sugar
1 teaspoon salt

Place cucumbers in bowl; add remaining ingredients and stir to combine.
Refrigerate for at least 2 hours. Makes 8 servings.

FLUTED MUSHROOMS

Use 2 cups uniform well-shaped mushrooms. Refer to page 14 for directions for preparation of Fluted Mushrooms. Sprinkle finished mushrooms with lemon juice; chill. Makes 8 servings.

For an even more decorative effect, scoop small circle out of center of each fluted mushroom cap. Fill each with a small piece of lemon rind or a caper.

If desired, mushrooms may be cooked in acidulated water (2 cups water and 1 tablespoon lemon juice), drained, and refrigerated until ready to serve.

TOMATO ASPIC IN A SEA OF CRUDITÉS

Use Crudités as dippers for Red Russian and Dill Dressings (see recipes, below and page 46).

1 envelope unflavored gelatin
2 cups tomato juice, divided
Artificial sweetener to equal ½ teaspoon sugar (optional)
½ teaspoon onion powder
½ teaspoon Worcestershire sauce
Dash hot sauce
4 cups crisp fresh vegetables (crudités)
Choice of:
broccoli florets
celery frills (refer to page 14)

Chinese cabbage leaves, formed into cups
cucumbers, scored and sliced
green peppers, seeded and cut into 1½ × 2-inch pieces
mushrooms, sliced lengthwise through cap and stem
radish roses (refer to page 17)
white turnips, pared and cut into thin semicircles
zucchini, well scrubbed and cut into thin strips

In saucepan sprinkle gelatin over ½ cup tomato juice; allow to stand a few minutes to soften. Add remaining tomato juice and all remaining ingredients except vegetables; bring to a boil. Reduce heat and simmer for 10 minutes. Pour into 2-cup mold. Chill about 2 hours or until firm. Unmold onto serving platter or tray. Surround with fresh vegetables. Makes 8 servings.

RED RUSSIAN DRESSING

Serve with Crudités (see recipe, above).

½ cup plain unflavored yogurt
¼ cup chili sauce
½ medium dill pickle, diced
Artificial sweetener to equal 2 teaspoons sugar

1 teaspoon dehydrated onion flakes
Dash hot sauce
Salt to taste

Combine all ingredients in small bowl; chill. Makes 8 servings.

DILL DRESSING

Serve with Crudités (see recipe, page 45).

1 cup plain unflavored yogurt
2 tablespoons minced fresh
  parsley
1 teaspoon dill weed, or 1
  tablespoon chopped fresh dill

¼ teaspoon garlic powder
¼ teaspoon onion powder
¼ teaspoon white pepper

Combine all ingredients in small bowl; chill. Makes 8 servings.

TANGY BEAN SALAD

1½ cups drained, canned cut
  green beans
1½ cups drained, canned cut wax
  beans
1 cup minced celery
2 tablespoons diced onion
¼ cup red wine vinegar

2 tablespoons water
Artificial sweetener to equal 3
  teaspoons sugar (optional)
1½ teaspoons prepared mustard
Salt, pepper, garlic powder, and
  paprika to taste

Combine vegetables in medium bowl. Combine remaining ingredients in small bowl or measuring cup; mix well. Pour dressing over vegetables; toss to coat. Chill at least 2 hours. Makes 8 servings.

ELBOW MACARONI SALAD

2⅔ cups cooked enriched elbow
  macaroni
½ cup diced celery
½ cup diced, pared cucumber
¼ cup chopped onion

¼ cup imitation mayonnaise
⅛ teaspoon garlic powder
⅛ teaspoon celery seed
Salt and pepper to taste

Combine elbow macaroni, celery, cucumber, and onion in salad bowl. Combine remaining ingredients in measuring cup; mix well. Stir gently into vegetable mixture. Makes 8 servings.

JULIENNE ZUCCHINI WITH ANCHOVY DRESSING

4 cups julienne zucchini
2 ounces drained canned
  anchovies, minced
1 tablespoon plus 1 teaspoon
  minced shallots

1 tablespoon plus 1 teaspoon
  vegetable oil
1 tablespoon plus 1 teaspoon
  lemon juice

Place zucchini in saucepan with boiling water to cover. Cover and cook 4 to 5 minutes or until zucchini is just tender. Drain thoroughly and cool.

Arrange zucchini attractively in serving dish. Combine remaining ingredients in small bowl; mix well and pour over zucchini. Chill. Makes 8 servings.

SMOKED SALMON CANAPÉS

3 ounces smoked salmon, cut
into very thin strips
1 medium cucumber, cut into
24 slices
24 capers

2 cups crisp, torn spinach leaves,
bite-size pieces
8 lemon wedges
Pepper mill filled with
peppercorns

Place an equal amount of salmon on each cucumber slice. Top each with a caper and arrange on serving tray. Surround canapés with spinach and garnish spinach with lemon wedges. Invite guests to squeeze lemon and grind pepper over their canapés. Makes 8 servings.

DILL-FLAVORED CREAMY HERRING

½ cup cider vinegar
1½ teaspoons pickling spice
1 teaspoon salt
1 bay leaf
3 cups water

8 ounces skinned herring fillets,
diced
½ cup plain unflavored yogurt
½ teaspoon dill weed or 2
teaspoons chopped fresh dill

In saucepan combine vinegar, pickling spice, salt, and bay leaf; add water. Bring to a boil; add herring fillets. Reduce heat and simmer for 15 minutes; drain. Place fillets in small bowl. Add remaining ingredients; chill. Makes 8 servings.

TURKEY ROLLS WITH PINEAPPLE-BEAN SPROUT SALAD

8 slices cooked turkey, 1 ounce
each
8 cooked, medium, white
asparagus spears

Pineapple-Bean Sprout Salad
(see following recipe)

Roll 1 slice of turkey around each asparagus spear; chill. Arrange Pineapple-Bean Sprout Salad in center of serving platter. Surround salad with turkey rolls. Makes 8 servings.

Pineapple-Bean Sprout Salad

2 cups well-drained canned bean
sprouts, rinsed
1 cup diced celery
½ cup diced green pepper
½ cup diced carrot
½ cup canned pineapple chunks,
no sugar added

3 medium prunes, pitted and
diced
2 tablespoons imitation
mayonnaise
1 tablespoon white vinegar
1 teaspoon prepared mustard
Salt to taste

Combine bean sprouts, celery, green pepper, and carrot in medium bowl. Drain pineapple chunks and reserve juice. Add pineapple chunks and prunes to vegetable mixture. In small bowl combine reserved pineapple juice, mayonnaise, vinegar, mustard, and salt; mix well. Add to bean sprout mixture. Toss to coat vegetables and fruit with dressing. Serve as directed in recipe for Turkey Rolls (see recipe, page 47)

TUNA-STUFFED PEPPERS

½ cup plain unflavored yogurt
2 tablespoons Dijon mustard
2 tablespoons ketchup
2 teaspoons prepared horseradish
½ teaspoon Worcestershire sauce
8 ounces drained canned tuna, flaked

½ cup chopped onion
½ cup chopped celery
4 medium green peppers, cut into halves and seeded

In medium bowl combine yogurt, mustard, ketchup, horseradish, and Worcestershire sauce; mix well. Add tuna, onion, and celery; stir to combine. Divide mixture into 8 equal portions. Stuff each pepper half with 1 portion tuna mixture. Makes 8 servings.

SARDINES IN ASPIC

1 envelope unflavored gelatin
¼ cup cold water
½ cup boiling water
1 cup plain unflavored yogurt
2 tablespoons imitation mayonnaise
1 tablespoon Worcestershire sauce
1 teaspoon red wine vinegar

⅛ teaspoon each garlic powder and dry mustard
4 ounces drained canned sardines, chopped
Garnishes: Choice of carrot curls, celery frills, cucumber cartwheels, radish roses (refer to section on garnishing, page 13)

In bowl sprinkle gelatin over cold water; let stand a few minutes to soften. Add boiling water and stir until gelatin is dissolved. Using a wire whisk, beat in yogurt, mayonnaise, Worcestershire, vinegar, garlic powder, and dry mustard. Gently stir in sardines. Transfer mixture to 2-cup ring-shaped mold that has been rinsed in cold water. Chill until firm. Unmold onto round serving platter. Fill center with garnishes. Makes 8 servings.

POTATO SALAD WITH WHITE GARLIC DRESSING

Salad:

1 pound cooked pared potatoes, cut into thin strips
2 cups sliced, drained, canned hearts of palm, 1-inch pieces

1 cup diced celery

Dressing:

1 cup plus 2 tablespoons plain
    unflavored yogurt
¼ cup plus 2 tablespoons
    evaporated skimmed milk
1 tablespoon prepared mustard

1 tablespoon prepared
    horseradish
1½ teaspoons dehydrated onion
    flakes
¾ teaspoon garlic powder

To Prepare Salad: Combine potatoes and vegetables in large bowl. Toss
to combine; chill.

To Prepare Dressing: In small bowl combine remaining ingredients; mix
well. Chill.

To Serve: Add dressing to salad; toss to coat. Makes 8 servings.

HOT BLUEBERRY DESSERT

4 cups frozen blueberries, no
    sugar added
Artificial sweetener to equal 24
    teaspoons sugar
1 tablespoon lemon juice
1 teaspoon each vanilla and
    almond extracts

¾ teaspoon cinnamon
1½ quarts water
1 tablespoon cornstarch,
    dissolved in 2 tablespoons
    water

Combine first 5 ingredients in saucepan; add water. Bring to a boil; reduce
heat and simmer 30 minutes, stirring occasionally. Stir in cornstarch. Cook
for 10 minutes longer or until slightly thickened. Serve hot in coffee cups.
Makes 8 servings.

DECORATIVE ICE MOLDS

1. Use a decorative mold—ring, bombe, etc. Fill it with boiled water;
freeze. Unmold onto a tray or platter that is deep enough to hold melt-
ing ice. To unmold easily, place mold upside down onto tray. Wrap a hot
towel around mold; lift mold away from ice. Return ice to freezer until
needed. Use as a decorative base for vegetable garnishes.
2. The center of a solid ice mold can be hollowed out to hold a bowl
of salad dressing or dip. Prepare ice mold as directed above; unmold. Chip
a tiny hollow in the center of mold. Set a heatproof bowl, about the same
size as your serving bowl, in the center of ice over hollow. Fill bowl with
hot water; keep replacing water as it cools. The hot water will melt the
ice. When ice is sufficiently melted, remove bowl. Return mold to freezer
until needed.
3. Handsome floral or vegetable arrangements can be made in ice molds.
Pour a thin layer of boiled water into a decorative mold; freeze. Add your
choice of flowers, leaves, lemon slices, mint sprigs, watercress, or any-

thing else your imagination can dream up. Arrange in an attractive design. Cover with a thin layer of boiled water; freeze. Repeat procedure, building up decorative layers until mold is filled. Keep frozen until needed. Unmold as directed above.

APRÈS SKATING OR SKIING FOR FOUR

Hot Tomato Soup
Pearfect Meat Loaf
Piquant Green Beans
Cabbage-Carrot Salad
Sesame-Rye Sticks
Apple-Peach Bake
Mocha Milk

Slaloming down the slopes or cutting nifty figures on the ice works up healthy appetites in the brisk winter air. Take the chill off the occasion by providing a welcome flask of hot soup, zestily seasoned. Then back to the lodge or house for this energy-fueling feast that sports easy do-it-ahead dishes that free you to join the fun. Everything except the bread, beverage, and salad can conveniently be served either hot or chilled. Meat loaf is a budget booster that doesn't have to be dull—as proven by our "*pear*-fect" addition of fruit to give the meat an unusual sweet taste. Adding soy and hot sauce to beans is another simple way to provide interesting flavor combinations. Prepare the ingredients for the Sesame-Rye Sticks ahead of time too, so they can bake in the brief time it takes guests to thaw out. Warm up wintry spirits with nutritious Mocha Milk, along with a juicy Apple-Peach Bake. You just might win a trophy for champion serving designed to help everyone stay in shape for the sporting life!

———————— •❖• ————————

SUGGESTED SHOPPING LIST

Staples and Miscellaneous

Artificial sweetener
Cinnamon
Garlic powder
Instant chicken broth and seasoning
  mix
Marjoram
Nutmeg
Paprika
Salt
Sesame seeds
White pepper

Hot sauce
Prepared mustard
Soy sauce

Instant coffee
Unflavored gelatin
Unsweetened cocoa

Margarine

Enriched white bread
Rye bread

[51]

Additional Items

Ground beef, 1½ pounds

Apples, 2 small
Lemon, 1
Pear, 1 small

Cabbage, 1 small head
Carrots, 3 medium
Celery, 1 rib
Ginger root, 1
Green beans, ½ pound
Green peppers, 1 medium

Onion, 1 small
Parsley, 1 bunch
Scallions, 1 bunch

Canned sliced peaches, no sugar
    added, 2 16-ounce cans

Canned crushed tomatoes, 1 28-ounce
    can
Tomato puree, 1 16-ounce can

Evaporated skimmed milk, 2 13-fluid-
    ounce cans

SUGGESTED EQUIPMENT LIST

Baking pan
Baking sheet
Blender
Bowls (small, medium, large)
Chef's knife
Colander
Corer
Cutting board
Electric mixer
Grater
Measuring cups

Measuring spoons
Pot holder
Rack
Roasting pan
Saucepans (small and medium) with
    covers
Scale
Toaster
Vegetable peeler
Wooden spoons

HOT TOMATO SOUP

This soup can be carried in a thermal flask to the rink or the slopes.

1 cup sliced onion
½ cup diced celery
*2 packets instant chicken broth
    and seasoning mix*
1 quart water

2 cups canned crushed tomatoes
1 teaspoon chopped fresh parsley
⅛ teaspoon garlic powder
Salt and pepper to taste

Combine onion, celery, and broth mix in medium saucepan. Cook over low heat for 3 to 5 minutes or until onion is transparent. Add remaining ingredients; simmer 20 minutes, stirring occasionally. Transfer to blender container and process until smooth. Add additional water to adjust consistency, if desired. Return to saucepan and reheat. Makes 4 servings.

PEARFECT MEAT LOAF

May be served hot or chilled.

1½ pounds ground beef
1 small pear, pared, cored, and grated
1 slice enriched white bread, made into crumbs
2 tablespoons tomato puree
½ teaspoon finely chopped fresh ginger root
½ teaspoon each marjoram and chopped fresh parsley
⅛ teaspoon pepper
Salt to taste
Parsley sprigs to garnish

Combine all ingredients in large bowl. Shape meat mixture into loaf; place on rack that has been sprayed with nonstick cooking spray. Place rack in roasting pan and bake at 350°F. for 1 hour or until done. Transfer to serving platter and garnish with parsley. Makes 4 servings.

PIQUANT GREEN BEANS

Serve hot or chilled.

2 cups green beans
2 tablespoons soy sauce
¼ teaspoon hot sauce

In saucepan cook beans in boiling water about 6 minutes or until tender-crisp. Drain immediately and cool under cold running water. Drain beans again and transfer to a medium bowl. Add soy and hot sauce; toss to combine. Makes 4 servings.

CABBAGE-CARROT SALAD

2 cups grated cabbage
1½ cups grated carrots
½ cup chopped green pepper
¼ cup finely chopped scallions
1½ teaspoons unflavored gelatin
¼ cup water
¼ cup evaporated skimmed milk, chilled
2 tablespoons prepared mustard
2 teaspoons lemon juice
½ teaspoon salt

Combine vegetables in medium bowl; chill. In small saucepan sprinkle gelatin over water; let stand a few minutes to soften. Heat, stirring constantly, until gelatin is dissolved. Pour into medium mixing bowl and refrigerate until syrupy. Add milk, mustard, lemon juice, and salt. Beat with electric mixer until thick and foamy. Add chilled vegetables and stir to combine. Serve immediately. Makes 4 servings.

SESAME-RYE STICKS

> 3 slices rye bread, toasted
> 1 tablespoon margarine
>
> ¾ teaspoon sesame seeds

Spread 1 teaspoon margarine on each slice of toast. Sprinkle each with ¼ teaspoon sesame seeds and place on baking sheet, margarine side up. Bake at 350°F. for 7 to 10 minutes. Cut each slice into 4 equal strips and serve immediately. Makes 4 servings.

APPLE-PEACH BAKE

May be served warm or chilled.

> 1½ cups canned sliced peaches,
>   no sugar added
> 2 small apples, pared, cored, and
>   sliced
>
> 1 teaspoon lemon juice
> ½ teaspoon cinnamon
> ¼ teaspoon nutmeg

In medium baking pan combine all ingredients. Cover and bake at 350°F. for 20 to 30 minutes or until apples are tender. Makes 4 servings.

MOCHA MILK

> 2 tablespoons unsweetened cocoa
> Artificial sweetener to equal 8
>   teaspoons sugar
>
> 1½ teaspoons instant coffee
> 1 cup water
> 2 cups evaporated skimmed milk

In saucepan combine cocoa, sweetener, and coffee. Add water and stir until cocoa is dissolved. Cook over medium heat, stirring constantly, for 3 to 4 minutes or until just below boiling. Stir in milk; continue to stir and cook until milk is heated. Divide evenly into 4 mugs. Serve immediately. Makes 4 servings.

SLUMBER PARTY FOR EIGHT

Chili Dip with Vegetables
"Sloppy Joes"
Vegetable and Spiral Macaroni Salad
Chocolate Sundae
Orange "Candy"
Beverage

Slumber parties rate high on the teen and pre-teen scene—and so does each of these popular dishes, deliberately chosen to please the young set, or anyone young in *heart*. Chili is a red-hot favorite, and there'll be no struggle to get anyone to eat vegetables when they're dipped into this spicy mix. "Sloppy Joes" are always big hits. So are "roller coasters," as the youngsters dub macaroni spirals. (What a fun way to eat pasta!) Add a Chocolate Sundae—and chewy Orange "Candy"—they're all okay on a weight-loss plan?—and you'll turn the young crowd into your ardent fans!

SUGGESTED SHOPPING LIST

Staples and Miscellaneous

Artificial sweetener
Chili powder
Garlic powder
Onion powder
Oregano
Paprika
Parsley flakes
Salt
Sesame seeds
Vanilla extract
White pepper

Hot sauce
White vinegar

Cornstarch
Unflavored gelatin
Unsweetened cocoa

Imitation mayonnaise
Sesame oil
Vegetable oil

Hamburger rolls

Ground beef, 1½ pounds

Plain unflavored yogurt, 1 8-ounce container

Broccoli, 1 bunch
Carrots, 6 medium
Cauliflower, 1 head
Celery, 4 ribs
Cucumbers, 3 medium
Green chili peppers, 6 small
Mushrooms, 1 pound
Onion, 1 medium
Parsley, 1 bunch
Zucchini, 2 medium

Frozen orange juice concentrate, 1 12-fluid-ounce can box
Vanilla-flavored dietary frozen dessert, 1 64-ounce package

Canned kidney beans, 3 16-ounce cans
Canned tomatoes, 1 28-ounce can
Tomato sauce, 2 28-ounce cans

Evaporated skimmed milk, 1 13-fluid-ounce can

Enriched spiral macaroni, 1 16-ounce box

SUGGESTED EQUIPMENT LIST

Baking pan (8 x 8 x 2½ inches)
Blender or food processor
Bowls (medium and large)
Broiling pan
Can opener
Colander
Chef's knife
Cutting board
Electric mixer

Ice cream scoop
Measuring cups
Measuring spoons
Pot holder
Saucepans (medium and large)
Scale
Vegetable peeler
Wooden spoon

CHILI DIP WITH VEGETABLES

3 cups drained canned tomatoes
½ cup chopped onion
¼ cup parsley sprigs
¼ cup green chili peppers, seeded
1 tablespoon white vinegar
1 tablespoon oregano

½ teaspoon salt
2 cups cauliflower florets
2 cups whole mushrooms
4 celery ribs, cut into sticks
3 medium cucumbers, cut into sticks

Combine first 7 ingredients in blender container or food processor; process until pureed. Chill at least 2 hours. Arrange vegetables on serving platter. Serve with chilled dip. Makes 8 servings.

"SLOPPY JOES"

1½ pounds ground beef
1½ teaspoons garlic powder, divided
2 teaspoons salt, divided
¾ teaspoon pepper, divided
½ teaspoon dehydrated parsley flakes
1½ pounds drained canned kidney beans

1 quart tomato sauce
1 tablespoon chili powder
1 teaspoon paprika
½ teaspoon onion powder
½ teaspoon hot sauce, or to taste
4 hamburger rolls, 2 ounces each, cut into halves and toasted

Combine ground beef, 1 teaspoon each garlic powder and salt, ½ teaspoon pepper, and parsley flakes in medium bowl; form into 8 patties. Broil on rack for 15 minutes, turning once. In blender container or food processor combine ½ of the beans and ½ of the tomato sauce; process until smooth. Transfer to large saucepan. Repeat with remaining beans and tomato sauce. Crumble patties; add meat and remaining ingredients except rolls to saucepan. Simmer, stirring frequently, for 20 minutes. Divide meat mixture into 8 equal portions. Serve 1 portion over each roll half. Makes 8 servings.

VEGETABLE AND SPIRAL MACARONI SALAD

½ cup plain unflavored yogurt
¼ cup imitation mayonnaise
2 tablespoons vegetable oil
2 teaspoons sesame oil
2 teaspoons sesame seeds, toasted
Salt and white pepper to taste
5⅓ cups cooked enriched spiral macaroni

2 cups sliced zucchini, blanched and chilled
2 cups sliced carrots, blanched and chilled
2 cups broccoli florets, blanched and chilled

In large bowl combine yogurt, mayonnaise, vegetable oil, sesame oil, sesame seeds, salt, and white pepper; mix well. Add remaining ingredients. Toss to coat all ingredients. Makes 8 servings.

CHOCOLATE SUNDAE

2 tablespoons unsweetened cocoa
2 tablespoons water
1 tablespoon plus 1 teaspoon cornstarch
1 cup evaporated skimmed milk

Artificial sweetener to equal 8 teaspoons sugar
8 scoops vanilla-flavored dietary frozen dessert, 3 ounces each
4 recipes Whipped Topping (see page 30)

Combine cocoa, water, and cornstarch in measuring cup and stir until cocoa and cornstarch are dissolved. In saucepan bring milk to boiling point. Stirring constantly, add cocoa mixture; continue to stir and cook

2 to 3 minutes or until thickened. Remove from heat; add sweetener. Chill. Place 1 scoop of frozen dessert into each of 8 dessert glasses. Divide syrup into 8 equal portions. Pour 1 portion of syrup over each dessert. Top each with ⅛ of the Whipped Topping. Makes 8 servings.

ORANGE "CANDY"

3 cups orange juice	Artificial sweetener to equal 2
3 envelopes unflavored gelatin	teaspoons sugar

Pour orange juice into medium saucepan. Sprinkle gelatin over orange juice; let stand a few minutes to soften. Cook over low heat, stirring constantly, until gelatin is dissolved. Stir in sweetener. Pour into 8 × 8 × 2½ inch baking pan. Chill until firm. Cut into small squares. Makes 8 servings

TEEN SCENE BREAKFAST FOR EIGHT

Tomato Juice
Teen Scene "Granola"
Cinnamon-Raisin Toast
Hot Mocha Koca

Follow up slumber party fun with a dream of a breakfast menu. Start off by dipping edible stirrers of celery into nutritious "morning after" glasses of tomato juice. Wake up sleepyheads with a warm treat: Hot Mocha Koca. Granola rates high on teen popularity polls, so delight your youthful guests with a slimming version that combines a potpourri of tastes: sesame, cinnamon, allspice, vanilla, coconut, and banana. What a delicious way to season a party! Then treat sweet teeth to another welcome surprise: cinnamon-raisin bread delectably topped by apricot preserves. A morning scene to savor—and you'll feast all day on the raves from weight-conscious teens!

———— ◆•◆ ————

SUGGESTED SHOPPING LIST

Staples and Miscellaneous

Allspice
Artificial sweetener
Cinnamon
Coconut extract
Nutmeg
Salt
Sesame seeds
Vanilla extract

Coffee
Nonfat dry milk powder
Unflavored gelatin
Unsweetened cocoa

Imitation (or diet) margarine

Cinnamon-raisin bread

Low-calorie apricot preserves

Additional Items

Skim milk, 1 quart

Apples, 2 small
Bananas, 4 medium

Celery, 8 ribs

Tomato juice, 2 1-quart jars

Buckwheat flake cereal, 1 15-ounce box
Oatmeal, 1 18-ounce box
Raisin bran, 1 20-ounce box

[59]

Baking pan, nonstick (9 x 13 x 2 inches)
Bowls (small, medium)
Corer
Fork
Measuring cups
Measuring spoons
Metal spoon

Pot holder
Saucepan
Scale
Spatula
Spreading knife
Toaster
Vegetable peeler
Wooden spoons

TOMATO JUICE

1½ quarts tomato juice　　　　8 celery ribs

Chill tomato juice. Divide evenly into eight 6-ounce glasses. Clean and trim celery ribs. Place 1 rib in each glass to be used as a stirrer. Makes 8 servings.

TEEN SCENE "GRANOLA"

3 ounces uncooked oatmeal
1½ ounces buckwheat flake cereal
1½ ounces raisin bran cereal
1 tablespoon plus 1 teaspoon sesame seeds, toasted
½ teaspoon cinnamon
¼ teaspoon each allspice, nutmeg, and salt
2 small apples, pared, cored, and finely chopped

⅔ cup nonfat dry milk powder
4 envelopes unflavored gelatin
Artificial sweetener to equal 8 teaspoons sugar
¾ cup boiling water
2 tablespoons plus 2 teaspoons imitation (or diet) margarine
½ teaspoon each vanilla and coconut extracts
4 medium bananas, cut into ¼-inch slices

Preheat oven to 350°F. In bowl combine first 6 ingredients. Add apples and toss to combine. Spread evenly in 9 × 13 × 2-inch nonstick baking pan. Bake for 45 minutes. Remove from oven and broil, 2 inches from source of heat, for 2 minutes or until golden brown. In small bowl combine dry milk, gelatin, and sweetener. Stir into cereal mixture. In same small bowl combine water, margarine, and extracts, stirring until margarine melts. Pour over cereal mixture, stirring quickly with a fork to combine. Mixture will be lumpy. Cool. Divide into 8 equal portions. Top each portion with ⅛ of the banana slices. Makes 8 servings.

CINNAMON-RAISIN TOAST

Serve each person 1 slice toasted cinnamon-raisin bread, which has been spread with 2 teaspoons low-calorie apricot preserves.

HOT MOCHA KOCA

2 tablespoons plus 2 teaspoons
  unsweetened cocoa
2 cups hot coffee
1 quart skim milk

Artificial sweetener to equal 10
  teaspoons sugar
1 teaspoon vanilla extract

Place cocoa in medium saucepan. Pour hot coffee over cocoa; stir to dissolve cocoa. Stir in milk. Cook until thoroughly heated. Stir in sweetener and vanilla. Divide evenly into eight 6-ounce mugs. Makes 8 servings.

HEARTY WINTER LUNCHEON FOR FOUR

Onion Bouillon
Creamed Salmon with Vegetables
Hominy Grits and Carrots
Apple Dessert with Creamy Cheese Topping
Hot Coffee or Tea

Here's a hot, hearty, and healthy luncheon that will draw hurrahs from your family. You'll rate extra accolades when they realize it's also economical, since canned salmon goes far when nutritiously combined with cottage cheese and vegetables in a filling casserole. Hominy grits add a warm southern note to your winter scene—and how eye-appealing the grits look when combined with golden carrots and spring-green parsley. (This useful herb is probably the most widely used one in the world!) Wind up this filling meal with a homey apple dessert "topped" by an easily blended creamy cheese crust. The pie and grits bake in the oven at the same temperature—an energy-saving plus. Here's a swift-cooking and easy-to-prepare meal that thriftily serves weight-loss efforts, too.

* * * * *

SUGGESTED SHOPPING LIST

Staples and Miscellaneous

Apple pie spice	Flour
Artificial sweetener	Nonstick cooking spray
Cinnamon	
Instant onion broth and seasoning mix or bouillon cubes	Margarine
Paprika	Raisin bread
Pepper	
Salt	
Vanilla extract	

Additional Items

Canned salmon, 1 15¼-ounce can	Carrots, 4 medium
	Celery, 1 rib
Cottage cheese, 1 16-ounce container	Parsley, 1 bunch
Skim milk, 1 cup	
	Canned sliced mushrooms, 1 8-ounce can
Apples, 4 small	
Broccoli, 1 pound	Hominy grits, 1 16-ounce container

Blender or food processor
Can opener
Casseroles, 2 (1-quart)
Casserole, 1 (1-quart, shallow,
  flameproof)
Chef's knife
Cutting board
Double boiler
Measuring cups

Measuring spoons
Pot holder
Saucepans
Scale
Spatula
Vegetable peeler
Wire whisk
Wooden spoon

ONION BOUILLON

Dissolve 4 packets instant onion broth and seasoning mix or 4 onion bouillon cubes in 3 cups boiling water. Slice 1 celery rib into 4 equal sticks. Pour ¾ cup bouillon into each of 4 mugs. Serve each portion with a celery-stick stirrer. Makes 4 servings.

CREAMED SALMON WITH VEGETABLES

1 tablespoon margarine
1 tablespoon flour
1 cup skim milk
⅔ cup cottage cheese
1½ cups cooked chopped
  broccoli

8 ounces drained canned salmon,
  flaked
½ cup drained, canned sliced
  mushrooms
¼ cup diced celery
Salt, pepper, and paprika to taste

Melt margarine in top of double boiler, over boiling water. Using wire whisk, stir in flour. Stirring constantly, gradually add milk and cook until smooth. Continue to cook, stirring often, until sauce thickens. Stir in cottage cheese. Add remaining ingredients; cook for 5 minutes. Transfer to shallow, flameproof 1-quart casserole and broil for 1 minute. Makes 4 servings.

HOMINY GRITS AND CARROTS

2 cups sliced carrots, blanched
1½ cups cooked enriched
  hominy grits
Artificial sweetener to equal 4
  teaspoons sugar (optional)

1 tablespoon chopped fresh
  parsley
¼ teaspoon cinnamon

Combine all ingredients in 1-quart casserole. Bake at 350°F. for 20 minutes or until thoroughly heated. Makes 4 servings.

APPLE DESSERT WITH CREAMY CHEESE TOPPING

4 small apples, pared, cored, and
cut into thin slices
Artificial sweetener to equal 2
teaspoons sugar
1½ teaspoons apple pie spice

½ teaspoon vanilla extract
⅔ cup cottage cheese
2 slices raisin bread, torn into
pieces

Place apples in 1-quart casserole that has been sprayed with nonstick cooking spray. Stir in sweetener, apple pie spice, and vanilla. Combine cottage cheese and bread in blender container or food processor; process until smooth. Spoon cheese topping evenly over apple mixture. Bake at 350°F. for 45 minutes or until apples are tender. Makes 4 servings

February

What could be more enjoyable during the heart of winter than our February fare? Featured are creamy hot soups, fruit desserts, even a "trip to the Orient"! A winter wonderland awaits you and your guests!

A MIDDAY MEAL FOR WINTER WEEKEND GUESTS FOR FOUR

Creamed Cauliflower Soup
Egg "Cupcakes" with Ham
Scalloped Tomatoes □ Onion Surprise
Cucumbers in Yogurt Dressing
Apple-Pineapple Pie
Hot Cocoa

Mark Twain jestingly called cauliflower "cabbage with college education"! Show off how smart *you* are by treating weekend guests to a few well-thought-out culinary surprises. Begin by "graduating" cauliflower into a warming creamed soup garnished with parsley for eye appeal. These colors are picked up again in the green cucumber salad with its snow-white yogurt dressing. Cleverly transform routine ham-and-eggs into "cupcakes" baked in muffin tins! This unexpected treat is accompanied by a few other eye-openers, such as onions with a sweet glaze of apricot preserves and tomatoes topped with crunchy diced toast for a texture contrast. You're also cannily conserving energy by choosing dishes that bake in the oven at the same temperature. The pie should be made ahead of time and chilled to give the gelatin base time to firm. Of course, the most intelligent thing is that all these luscious dishes are amazingly helpful in weight control!

———◆·◆·———

SUGGESTED SHOPPING LIST

Staples and Miscellaneous

Apple pie spice	Flour
Artificial sweetener	Nonstick cooking spray
Dehydrated onion flakes	Unflavored gelatin
Garlic powder	Unsweetened cocoa
Nutmeg	
Salt	Imitation (or diet) margarine
Vanilla extract	Sesame oil
White pepper	
	Whole wheat bread
Soy sauce	
Worcestershire sauce	Low-calorie apricot preserves

Cooked ham, 6 ounces

Eggs, 4

Plain unflavored yogurt, 2 16-ounce containers

Skim milk, 1 quart

Apples, 4 small

Cauliflower, 1 head
Cucumbers, 2 medium
Lettuce, 1 head
Parsley, 1 bunch

Frozen small white onions, 1 16-ounce bag

Canned crushed pineapple, no sugar added, 1 20-ounce can

Canned tomatoes, 1 28-ounce can

Lemon-lime-flavored dietetic soda, 1 12-fluid-ounce can

SUGGESTED EQUIPMENT LIST

Bowls
Casseroles, 2 (1-quart)
Chef's knife
Cutting board
Double boiler
Fork
Grater
Measuring cups
Measuring spoons

Muffin tin
Pie plate (9-inch)
Pot holder
Saucepan (large)
Toaster
Vegetable peeler
Wire whisk
Wooden spoon

CREAMED CAULIFLOWER SOUP

1 tablespoon imitation (or diet) margarine
2 tablespoons flour
¼ teaspoon nutmeg
1 cup skim milk

1 cup water
2 cups cooked cauliflower florets
Salt and white pepper to taste
Chopped fresh parsley to garnish

Melt margarine in top of double boiler, over boiling water. Add flour and nutmeg; stir to combine. Using wire whisk, gradually stir in milk and water; cook, stirring constantly, until smooth. Stir in cauliflower; cook until thoroughly heated. Season with salt and white pepper and garnish with chopped parsley. Makes 4 servings.

EGG "CUPCAKES" WITH HAM

4 eggs
Salt and white pepper to taste

6 ounces diced cooked ham

Spray 4 cups of a muffin tin with nonstick cooking spray. Carefully crack and slide 1 egg into each muffin cup. Season to taste. Bake at 375°F. for 10 minutes or until set. Remove eggs from tin. Top each egg with 1½ ounces diced cooked ham. Makes 4 servings.

SCALLOPED TOMATOES

2 cups canned tomatoes, diced
2 tablespoons dehydrated onion
  flakes, reconstituted in 2
  tablespoons water
Artificial sweetener to equal 2
  teaspoons sugar (optional)

¼ teaspoon garlic powder
¼ teaspoon salt
⅛ teaspoon pepper
4 slices whole wheat bread,
  toasted and diced

In bowl combine tomatoes, onion flakes, sweetener if desired, garlic powder, salt, and pepper; mix well. Spoon ½ of tomato mixture into 1-quart casserole; top with ½ of diced toast. Repeat layers. Bake at 375°F. for 30 minutes. Makes 4 servings.

ONION SURPRISE

2 cups cooked small white onions
2 tablespoons low-calorie apricot
  preserves, heated

1 tablespoon imitation (or diet)
  margarine

Combine all ingredients in 1-quart casserole. Bake at 375°F. for 25 minutes. Stir to coat onions with sauce. Makes 4 servings.

CUCUMBERS IN YOGURT DRESSING

2 cups plain unflavored yogurt
1 tablespoon soy sauce
1 teaspoon sesame oil
1 teaspoon Worcestershire sauce
⅛ teaspoon garlic powder

2 medium cucumbers, pared,
  scored, and cut into ¼-inch
  slices
2 cups lettuce leaves

In medium bowl combine yogurt, soy sauce, sesame oil, Worcestershire, and garlic powder. Add cucumbers; toss to combine. Serve on bed of lettuce leaves. Makes 4 servings.

APPLE-PINEAPPLE PIE

1 cup lemon-lime-flavored
  dietetic soda
1 envelope unflavored gelatin
4 small apples, pared, cored, and
  sliced
1 cup canned crushed pineapple,
  no sugar added

Artificial sweetener to equal 12
  teaspoons sugar
1 teaspoon vanilla extract
¼ teaspoon apple pie spice

Pour lemon-lime soda into large saucepan. Sprinkle gelatin over soda and allow to soften; cook over low heat, stirring constantly, until gelatin is dissolved. Remove from heat; stir in remaining ingredients. Transfer to a 9-inch pie pan. Bake at 350°F. for 1 hour. Chill until firm. Makes 4 servings.

HOT COCOA

3 cups skim milk
Artificial sweetener to equal 12
  teaspoons sugar

1 tablespoon plus 1 teaspoon
  unsweetened cocoa
1 teaspoon vanilla extract

Combine all ingredients in saucepan. Heat, stirring constantly, until cocoa is dissolved and mixture is hot. Makes 4 servings.

HEARTY NEW ORLEANS BREAKFAST
FOR EIGHT

Chicken Bouillon
Chicken Florentine
Fruit à l'Orange
Coffee or Tea

New Orleans's famed French Quarter is a mecca for gourmets. Dining in style begins soon after dawn there, for its world-renowned restaurants specialize in memorable breakfast menus. Delight your own visitors with this slimming adaptation of a New Orleans favorite—Chicken Florentine—a dish brought to the New World from France by marriageable mademoiselles who knew the culinary way to a man's heart! Sweeten the meal with Fruit à l'Orange, a Gallic treat. What a gourmet way to start the day!

SUGGESTED SHOPPING LIST

Staples and Miscellaneous

Artificial sweetener
Garlic powder
Instant chicken broth and seasoning
  mix or bouillon cubes
Nutmeg
Pepper
Salt
Vanilla extract

Cornstarch
Flour

Imitation (or diet) margarine

English muffins

Additional Items

Chicken breasts, skinned and boned,
  12 ounces

Lemon, 1
Papayas, 2 medium

Frozen orange juice concentrate,
  1 6-fluid-ounce can

Frozen chopped spinach, 1 10-ounce
  package

Evaporated skimmed milk, 1 13-fluid-
  ounce can

Prunes, medium, 1 16-ounce box

Bowls
Can opener
Casseroles, 8 (small)
Chef's knife
Double boiler
Measuring cups
Measuring spoons

Metal spoon
Paring knife
Pot holder
Saucepans (small and large)
Strainer
Toaster
Wooden spoon

CHICKEN BOUILLON

Dissolve 8 packets instant chicken broth and seasoning mix or 8 chicken bouillon cubes in 1½ quarts boiling water. Divide evenly into 8 mugs. Makes 8 servings.

CHICKEN FLORENTINE

*12 ounces skinned and boned
    chicken breasts
1 quart water
1 tablespoon lemon juice
¼ teaspoon garlic powder
Salt and pepper to taste
1 tablespoon plus 1 teaspoon
    imitation (or diet) margarine*

*1 tablespoon plus 1 teaspoon
    flour
⅛ teaspoon nutmeg
1 cup evaporated skimmed milk
8 English muffins, split into
    halves and toasted
1 cup cooked frozen chopped
    spinach*

Dice chicken breasts. In saucepan combine water, lemon juice, garlic powder, salt, and pepper; bring to a boil. Add diced chicken; reduce heat and simmer 10 minutes. Drain and set chicken aside. In top of double boiler, over boiling water, melt margarine. Add flour and nutmeg; stir to combine. Stirring constantly, gradually add milk and cook until thickened. Remove from heat. Place 2 English muffin halves in each of 8 small casseroles. Top each serving of muffins with 2 tablespoons of spinach, 1 ounce of chicken, and ⅛ of the white sauce; bake at 350°F. for 10 minutes or until heated. Makes 8 servings.

FRUIT À L'ORANGE

*1 cup orange juice
1 tablespoon lemon juice
1 tablespoon plus 1 teaspoon
    cornstarch, dissolved in 2
    tablespoons water
Artificial sweetener to equal 2
    teaspoons sugar (optional)*

*1 teaspoon vanilla extract
2 medium papayas, pared,
    seeded, and diced
6 medium prunes, pitted and
    quartered*

[72]

Combine orange and lemon juices in small saucepan; bring to a boil. Stirring constantly, add dissolved cornstarch and cook until thickened. Stir in sweetener if desired, and vanilla. Remove from heat. Place papayas and prunes in serving bowl. Pour orange sauce over fruit; stir to combine. Chill at least 2 hours. Makes 8 servings.

CAMPUS PARTY FOR SIX

Vegetable Soup
Chicken Livers Harlequin
Bean Sprout Salad
Orange Sherbet
Beverage

The savvy college crowd knows that liver rates A+ in nutrition. You'll rate high marks yourself when you serve chicken livers with the imaginative harlequin colors of celery, carrots and green peppers. For an off-beat touch, serve the chicken livers on barley. Let your entrée keep company with a dish popular among health-conscious youths: Bean Sprout Salad. For a sure-fire crowd-pleaser, top off the evening with sherbet. Everything except the swift-cooking livers can be prepared ahead of time and easily reheated—smart thinking, especially if you're whipping up dinner on a two-burner in a dorm. The menu's easy on a slender purse (as well as on your hopefully slender friends)! You don't have to worry about providing a dining table or chairs, either. Since every dish is fork-food, your guests can sprawl anywhere.

———— •••• ————

SUGGESTED SHOPPING LIST

Staples and Miscellaneous

Artificial sweetener
Cinnamon
Garlic powder
Ginger
Instant beef broth and seasoning mix
Oregano
Peppercorns
Salt
Vanilla extract
White pepper

Cider vinegar

Vegetable oil

Chicken Stock, 1 quart plus ½ cup
(see page 31) or 6 packets instant
chicken broth and seasoning mix or
bouillon cubes

Additional Items

Chicken livers, 2¼ pounds

Lemons, 3

Bean sprouts, 1 pound
Carrots, 2 medium
Celery, 6 ribs
Garlic clove, 1
Green beans, ½ pound
Green peppers, 2 medium
Onions, 2 large

Frozen orange juice concentrate,
1 6-fluid-ounce can

Tomato sauce, 1 28-ounce can

Evaporated skimmed milk, 2 13-fluid-
ounce cans

Barley, 1 16-ounce box

SUGGESTED EQUIPMENT LIST

Bowls
Can opener
Chef's knife
Cutting board
Measuring cups
Measuring spoons
Pepper mill

Pot holder
Saucepans
Scale
Strainer
Vegetable peeler
Wooden spoon

VEGETABLE SOUP

1 quart plus ½ cup Chicken
Stock (see page 31)*
1½ cups cut green beans, 1-inch
pieces

1½ cups thinly sliced celery
1 cup diced onions
Freshly ground pepper to taste

Combine all ingredients in saucepan. Bring to a boil; reduce heat and simmer until vegetables are tender. Divide evenly into 6 mugs. Makes 6 servings.

* If stock is not available, use 6 packets instant chicken broth and seasoning mix or 6 chicken bouillon cubes, dissolved in 1 quart plus ½ cup hot water.

CHICKEN LIVERS HARLEQUIN

2¼ pounds chicken livers
1 cup diced onions
1 cup finely diced celery
1 cup finely diced carrots
2 medium green peppers, seeded
and diced
2 packets instant beef broth and
seasoning mix

1 garlic clove, minced
⅛ teaspoon each ginger and
cinnamon
2 cups tomato sauce
2 tablespoons lemon juice
3 cups cooked barley (see Note)

Place livers in bowl with boiling water to cover. Let stand 3 minutes; drain. Repeat process and set livers aside. In saucepan combine next 7 ingredients; cook 3 to 5 minutes. Add tomato sauce and lemon juice; simmer until vegetables are tender. Add livers; simmer 10 minutes or until livers are done to taste. Serve over hot barley. Makes 6 servings.

Note. Barley can be prepared in advance and reheated. To reheat, use any of the following methods:

1. Place barley in a strainer. In medium saucepan, bring ½ cup water to a boil. Place strainer in saucepan, over boiling water. Cover and steam over medium heat about 5 minutes or until thoroughly heated. Be sure that water does not boil out; add more if necessary.

2. Combine barley and ¼ cup plus 2 tablespoons water in saucepan. Cover and cook over low heat for about 4 minutes or until thoroughly heated.

3. Place barley in top half of double boiler, over boiling water. Cover and cook about 10 minutes or until thoroughly heated.

BEAN SPROUT SALAD

5 cups bean sprouts
1 cup grated carrots
¼ cup vegetable oil
2 tablespoons cider vinegar

2 tablespoons lemon juice
1 teaspoon oregano
Dash garlic powder
Salt and white pepper to taste

In bowl combine all ingredients; toss to coat vegetables with dressing. Chill. Makes 6 servings.

ORANGE SHERBET

2 cups evaporated skimmed milk
Artificial sweetener to equal 18 teaspoons sugar
¼ cup frozen orange juice concentrate, thawed

1 tablespoon lemon juice
1 teaspoon vanilla extract

Chill 6 glasses. In bowl combine all ingredients. Freeze, stirring often, until ice crystals form throughout and mixture is firm. If mixture becomes solid, allow to soften in refrigerator for about 20 minutes before serving. Divide evenly into chilled glasses. Makes 6 servings.

AN ELEGANT WINTER LUNCHEON
FOR FOUR

"Crème" of Spinach Soup
Veal Kidneys in Mustard Sauce
Potatoes Bonne Femme
Orange Beets
Braised Celery
Strawberry Bavarian
Herb Tea

Even if the weather outside is frightful, your menu can be delightful if you're determined not to let snowed-in afternoons become humdrum. Enchant your friends (or family) with this elegant French-style menu. Veal has been prized by Parisians for centuries. Our choice veal kidney entrée is accompanied by a savory sauce that blends in the famed mustard of the Dijon region of France. Potatoes take on a special look when they're served "*bonne femme*," and ordinary vegetables are transformed into distinctive Orange Beets and Braised Celery. And how chic to serve fresh strawberries in winter. *Voilà!* You've created a February feast that's bound to draw appreciative cries of "encore"!

———————— ◆◆◆ ————————

SUGGESTED SHOPPING LIST

Staples and Miscellaneous

Artificial sweetener	Cornstarch
Chopped chives	Unflavored gelatin
Instant beef broth and seasoning mix or bouillon cubes	
Instant chicken broth and seasoning mix or bouillon cubes	Imitation (or diet) margarine
Nutmeg	Cider vinegar
Paprika	Dijon mustard
Salt	
Vanilla extract	Low-calorie orange marmalade
White pepper	

Trimmed veal kidneys, 1½ pounds

Plain unflavored yogurt, 1 8-ounce
  container

Lemon, 1
Orange, 1 small
Strawberries, 2 pints, very ripe

Celery, 1 stalk
Onion, 1 small
Parsley, 1 bunch
Potatoes, 1 pound
Shallots, 2 1-ounce packages

Frozen chopped spinach, 2 10-ounce
  packages

Canned sliced beets, 1 16-ounce can

Evaporated skimmed milk, 1 13-fluid-
  ounce can

SUGGESTED EQUIPMENT LIST

Blender
Bowl (small)
Can opener
Casserole (1-quart)
Casserole (1½-quart, shallow)
Chef's knife
Colander
Cutting board

Double boiler
Measuring cups
Measuring spoons
Pot holder
Saucepans, 3 (medium) with covers
Scale
Vegetable peeler
Wooden spoon

"CRÈME" OF SPINACH SOUP

2 cups chicken bouillon
1 cup cooked, frozen chopped
  spinach
⅛ teaspoon nutmeg

Salt and white pepper to taste
½ cup evaporated skimmed milk
1 tablespoon chopped chives

Combine bouillon and spinach in blender container; process until smooth.
Pour into medium saucepan. Season with nutmeg, salt, and white pepper.
Bring to a boil; remove from heat. Slowly pour in milk; cook for 2 minutes longer, stirring constantly. Remove from heat and stir in chives. Makes
4 servings.

VEAL KIDNEYS IN MUSTARD SAUCE

2 tablespoons imitation (or diet)
  margarine
2 tablespoons finely chopped
  shallots

½ cup chicken bouillon
1 teaspoon Dijon mustard
1 pound cooked veal kidneys,
  cut into ¼-inch-thick slices

In top of double boiler, over boiling water, melt margarine. Add shallots;
cook until shallots are tender. Add bouillon and mustard. Cook until hot;
add kidneys. Cook, stirring often, for about 5 minutes or until heated
throughout. Makes 4 servings.

POTATOES BONNE FEMME

1 pound cooked pared
   potatoes, cut into ¼-inch dice
2 tablespoons diced onion
2 tablespoons imitation (or diet)
   margarine, melted

½ teaspoon paprika
Salt and white pepper to taste

Combine all ingredients in shallow 1½-quart casserole. Bake at 400°F. for 30 minutes or until lightly browned. Makes 4 servings.

ORANGE BEETS

1¾ cups drained, canned sliced
   beets; reserve ½ cup beet
   liquid
2 tablespoons low-calorie orange
   marmalade
1 tablespoon cider vinegar

Artificial sweetener to equal 2
   teaspoons sugar (optional)
1 tablespoon cornstarch,
   dissolved in 1 tablespoon
   water
1 teaspoon grated orange rind

In medium saucepan combine reserved liquid from beets, marmalade, vinegar, and sweetener if desired. Cook, stirring occasionally, until hot. Stirring constantly, add cornstarch and cook until thickened. Stir in beets and cook, stirring often, until thoroughly heated. Serve garnished with grated orange rind. Makes 4 servings.

BRAISED CELERY

2 cups celery sticks
½ cup beef bouillon
2 tablespoons chopped fresh
   parsley

1 tablespoon plus 1 teaspoon
   imitation (or diet) margarine

Combine all ingredients in 1-quart casserole. Bake at 400°F. for 30 minutes. Makes 4 servings.

STRAWBERRY BAVARIAN

1 envelope unflavored gelatin
½ cup water
3 cups very ripe strawberries,
   divided
Artificial sweetener to equal 12
   teaspoons sugar

2 teaspoons vanilla extract,
   divided
2 teaspoons lemon juice, divided
½ cup plain unflavored yogurt

In medium saucepan sprinkle gelatin over water; let stand 5 minutes. In blender container puree 2 cups strawberries. Add strawberry puree, sweetener, and 1 teaspoon each vanilla and lemon juice to saucepan. Cook, stirring often, for 10 minutes. Remove from heat; cool to room temperature. Slice remaining berries; combine in small bowl with remaining vanilla and lemon juice. Stir yogurt into cooled puree mixture. Divide evenly into four ¾-cup dessert glasses. Top each portion with ¼ of the sliced strawberries. Chill for at least 4 hours. Makes 4 servings.

A FRANKLY DELICIOUS WASHINGTON'S
BIRTHDAY MENU FOR SIX

Spiked Vegetable Juice on the Rock·
Cherry Red Franks 'n' Noodles
Poppy-Kraut
Minted Zucchini and Carrot Mélange
Puree of Peas
Chilled Fruit Pudding
Spiced Coffee

To perk up mid-winter doldrums, host a birthday party, by George! Celebrate Washington's Birthday in merry style by letting your imagination run riot. Fittingly serve franks because (in case your guests can't guess) our first President was so *frank!* Instead of beans, add a revolutionary accompaniment: noodles. Of course, the sauce gives a nod to the famous cherry tree! Give Old World sauerkraut a new world of taste by seasoning it into "Poppy-Kraut." (If you dare, quip that it's for the "poppy" of his country!) A colorful fruit pudding proves it's no lie that you can enjoy dessert on a weight-loss program. You'll probably want to decorate colorfully too, in meaningful shades of red, white, and blue—to set the tone for a high-jinks party that's low scoring on the scale.

------- •◦• -------

SUGGESTED SHOPPING LIST
Staples and Miscellaneous

Allspice
Artificial sweetener
Chopped chives
Cinnamon
Cloves
Cumin
Curry powder
Dried mint
Ground cloves
Instant chicken broth and seasoning
  mix
Peppercorns
Poppy seeds
Salt

Coffee
Cornstarch

Hot sauce
Worcestershire sauce

Frankfurters, 1 pound 2 ounces

Plain unflavored yogurt, 1 16-ounce container

Strawberries, 1 pint

Carrots, 4 medium
Celery, 2 ribs
Parsley, 1 bunch
Zucchini, 2 medium

Frozen peas, 2 10-ounce packages

Canned crushed pineapple, no sugar added, 1 20-ounce can

Canned pitted cherries, no sugar added, 1 16-ounce can

Canned plums, no sugar added, 2 8½-ounce cans

Pimientos, 1 4-ounce jar
Sauerkraut, 2 16-ounce cans

Evaporated skimmed milk, 1 13-fluid-ounce can

Mixed vegetable juice, 2 12-fluid-ounce cans

Enriched broad noodles, 1 16-ounce box

SUGGESTED EQUIPMENT LIST

Blender
Bowls
Can opener
Casserole (2½-cup)
Chef's knife
Coffee pot
Cutting board
Double boiler

Measuring cups
Measuring spoons
Pepper mill
Pot holder
Saucepans and covers
Scale
Strainer
Wooden spoon

SPIKED VEGETABLE JUICE ON THE ROCKS

3 cups mixed vegetable juice
¼ cup plus 2 tablespoons chopped celery
2 teaspoons Worcestershire sauce
1½ teaspoons chopped fresh parsley

¼ teaspoon hot sauce, or to taste
Salt and pepper to taste
Ice cubes

Combine all ingredients except ice cubes in blender container; process for 30 seconds. Partially fill 6 glasses with ice. Pour an equal amount of juice mixture into each glass. Makes 6 servings.

CHERRY RED FRANKS 'N' NOODLES

1 pound 2 ounces sliced
   frankfurters
1½ cups canned pitted cherries,
   no sugar added
¼ cup water
Artificial sweetener to equal 4
   teaspoons sugar

⅛ teaspoon cinnamon
1 tablespoon cornstarch,
   dissolved in 1 tablespoon water
3 cups hot, cooked enriched
   broad noodles

In saucepan combine frankfurters, cherries, water, sweetener, and cinnamon. Bring to a boil. Reduce heat and simmer 15 minutes. Stir in cornstarch; cook, stirring constantly, for 5 minutes. Place noodles in serving dish. Serve frankfurters and cherry sauce over noodles. Makes 6 servings.

POPPY-KRAUT

2 cups drained canned
   sauerkraut
¾ cup chicken bouillon
½ cup diced pimientos

1 tablespoon poppy seeds
½ teaspoon chopped chives
⅛ teaspoon cumin

Combine all ingredients in saucepan. Cook, stirring occasionally, until thoroughly heated. Makes 6 servings.

MINTED ZUCCHINI AND CARROT MÉLANGE

2 cups thinly sliced carrots
¾ cup chicken bouillon
2 cups thinly sliced zucchini

½ teaspoon dried mint
Salt and pepper to taste

In saucepan combine carrots and bouillon. Bring to a boil; reduce heat and simmer 5 minutes. Add zucchini; cover and cook 5 minutes longer. Season with mint, salt, and pepper. Makes 6 servings.

PUREE OF PEAS

3 cups cooked frozen peas
¼ cup evaporated skimmed milk
1 packet instant chicken broth
   and seasoning mix

¼ teaspoon curry powder
Salt and freshly ground pepper
   to taste

Combine all ingredients in blender container; process until smooth. Transfer to 2½-cup casserole. Bake at 350°F. for 15 minutes. Makes 6 servings.

CHILLED FRUIT PUDDING

6 canned plums with ¼ cup plus
   2 tablespoons juice, no sugar
   added
1 cup canned crushed pineapple,
   no sugar added
1½ cups plain unflavored yogurt
2 tablespoons water

2 tablespoons cornstarch,
   dissolved in 2 tablespoons
   water
Artificial sweetener to equal 4
   teaspoons sugar
1 cup strawberries, sliced

Dice plums and set aside. Drain juice from pineapple into top of double boiler, over boiling water. Add plum juice, yogurt, and water; cook until hot, stirring often. Stirring constantly, add cornstarch and sweetener and cook until thickened. Divide mixture in half. Stir pineapple into one half of mixture; stir plums into the other half. Spoon pineapple mixture into 1-quart glass bowl; top with strawberries. Spoon plum mixture over strawberries. Chill overnight. Makes 6 servings.

SPICED COFFEE

1½ quarts hot coffee
Ground cloves, cinnamon,
   allspice, and artificial
   sweetener to taste

½ cup evaporated skimmed
   milk, heated

Divide coffee into 6 mugs. Invite each guest to sprinkle coffee with desired amount of cloves, cinnamon, allspice, and sweetener. Pour an equal amount of heated milk into each mug. Makes 6 servings.

THE CHINESE FIRE POT FOR FOUR

Assorted Seafood and Vegetables
cooked in simmering Chinese Chicken Broth

Condiments for Dipping
Chinese Mustard ☐ Plum Sauce ☐ Red Sauce

Fluffy White Rice

Chicken-Rice Soup
made from the broth in
which foods were cooked

Tangerine Sections
Chinese Tea

Eating becomes an experience when it's a Chinese Fire Pot dinner. This Oriental answer to the chafing dish blends fun with feasting as each diner dips portions of food into broth on a cook-it-yourself basis, and then samples a tantalizing array of mustards and sauces. We've supplied easy directions for this intriguing style of dining, and our menu adaptations are true to the spirit of Chinese cuisine. Seafood is featured, since fish is to the East what beef is to the West. Vegetables also appear in abundance and should be cut into uniform-size pieces, since the Chinese wisely value eye appeal. Serve our colorful version of Red Sauce—so-called because in certain areas of China the soy is so dark it imparts a reddish color to foods cooked in it. Plum Sauce is our adaptation of sweet-and-sour sauce, converted into sweetly slimming fare. A fruit dessert is also traditional. We suggest tangerines, which originated in China.

Staples and Miscellaneous

Artificial sweetener
Dry mustard
Instant chicken broth and seasoning
  mix
Salt

Cider vinegar
Hot sauce
Ketchup
Red wine vinegar
Soy sauce
Worcestershire sauce

Cornstarch
Chinese tea

Additional Items

Shucked clams, 6 ounces
Fish fillets, 6 ounces
Scallops, 6 ounces
Shrimp or shelled lobster, 6 ounces

Chinese cabbage, 1 small head
Garlic clove, 1
Ginger root, 1
Green beans, ½ pound

Lemon, 1
Pear, 1 small
Tangerines, 4 large

Canned plums, no sugar added, 1 8½-
  ounce can

Broccoli, 1 small bunch
Carrots, 3 medium
Cauliflower, 1 small head
Celery, 4 ribs

Tomato puree, 1 16-ounce can

Dried Chinese mushrooms, ½ pound
Enriched white rice, 1 16-ounce box

SUGGESTED EQUIPMENT LIST

Blender
Bowls (small)
Can opener
Chef's knife or cleaver
Chinese fire pot, fondue pot, or
  electric skillet
Colander
Corer
Cutting board

Measuring cups
Measuring spoons
Paring knife
Pot holder
Saucepans and covers (small and
  medium)
Scale
Vegetable peeler
Wooden spoon

THE FIRE POT

One of the most unusual yet outstanding of Chinese specialties is the fire pot. This is not merely a piece of equipment but an entire style of dining. Our adaptation of this unique method can utilize the authentic apparatus, which is a pot that stands in the middle of a round table and has a chimneylike extension in the middle Charcoal is burned in its base to heat the liquid in the pot. If you are unable to acquire this cooking–serving piece, a fondue pot or electric skillet makes an acceptable substitute.

The table setting for each person should include:

—a plate
—a dinner fork or chopsticks
—a small fork, tongs, or wire strainer
—3 small dishes—1 filled with 1 serving Chinese Mustard (see recipe, page 89), 1 filled with 1 serving Plum Sauce (see recipe, page 89), and 1 filled with 1 serving Red Sauce (see recipe, page 89)
—a bowl filled with ½ cup Fluffy White Rice (see page 32)
—a soup spoon

Pour Chinese Chicken Broth (see recipe, page 88) into the pot; keep liquid simmering throughout the meal. As liquid reduces, add more boiling water. Using the small fork, tongs, or wire strainer, each guest dips a piece of seafood or vegetable into the broth and allows it to cook until done to taste. The food is then transferred to a dinner fork or chopsticks and dipped into either the mustard or one of the sauces. The rice is eaten throughout the meal. After all guests have finished their portions of fish and vegetables, Chicken-Rice Soup is made by ladling an equal amount of the remaining broth into each rice bowl. Any remaining rice in the bowl is then consumed with the broth.

SEAFOOD FOR FIRE POT

6 ounces skinned and boned fish,
  cut into 1-inch pieces
6 ounces shucked clams

6 ounces peeled and deveined
  shrimp or shelled lobster, cut
  into 1-inch pieces
6 ounces scallops

Place 6 ounces of mixed seafood on each plate. Follow preceding directions for cooking. Makes 4 servings.

VEGETABLES FOR FIRE POT

A variety of colorful and crisp fresh vegetables are a traditional and important part of Chinese cuisine. Careful preparation of these vegetables is a key to success. Follow these preparation directions for the assortment given and place an equal amount on each plate. Follow preceding directions for cooking. Makes 4 servings.

Broccoli

Trim away leaves and tough stalks. Cut into florets; measure 1 cup. Place in medium saucepan with boiling salted water to cover; simmer for 5 minutes. Run under cool water; drain. Pat dry and refrigerate until needed.

Cauliflower

Cut off tough end of stem; remove and discard leaves. Break into florets; measure 1 cup. Place in medium saucepan with boiling salted water to cover; simmer for 6 minutes. Run under cool water; drain. Pat dry and refrigerate until needed.

Carrots

Scrape and cut into thin strips; measure 1 cup. Place in medium saucepan with boiling salted water to cover; simmer for 5 minutes. Run under cool water; drain. Pat dry and refrigerate until needed.

Chinese Cabbage

Wash well; cut crosswise into 1½-inch strips. Measure 1 cup. Place in medium saucepan with boiling salted water to cover; simmer for 5 minutes. Run under cool water; drain. Pat dry and refrigerate until needed.

Green Beans

Snip off ends; measure 1 cup. Place in medium saucepan with boiling salted water to cover; simmer for 5 minutes. Run under cool water; drain. Pat dry and refrigerate until needed.

Celery

Separate ribs by cutting off root end; trim away leaves. Remove stringy fibers with vegetable peeler. Slice diagonally; measure 1 cup. Place in medium saucepan with boiling salted water to cover; simmer for 5 minutes. Run under cool water; drain. Pat dry and refrigerate until needed.

CHINESE CHICKEN BROTH

¼ cup dried Chinese mushrooms
1 quart water
2 tablespoons soy sauce
5 packets instant chicken broth
and seasoning mix

1 slice fresh ginger root,
shredded

In small bowl soak mushrooms in hot water to cover for about 20 minutes or until soft. Drain. Remove and discard mushroom stems; slice caps. Place in large saucepan; add 1 quart water and remaining ingredients. Bring to a boil; transfer to fire pot and use as directed on page 86. Makes 4 servings.

CHINESE MUSTARD

2 tablespoons hot tea
1 tablespoon dry mustard

Artificial sweetener to equal 1
teaspoon sugar

In small bowl combine all ingredients. Serve at room temperature. Makes 4 servings.

PLUM SAUCE

4 canned plums with ¼ cup
juice, no sugar added
1 small pear, pared, cored, and
diced
2 tablespoons red wine vinegar
Artificial sweetener to equal 2
teaspoons sugar

1 slice fresh ginger root, minced
1 garlic clove, minced
½ teaspoon soy sauce
¼ teaspoon lemon juice
2 teaspoons cornstarch,
dissolved in 2 tablespoons
water

Remove and discard pits from plums. In blender container combine plums with remaining ingredients except cornstarch; process until smooth. Pour mixture into small saucepan. Bring to a boil; reduce heat. Stir in dissolved cornstarch. Simmer for 10 minutes or until mixture thickens, stirring occasionally. Serve at room temperature. Makes 4 servings.

RED SAUCE

½ cup tomato puree
2 tablespoons plus 2 teaspoons
ketchup
2 tablespoons cider vinegar

1 tablespoon Worcestershire
sauce
Dash hot sauce

Combine all ingredients in small saucepan; cover and simmer for 10 minutes. Serve at room temperature. Makes 4 servings.

TANGERINE SECTIONS

Peel and section 4 large tangerines, placing each tangerine on an individual dessert plate. Makes 4 servings.

March

Looking for new ways to serve readily
available vegetables? Our March menus
offer an array of appetizers using
eggplant, as well as mushrooms, in a
variety of forms, such as steamed,
stuffed, marinated, and as a topping!
Welcome spring with these
new taste treats!

SIMPLE SOIREE FOR SIX

Eggplant Caviar in Cherry Tomatoes
Veal with Lemon Sauce and Noodles
Tiny Peas Cooked in Lettuce
Poached Pears in Lemon Gelatin
Sparkling Mineral Water with Lime Slice

A "soiree"—according to Webster—is a social gathering, "especially one held for a particular purpose." The aim of this soiree is to enjoy feasting along with friendship in friendly weight-controlling style. The menu looks impressive, but behind the scenes it's rewardingly easy and economical. Advance preparation is the key that frees you to spend more time with your guests. Eggplant Caviar should be made the night before and chilled. Dessert can also be made in advance and safely stored in the refrigerator. No one seeing the savory result would believe the elegant-looking Poached Pears are just an in-season fruit and packaged gelatin. *Petit pois* (small peas) were the rage of seventeenth-century Parisian nobles, and they'll score regally on your dining table when cleverly cooked with lettuce leaves in what is actually an easy, one-pot recipe. The vegetables and gourmet-style entrée actually take less than half an hour to prepare! So when the doorbell rings, you're ready to greet your guests in relaxed form—proving that successful hosting doesn't have to be a hassle.

———— •◆• ————

SUGGESTED SHOPPING LIST

Staples and Miscellaneous

Cinnamon
Instant chicken broth and seasoning
   mix
Marjoram
Paprika
Peppercorns
Salt
White pepper

Capers

Imitation (or diet) margarine

Veal cutlets, 2¼ pounds

Plain unflavored yogurt, 1 8-ounce container

Lemons, 3
Lime, 1
Pears, 6 small, firm

Carrot, 1 medium
Celery, 1 rib
Cherry tomatoes, 2 pints
Eggplant, 1 small (approximately 12 ounces)
Garlic cloves, 2
Lettuce, 1 medium head
Mint, 1 bunch

Parsley, 1 bunch
Scallions, 1 bunch

Frozen tiny peas, 2 10-ounce packages

Canned button mushrooms, 1 16-ounce can

Enriched broad noodles, 1 16-ounce box

Lemon-flavored low-calorie gelatin, 1⅝-ounce box

Cream-flavored dietetic soda, 1 28-fluid-ounce bottle

Sparkling mineral water, 1 48-fluid-ounce bottle

SUGGESTED EQUIPMENT LIST

Baking pan
Bowls (small)
Can opener
Chef's knife
Colander
Cutting board
Fork
Kitchen hammer (pounder)
Large nonstick skillet
Measuring cups

Measuring spoons
Pepper mill
Pot holder
Rack
Saucepans (small, medium, large)
Scale
Serving dish (1-quart, shallow)
Vegetable peeler
Wooden spoon

EGGPLANT CAVIAR IN CHERRY TOMATOES

1 small eggplant, about 12 ounces
¼ cup finely diced celery
¼ cup finely diced carrot
2 tablespoons plain unflavored yogurt

1 teaspoon lemon juice
¼ teaspoon marjoram
⅛ teaspoon minced fresh garlic
24 medium cherry tomatoes
24 capers

Pierce eggplant all over with prongs of fork. Place on rack in baking pan. Bake at 425°F. for 1 hour or until very tender and skin is shriveled. Remove from oven; cool slightly. Cut open and measure ½ cup eggplant pulp.* Place in small bowl; mash with fork. Add celery, carrot, yogurt, lemon juice, marjoram, and garlic. Stir well to combine. Chill overnight or at least 3 hours. Cut off thin slice from stem end of each cherry tomato. Scoop out and discard seeds and pulp, leaving firm shell. Divide eggplant mixture into 24 equal portions, about 1½ teaspoons each. Stuff each portion of eggplant into a cherry tomato. Garnish each with a caper. Chill until ready to serve. Makes 6 servings.

* Reserve remaining eggplant for use at another time.

VEAL WITH LEMON SAUCE AND NOODLES

2¼ pounds veal cutlets
1 cup drained canned button
  mushrooms
1 cup water
2 packets instant chicken broth
  and seasoning mix
¼ cup imitation (or diet)
  margarine
2 tablespoons lemon juice

1 tablespoon chopped fresh
  parsley
1 garlic clove, crushed
Salt and white pepper to taste
3 cups cooked enriched broad
  noodles
Paprika and parsley sprigs to
  garnish
1 lemon, cut into 6 slices

Pound veal into ¼-inch thickness; cut into 1-inch-wide strips. In large nonstick skillet brown veal for 3 minutes on each side; add mushrooms, water, and broth mix. Cook for 10 minutes. Keep warm until ready to serve. Melt margarine in small saucepan; add lemon juice, chopped parsley, garlic, salt, and pepper. Remove from heat. Place ½ cup noodles on each of 6 plates. Divide veal–mushroom mixture into 6 equal servings. Top each portion of noodles with 1 serving veal mixture. Spoon ⅙ of the lemon sauce over each serving and sprinkle each with paprika. Garnish with parsley sprigs and lemon slices. Makes 6 servings.

TINY PEAS COOKED IN LETTUCE

½ medium head lettuce,
  shredded
2⅔ cups frozen tiny peas
⅓ cup finely chopped scallions

¼ teaspoon salt
Dash freshly ground pepper
¾ cup water

Line bottom of medium saucepan with lettuce. Add peas and scallions. Season with salt and pepper. Add water. Bring to a boil. Cover; reduce heat and simmer 5 to 7 minutes or until peas are tender. Makes 6 servings.

POACHED PEARS IN LEMON GELATIN

3 cups cream-flavored dietetic
  soda
6 firm, small pears with stems,
  pared
1 envelope lemon-flavored low-
  calorie gelatin (4 servings)

½ cup water
1 tablespoon cinnamon
Lemon twists and mint leaves to
  garnish

In large saucepan bring soda to a boil. Add pears; reduce heat and simmer, turning occasionally, for 15 minutes or until pears are soft. Transfer pears to a plate; measure and reserve 1½ cups cooking liquid. In saucepan sprinkle gelatin over ½ cup water; let stand a few minutes to soften. Add reserved cooking liquid; cook over low heat, stirring constantly, until gelatin is dissolved. Pour into shallow 1-quart serving dish; chill for 30 minutes. Stand pears in gelatin; sprinkle with cinnamon. Refrigerate for at least 3 hours. When ready to serve, garnish with lemon twists and mint leaves. Makes 6 servings.

ANNIVERSARY PARTY FOR EIGHT

Hot Garlic-Cucumber Soup
Piquant Liver and Noodles
Steamed Mushrooms and Turnips
Green Salad with Sesame Dressing
Piña Whip
Beverage

Novelty is the ingredient that's said to add interest to a marriage . . . and novelty certainly adds zest to this Anniversary Party menu. It's filled with unexpected delights, such as cucumbers served in a hot soup enhanced with a whisper of garlic. The occasion merits a special entrée like Piquant Liver —and you'll *pique* your guests' interest when you serve it casserole style, "married" to a rich vinegar sauce. (Adaptability, another feature of a good marriage, applies to this recipe too, for the casserole can be made with poultry instead of liver, and the versatile sauce can also accompany other meats.) Team mushrooms and turnips steamed—a cooking method that brings out vegetables' best color and taste. Sesame dresses up salad in distinctive style. Sweeten the occasion with a luscious Piña Whip that's an easy blender recipe. This fortunate combination of dishes is compatible with everyone's weight-loss efforts.

———————◆◆◆———————

SUGGESTED SHOPPING LIST

Staples and Miscellaneous

Artificial sweetener
Bay leaves
Dill weed
Garlic powder
Instant beef broth and seasoning mix
Instant chicken broth and seasoning mix
Oregano
Peppercorns
Pineapple extract

Salt
Thyme

Browning sauce
Red wine vinegar

Cornstarch
Nonfat dry milk powder
Unflavored gelatin

Imitation (or diet) margarine
Sesame oil

Calf liver, 3 pounds

Lemon, 1

Carrots, 4 medium
Cucumbers, 2 medium
Garlic cloves, 9
Iceberg lettuce, 1 medium head
Romaine lettuce, small head
Mint, 1 bunch
Mushrooms, 2 pounds
Onions, 3 large (about 1½ pounds)
Parsley, 1 bunch

Radishes, 1 bag
Turnips, 8 medium
Watercress, 1 bunch

Canned crushed pineapple, no sugar
added. 1 20-ounce can

Tomato puree, 1 16-ounce can

Evaporated skimmed milk. 1 13-fluid
ounce can

Enriched broad noodles, 1 16-ounce
box

SUGGESTED EQUIPMENT LIST

Blender
Bowl (small)
Can opener
Chef's knife
Cutting board
Grater
Measuring cups
Measuring spoons
Large pot

Pepper mill
Pot holder
Saucepans (small, medium)
Scale
Steamer insert and 2-quart saucepan
Towel
Vegetable peeler
Wooden spoon

HOT GARLIC-CUCUMBER SOUP

2 cups grated, pared cucumbers
8 packets instant chicken broth
 and seasoning mix
4 garlic cloves, pressed

1 teaspoon dill weed
1½ quarts water
1 cup evaporated skimmed milk

Squeeze excess moisture from grated cucumbers. In saucepan combine cucumbers, broth mix, garlic, and dill. Cook, stirring often, for 5 minutes. Add water; simmer for 10 minutes. Remove from heat. Gradually add milk. Return to heat and cook until hot, but *do not boil*. Makes 8 servings.

PIQUANT LIVER AND NOODLES

3 pounds calf liver, cut into
 ½-inch strips
Salt, pepper, and garlic powder
 to taste
4 cups quartered mushrooms
3 cups diced onions, 1-inch dice
2 cups thinly sliced carrots
1 cup tomato puree
4 packets instant beef broth and
 seasoning mix
2 teaspoons browning sauce
4 large garlic cloves, minced

1 bay leaf
½ teaspoon thyme
Freshly ground pepper to taste
1¼ quarts water
¼ cup red wine vinegar
2 tablespoons plus 2 teaspoons
 cornstarch, dissolved in 3
 tablespoons water
4 cups hot, cooked enriched
 broad noodles
2 tablespoons plus 2 teaspoons
 imitation (or diet) margarine

Season liver with salt, pepper, and garlic powder. Place liver in small roasting pan; bake at 400°F. until firm. Set aside. Combine next 10 ingredients in large pot; cook for 10 minutes. Add water and vinegar; bring to a boil. Reduce heat and simmer until carrots are tender. Stir in dissolved cornstarch. Cook, stirring occasionally, until sauce thickens. Add liver; heat thoroughly. Remove and discard bay leaf. In large serving bowl combine hot noodles and margarine; toss lightly to coat noodles. Top noodles with liver-vegetable mixture. Makes 8 servings.

STEAMED MUSHROOMS AND TURNIPS

4 cups pared turnips, cut into
 thin strips
2 cups sliced mushrooms
2 cups water
2 tablespoons plus 2 teaspoons
 imitation (or diet) margarine,
 melted

½ teaspoon chopped fresh
 parsley
⅛ teaspoon garlic powder

Combine turnips and mushrooms in steamer insert. Pour water into 2-quart pan. Set insert in pan and place over medium heat. When water begins to boil, cover pan and steam for 6 to 8 minutes. Transfer vegetables to serving bowl. Add remaining ingredients; toss gently to combine. Makes 8 servings.

GREEN SALAD WITH SESAME DRESSING

1 medium head iceberg lettuce,
 separate leaves
1 small head romaine lettuce,
 separate leaves
1 bunch watercress, remove stems
1 cup small radishes, cut into
 halves

½ cup wine vinegar
2 tablespoons plus 2 teaspoons
 sesame oil
1½ teaspoons lemon juice
½ garlic clove, minced
⅛ teaspoon oregano

Wash vegetables; wrap greens loosely in clean, damp towel. Chill vegetables. In small bowl combine remaining ingredients; chill. Just before serving, tear lettuce into bite-size pieces. In large salad bowl combine lettuce with watercress and radishes; toss. Pour dressing over salad and toss again. Makes 8 servings.

PIÑA WHIP

2 cups canned crushed pineapple, no sugar added
1 tablespoon plus 1 teaspoon unflavored gelatin
⅔ cup nonfat dry milk powder
Artificial sweetener to equal 6 teaspoons sugar

1¼ teaspoons lemon juice
½ teaspoon pineapple extract
8 to 10 ice cubes
Mint leaves to garnish

Drain juice from pineapple into measuring cup; set pineapple aside. Place ¼ cup juice in blender container. Sprinkle gelatin over juice and let stand a few minutes to soften. Meanwhile, in small saucepan, heat ¼ cup juice to boiling. Add to blender container; process until gelatin is dissolved. Add enough cold water to remaining juice to equal ¼ cup liquid. Add the liquid, reserved pineapple, milk, sweetener, lemon juice, and pineapple extract to blender container; process until smooth. Add ice cubes, 1 at a time, processing after each addition. Divide evenly into 8 sherbet glasses; chill. Garnish each portion with mint leaves. Makes 8 servings.

BIRTHDAY FARE FOR EIGHT

Eggplant Puree
Minted Yogurt with Vegetable Dippers
Shoulder Steak Forestière
Carrot and Potato Velvet
Green Peas with Water Chestnuts
Apple Jelly Bars with Pineapple Tidbits
Beverage

Gift your guests with a rainbow-tinted dinner party that speaks volumes about your culinary imagination, for this menu wraps up a variety of textures and colors in one delectable birthday package. Pureed eggplant contrasts tastefully with the crunchiness of raw vegetable dippers. Let them come up "roses"—artistically arranged on a platter alongside a minted yogurt dip. Shoulder Steak Forestière gives an easy-to-prepare meat a gourmet look. (The term "forestière" indicates a mushroom garnish.) Make *any* age "golden" by adding carrot color and flavor to a hearty potato dish. Give green peas a distinctive appearance, too, by combining them with water chestnuts. Since this is a birthday party, treat your guests to a fun dessert: our version of old-fashioned jelly bars. How refreshing to enjoy a birthday party that gifts you on the scale as well!

———————◆•◆———————

SUGGESTED SHOPPING LIST

Staples and Miscellaneous

Bay leaves
Cinnamon sticks
Cloves
Dried mint
Dry mustard
Garlic powder
Instant beef broth and seasoning mix
Nutmeg
Onion powder
Oregano
Pepper

Peppercorns
Salt
Thyme

Browning sauce
Hot sauce
Wine vinegar

Flour
Unflavored gelatin

Imitation (or diet) margarine

Additional Items

Shoulder steaks, 4, 12 ounces each,
   boneless

Plain unflavored yogurt, 1 16-ounce
   container

Lemon, 1

Carrots, 8 medium
Cauliflower, 1 head
Cucumbers, 2 medium
Eggplants, 2 medium
Garlic cloves, 2
Green peppers, 2 medium
Lettuce, 1 small head
Mushrooms, 1½ pounds
Onions, 2 medium
Parsley, 1 bunch
Potatoes, 2 pounds

Radishes, 2 bags
Tomatoes, 4 medium
Zucchini, 1 medium (approximately
   5 ounces)

Frozen blueberries, no sugar added,
   1 16-ounce bag

Applesauce, no sugar added,
   1 15-ounce jar
Canned pineapple tidbits, no sugar
   added, 4 8-ounce cans

Canned peas, 1 17-ounce can
Canned water chestnuts, 1 8-ounce
   can

Lemon-flavored dietetic soda,
   1 16-fluid-ounce bottle

SUGGESTED EQUIPMENT LIST

Baking pan
Baking pan (2-quart)
Baking pan (shallow)
Blender
Bowls (small and large)
Chef's knife
Colander
Cutting board
Kitchen spoon
Masher
Measuring cups

Measuring spoons
Nonstick skillet
Pepper mill
Pot holder
Rack
Rectangular pan (1-quart, shallow)
Saucepans (medium)
Scale
Vegetable peeler
Wooden spoon

EGGPLANT PUREE

2 medium eggplants, about 1
   pound each
2 medium tomatoes, peeled and
   diced
¼ cup finely chopped onion
1 tablespoon lemon juice

½ teaspoon each oregano and
   salt
¼ teaspoon each garlic powder,
   pepper, and hot sauce
Lettuce leaves

Cut each eggplant in half lengthwise. Place, cut side down, in baking pan.
Bake at 400°F. for 15 minutes or until tender. Cool slightly; scoop out
pulp. Place pulp in blender container with remaining ingredients except
lettuce leaves; process until smooth. Chill. Serve on bed of lettuce leaves.
Makes 8 servings.

MINTED YOGURT WITH VEGETABLE DIPPERS

1 cup plain unflavored yogurt
1 tablespoon dried mint
1 teaspoon minced fresh parsley
¼ teaspoon salt
⅛ teaspoon garlic powder
2 cups cauliflower florets, chilled
2 cups radishes, made into roses (refer to page 17) and chilled

1 cup julienne zucchini, chilled
2 medium cucumbers, seeded and pared, cut into thin strips, and chilled
2 medium green peppers, seeded, cut into thin strips, and chilled
2 medium tomatoes, each cut into 8 wedges and chilled

Combine first 5 ingredients in serving bowl. Refrigerate for at least 1 hour before serving. Arrange chilled vegetables in sections on serving platter. Serve with yogurt mixture. Makes 8 servings.

SHOULDER STEAK FORESTIÈRE

½ cup wine vinegar
2 packets instant chicken broth and seasoning mix
1½ teaspoons thyme, divided
1 bay leaf
½ teaspoon each dry mustard, garlic powder, and browning sauce
4 boneless beef shoulder steaks, 12 ounces each

4 cups sliced mushrooms
1 cup diced onions
2 tablespoons chopped fresh parsley
2 garlic cloves, minced
1 tablespoon plus 1 teaspoon flour
Parsley sprigs to garnish

In shallow 5-quart baking pan combine vinegar, 1 packet broth mix, ½ teaspoon thyme, the bay leaf, mustard, garlic powder, and browning sauce. Cut each steak in half. Marinate steaks in vinegar mixture in refrigerator for 4 hours. Remove steaks from marinade; reserve marinade. Broil steaks on rack, 4 inches from source of heat, until done to taste, turning once and basting occasionally with reserved marinade. While steaks are broiling, in nonstick skillet combine mushrooms, onions, chopped parsley, garlic cloves, 1 teaspoon thyme, and remaining broth mix. Cook for 5 minutes; add flour. Cook 2 minutes longer, stirring constantly. Divide mushroom mixture into 8 equal portions. Top each ½ steak with 1 portion mushroom mixture. Garnish with parsley sprigs. Makes 8 servings.

CARROT AND POTATO VELVET

2 pounds peeled cooked potatoes, sliced
4 cups cooked sliced carrots
½ cup imitation (or diet) margarine

¾ teaspoon salt
½ teaspoon nutmeg
⅛ teaspoon onion powder
Dash freshly ground pepper

In large bowl mash together potatoes, carrots, and margarine. Season with salt, nutmeg, onion powder and pepper. Transfer to 1½- or 2-quart baking pan. Bake at 375°F. for 25 minutes. Makes 8 servings.

GREEN PEAS WITH WATER CHESTNUTS

2 cups drained canned peas, reserve liquid

¾ cup sliced, drained, canned water chestnuts

Pour liquid from peas into medium saucepan; bring to a boil. Reduce heat; add peas and water chestnuts. Heat thoroughly. Drain before serving. Makes 8 servings.

APPLE JELLY BARS WITH PINEAPPLE TIDBITS

4 cups canned pineapple tidbits, no sugar added

1½ cups lemon-flavored dietetic soda

2 envelopes unflavored gelatin

1 cup applesauce, no sugar added

1 cinnamon stick

2 cloves

1 cup frozen blueberries, no sugar added, thawed

Drain juice from pineapple tidbits into medium saucepan; set tidbits aside. Add soda. Sprinkle gelatin over juice mixture; let stand a few minutes to soften. Add applesauce, cinnamon, and cloves; heat, stirring constantly, until gelatin dissolves. Remove and discard cinnamon stick and cloves. Line the bottom of a shallow, rectangular, 1-quart pan with blueberries; top with gelatin mixture. Refrigerate overnight or until very firm. Cut "jelly" into bars; remove from pan with spatula. Arrange on serving platter with reserved pineapple tidbits in center. Makes 8 servings.

ERIN GO BRAGH FOR FOUR

Galway Bay Oyster Stew
Rolled Stuffed Fish Fillets
Colcannon
Steamed Spinach
"Irish Coffee"

"Everybody's a little bit Irish on St. Patrick's Day," according to an old American saying. Sure, and Irish is what you'll want to be when it means a convivial feast like this one. What else should star in your menu but stew—traditional for Erin. But for a surprise, make it with oysters. And why not, when Ireland's Galway Bay oysters are famed the world over? The potato is surely a symbol of the Emerald Isle and it provides a national dish—Colcannon, a mixture of potatoes and cabbage. Delight your guests with a charming Irish custom, especially popular at Halloween time, by hiding a ring inside the Colcannon—it's said that whoever finds it will be wed within the year! (In line with this, you might also point out to your guests that oysters are rumored to be aphrodisiacs!) Add to the spirit of the occasion with an extract version of "Irish Coffee."

For this background of feasting and fellowship, let your table wear a green cloth with shamrocks in a glass bowl or miniature leprechauns as an enchanting centerpiece. And isn't it the luck of the Irish to find a fun feast that's on the trimming side!

———————◆•◆———————

SUGGESTED SHOPPING LIST ·

Staples and Miscellaneous

Artificial sweetener
Brandy extract
Instant chicken broth and seasoning
  mix
Paprika
Peppercorns
Salt
White pepper

Instant coffee
Nonstick cooking spray

Margarine

Additional Items

Fillets of sole, 4, 3 ounces each
Shucked oysters, ¾ pound

Lemon, 1

Cabbage, 1 small head
Celery, 1 rib
Garlic clove, 1
Leeks, 2
Mushrooms, ¼ pound
Onions, 1 small
Parsley, 1 bunch

Potatoes, 1 pound
Spinach, 2 pounds

Dill pickles, 1 16-ounce jar
Tomato puree, 1 16-ounce can

Evaporated skimmed milk, 1 13-fluid-
ounce can

Low-calorie whipped topping, 1 2½-
ounce box

SUGGESTED EQUIPMENT LIST

Baking pan (2-quart, shallow)
Bowl (large)
Can opener
Casserole (1-quart, shallow)
Chef's knife
Cutting board
Electric mixer
Heatproof container
Measuring cups
Measuring spoons

Nonstick skillet (medium)
Pepper mill
Pot (large) with cover
Potato masher
Pot holder
Saucepans
Scale
Toothpicks
Wooden spoon

GALWAY BAY OYSTER STEW

1 cup evaporated skimmed milk
12 ounces shucked oysters,
reserve 2 tablespoons liquid
Salt and freshly ground pepper
to taste

¼ cup diced celery, parboiled
Paprika and minced fresh parsley
to garnish

In saucepan heat milk, but *do not boil*. Add oysters, reserved liquid, salt, and pepper. Poach oysters for 4 to 5 minutes or until edges curl. Pour ¼ of mixture into each of 4 mugs; add 1 tablespoon celery to each mug and garnish with paprika and parsley. Makes 4 servings.

ROLLED STUFFED FISH FILLETS

½ cup diced onion
½ cup chopped mushrooms
2 packets instant chicken broth
and seasoning mix
1 garlic clove, minced
½ cup tomato puree
½ cup diced dill pickle

Salt and freshly ground pepper
to taste
4 fillets of sole, 3 ounces each
½ cup water
2 lemon wedges
Parsley sprigs to garnish

In medium nonstick skillet combine onion, mushrooms, 1 packet broth mix, and garlic. Cook, stirring occasionally, until vegetables are tender. Stir in tomato puree, pickle, salt, and pepper. Place an equal amount of mixture on each fish fillet. Roll each fillet to enclose filling; secure each with a toothpick. Pour water into shallow, 2-quart baking pan. Add rolled fillets. Sprinkle ¼ packet broth mix over each fillet. Bake at 350°F. for 20 minutes. Remove toothpicks. Transfer fish rolls to serving platter and garnish with lemon wedges and parsley sprigs. Makes 4 servings.

COLCANNON

1 pound hot, cooked, pared
    potatoes
½ cup evaporated skimmed milk
1 tablespoon margarine
Salt and white pepper to taste

2 cups shredded cabbage
¾ cup shredded leeks, white
    portion only
2 packets instant chicken broth
    and seasoning mix

Combine potatoes, milk, margarine, salt, and pepper in large bowl; mash and set aside. Combine remaining ingredients in saucepan. Cook, stirring often, until vegetables are tender. Add to potatoes and mix well. Transfer potato mixture to shallow 1-quart casserole that has been sprayed with nonstick cooking spray. Bake at 350°F. for 20 minutes. Makes 4 servings.

STEAMED SPINACH

2 pounds spinach

Salt and pepper to taste

Trim off and discard stems. Rinse spinach in basin of water several times to remove sand. Lift from water and shake to remove excess moisture. Place in large pot. Cover and steam 3 to 5 minutes. Spinach will wilt but remain bright green. Drain; add salt and pepper. Makes 4 servings.

"IRISH COFFEE"

2 tablespoons plus 2 teaspoons
    instant coffee
Artificial sweetener to equal 4
    teaspoons sugar

½ teaspoon brandy extract
3 cups boiling water
¼ cup plus 2 tablespoons low-
    calorie whipped topping

Combine instant coffee, sweetener, and extract in heatproof container. Add water; stir well. Divide evenly into 4 warmed coffee mugs. Top each with 1½ tablespoons whipped topping; serve immediately. Makes 4 servings.

A CONTINENTAL DINNER FOR EIGHT

Endive Salad with Sauce Vinaigrette
Standing Rib Roast Au Jus
Horseradish Sauce
Oven-Roast Potatoes
Okra Creole
Medley of Fresh Fruit
Beverage

Treat your guests to a taste tour of Europe via this sophisticated menu. Standing Rib Roast Au Jus makes an expensive-looking and very English entrée. Display it on a platter, but do your carving in the privacy of the kitchen unless you're very adroit at this ticklish art. (Allowing the roast to "rest" for twenty minutes helps make carving easier.) Accompany the entrée with Horseradish Sauce, another English favorite, and carry on the British tradition by making it a "meat and potatoes" meal by serving miniature potatoes glowing with paprika and baked golden brown. Cross the Channel to borrow Endive Salad from the Belgians and add a specialty of the cuisine-wise French: Vinaigrette Sauce. Although spicy Okra Creole is a southern American dish, its ancestry is southern European. According to knowledgeable Europeans, a filling meal should end with a light, cool dessert, so our Medley of Fresh Fruit meets continental requirements. To top it all, the entire menu earns a "passport" to the slim world.

———————— •◦• ————————

SUGGESTED SHOPPING LIST

Staples and Miscellaneous

Artificial sweetener
Basil
Bay leaves
Chopped chives
Dried mint
Garlic powder
Instant beef broth and seasoning mix
Oregano
Paprika
Peppercorns
Salt
Thyme

Prepared horseradish
Red wine vinegar
Worcestershire sauce

Imitation (or diet) margarine
Imitation mayonnaise

Vegetable oil

Additional Items

Standing rib roast, 1 (5 to 6 pounds)	Green peppers, 3 medium
	Mint, 1 bunch
Plain unflavored yogurt, 1 16-ounce container	Onion, 1 small
	Parsley, 1 bunch
	Tomatoes, 4 medium
Bananas, 2 medium	
Kiwi fruits, 2 medium	Frozen okra, 1 1-pound bag
Lemon, 1 small	
Papaya, 1 medium	Canned whole potatoes, tiny, 2 28-ounce cans
Belgian endives, 6 medium	Tomato sauce, 1 8-ounce can
Celery, 1 rib	

SUGGESTED EQUIPMENT LIST

Blender
Bowls (small)
Can opener
Chef's knife
Cutting board
Measuring cups
Measuring spoons
Meat thermometer
Nonstick skillet (medium)

Ovenproof serving dish (9 x 13 x 2 inches)
Pepper mill
Pot holder
Roasting pan
Scale
Serving platter
Wooden spoons

ENDIVE SALAD WITH SAUCE VINAIGRETTE

Salad:

6 medium Belgian endives, sliced
4 medium tomatoes, sliced

2 medium green peppers, seeded and cut into rings

Sauce Vinaigrette:

¼ cup vegetable oil
2 tablespoons plus 2 teaspoons water
1 tablespoon plus 1 teaspoon wine vinegar

1 teaspoon basil
1 teaspoon chopped chives
½ teaspoon garlic powder

To Prepare Salad: Combine vegetables in large salad bowl.

To Prepare Sauce: Place remaining ingredients in blender container; process until combined.

To Serve: Pour Sauce Vinaigrette over salad. Makes 8 servings.

STANDING RIB ROAST AU JUS

Serve with Oven-Roast Potatoes and Horseradish Sauce (see recipes below).

5- to 6-pound standing rib roast
Salt and freshly ground pepper
  to taste
1½ cups water
1 celery rib, cut in half

2 packets instant beef broth and
  seasoning mix
½ teaspoon Worcestershire
  sauce
Parsley sprigs to garnish

Season roast with salt and pepper. Insert meat thermometer so that tip is in center of thickest part of meat but not touching fat or bone. Place meat on rack in roasting pan; roast at 325°F. Do not cover; add no water and do not baste. Allow about 23 to 25 minutes per pound, or until thermometer registers 140°F., for rare; about 27 to 30 minutes per pound, or until thermometer registers 160°F., for medium; about 32 to 35 minutes per pound, or until thermometer registers 170°F., for well-done. When done to taste, remove from oven; allow roast to "rest" at least 20 minutes before carving. While meat is "resting," prepare Au Jus. Combine water, celery, broth mix, and Worcestershire sauce in saucepan. Bring to a boil; reduce heat and simmer 5 minutes. Remove and discard celery. Transfer beef to serving platter. Surround with Oven-Roast Potatoes and garnish with parsley sprigs. To serve: slice, trim, and weigh eight 4-ounce portions. Pour an equal amount of Au Jus over each portion and serve with 4 ounces potatoes. Makes 8 servings.

HORSERADISH SAUCE

Serve with Standing Rib Roast Au Jus (see recipe above).

1 cup plain unflavored yogurt
2 tablespoons plus 2 teaspoons
  imitation mayonnaise
2 tablespoons prepared
  horseradish

½ teaspoon Worcestershire
  sauce
Artificial sweetener to taste
Chopped fresh parsley to garnish
  (optional)

Combine all ingredients except parsley in small mixing bowl; mix well. Cover and refrigerate 1 hour. Transfer to serving bowl; garnish with chopped parsley, if desired. Makes 8 servings.

OVEN-ROAST POTATOES

Serve with Standing Rib Roast Au Jus (see recipe above).

¼ cup imitation (or diet)
  margarine, melted
2 teaspoons vegetable oil
3 bay leaves, broken into halves
⅛ teaspoon paprika

⅛ teaspoon garlic powder
Salt and freshly ground pepper to
  taste
2 pounds drained, canned tiny
  whole potatoes

Combine all ingredients except potatoes in mixing bowl. Stir to dissolve paprika. Add potatoes; toss lightly. Transfer to 9 × 13 × 2-inch baking pan. Bake at 400°F. for 30 minutes or until golden brown. Serve as directed in recipe for Standing Rib Roast Au Jus.

OKRA CREOLE

⅔ cup diced onion, ½-inch dice
1 medium green pepper, seeded and cut into ½-inch dice
1 packet instant beef broth and seasoning mix

1 cup tomato sauce
½ teaspoon oregano
⅛ teaspoon thyme
⅛ teaspoon garlic powder
2⅓ cups cooked frozen okra

In medium nonstick skillet combine onion, green pepper, and broth mix. Cook, stirring occasionally, until vegetables are tender. Stir in tomato sauce, oregano, thyme, and garlic powder. Cook for 10 minutes, stirring often. Stir in okra and cook, stirring gently, for 5 minutes or until okra is hot. Makes 8 servings.

MEDLEY OF FRESH FRUIT

1 medium papaya, pared
2 medium kiwi fruits, pared and thinly sliced

2 medium bananas, thinly sliced
1 teaspoon lemon juice
Mint leaves to garnish

Cut papaya in half and remove seeds; dice into ½-inch pieces; place in serving bowl. Add kiwi fruits and bananas; toss with lemon juice. Divide evenly into 8 dessert glasses. Garnish each portion with mint leaf. Makes 8 servings.

COCKTAIL SUPPER PARTY FOR SIX

Eggplant Relish
Piquant Mushrooms and Green Beans
Marinated Carrots
Stuffed Artichokes
Lobster Salad
Sweet and Sour Meatballs
Lime "Soufflé"
Sparkling Mineral Water with Twist of Lemon

Party-time . . . and here's an inventive menu that takes you out of the kitchen and into the fun. Although it is designed as a sit-down dinner, our menu can be adapted to buffet style as well, and the serve-yourself dishes can easily be multiplied for a larger group. (If you are serving a buffet, set out small tables for your guests to rest their plates on, so they won't have to do a balancing act). Stuffed Artichokes are spectacular on any menu, and we've supplied explicit directions for preparing them properly. Every dish can conveniently be made ahead of time, except for the soufflé, which should be prepared earlier the same day. It's best to cook the meatballs and sauce separately, then mix them just before serving. A hot tray or fondue dish will keep them at the right temperature. The meatballs and carrots can be served either on platters or on toothpicks in easy cocktail style. It all adds up to a memorable party feast that won't put a strain on party fashions.

SUGGESTED SHOPPING LIST

Staples and Miscellaneous

Artificial sweetener
Basil
Bay leaves
Cinnamon
Cloves
Dehydrated onion flakes
Garlic powder
Nutmeg
Onion powder
Oregano
Pepper
Peppercorns
Salt

Capers
Hot sauce
Ketchup
Red wine vinegar
Steak sauce

Imitation mayonnaise
Margarine

Additional Items

Lobster meat, cooked, 12 ounces
or
Frozen lobster tails, 1½ pounds
Ground veal, 1 pound, 2 ounces

Plain unflavored yogurt, 1 8-ounce
  container

Lemons, 2
Lime, 1

Artichokes, 6 medium
Carrots, 6 large
Celery, 1 rib
Cucumber, 4 medium
Dill, 1 bunch or dill weed
Eggplant, 1 medium
Garlic clove, 2

Green beans, 1¼ pounds
Mushrooms, 1¼ pounds
Parsley, 1 bunch
Zucchini, 2 medium

Frozen orange juice concentrate,
  1 6-fluid-ounce can
Frozen spinach, 2 10-ounce packages

Pimientos, 1 4-ounce jar
Tomato sauce, 1 8-ounce can

Evaporated skimmed milk, 1 13-fluid-
  ounce can

Lime-flavored low-calorie gelatin,
  1 ⅝-ounce box

SUGGESTED EQUIPMENT LIST

Bowls (medium)
Baking pan (9 x 13 inches)
Can opener
Chef's knife
Colander
Cutting board
Electric mixer
Fork
Grapefruit knife
Grater
Measuring cups
Measuring spoons

Nonstick skillet
Pepper mill
Pot holder
Saucepans with covers (small,
  medium, large)
Scale
Scissors
Slotted spoon
Vegetable peeler
Wire whisk
Wooden spoon

EGGPLANT RELISH

2 cups diced, pared eggplant
2 tablespoons minced celery
2 tablespoons diced pimiento
1 tablespoon plus 2 teaspoons
 red wine vinegar
1½ teaspoons chopped fresh
 parsley
½ teaspoon capers, chopped
1 garlic clove, minced

¼ teaspoon basil
⅛ teaspoon oregano
Salt and freshly ground pepper
 to taste
4 medium cucumbers, cut into
 ¼-inch slices
Diced pimientos and chopped
 fresh parsley to garnish

Place eggplant in medium saucepan. Add salted water to cover. Bring to a boil; reduce heat and simmer 3 to 5 minutes or until tender. Drain. Transfer eggplant to medium bowl; mash with fork. Add next 9 ingredients; toss to combine. Chill at least 2 hours. Place approximately 1 teaspoon of eggplant relish on each cucumber slice. Garnish with diced pimientos and chopped parsley. Makes 6 servings.

PIQUANT MUSHROOMS AND GREEN BEANS

¾ cup red wine vinegar
½ cup water
Artificial sweetener to equal 6
 teaspoons sugar
1 teaspoon salt
½ teaspoon oregano
1 bay leaf

1 garlic clove, split
5 peppercorns
2 cloves
4 cups mushrooms, quartered
4 cups whole green beans,
 trimmed

In medium saucepan combine all ingredients except mushrooms and green beans. Bring to a boil; add mushrooms. Reduce heat, cover, and simmer 5 minutes. Using slotted spoon, remove mushrooms and transfer to serving dish. Add green beans to simmering mixture; cover and simmer about 15 minutes or until tender. Using slotted spoon remove green beans and combine with mushrooms in serving dish. Pour liquid over vegetables. Chill. Makes 6 servings.

MARINATED CARROTS

¼ cup imitation mayonnaise
2 teaspoons wine vinegar
2 teaspoons water
Artificial sweetener to equal 1
 teaspoon sugar

¼ teaspoon oregano
⅛ teaspoon garlic powder
Freshly ground pepper to taste
3 cups cooked carrot sticks

In medium bowl combine all ingredients except carrots. Mix well with wire whisk. Add carrots; stir to coat. Chill. Serve with cocktail picks. Makes 6 servings.

STUFFED ARTICHOKES

6 medium artichokes
1½ cups squeezed, cooked,
    chopped spinach
½ cup cooked mushroom halves
¼ cup ketchup
2 teaspoons dehydrated onion
    flakes

2 tablespoons margarine, melted
½ teaspoon each salt, garlic
    powder, and onion powder
Dash pepper
⅔ cup water

Wash artichokes thoroughly to remove all grit. Cut off stems and, with scissors, trim off sharp tips of leaves. Snap off tough bottom row of leaves by bending leaves back from core. Turn artichokes upside down and press hard to force leaves apart. Reverse artichokes; using a grapefruit knife, cut out and discard choke (spiny center growth) of each artichoke, leaving bottom intact. Place in large saucepan with about 1 inch boiling salted water. Reduce heat; cover and simmer for 20 minutes or until tender. Remove pan from heat and place under cold running water until artichokes are cooled. Drain artichokes and set aside. In bowl combine spinach and mushrooms. In small saucepan combine ketchup and onion flakes; heat until onion flakes are soft. Stir in remaining ingredients except water and add ketchup mixture to spinach; mix well. Divide mixture into 6 equal portions; stuff each artichoke with 1 portion. Place stuffed artichokes in 9x13-inch baking pan; add water. Bake at 350°F. for 15 to 20 minutes or until heated through. Makes 6 servings.

LOBSTER SALAD

½ cup plain unflavored yogurt
1 tablespoon chopped fresh dill or
    ¾ teaspoon dill weed
1 tablespoon lemon juice

1 teaspoon salt
12 ounces diced cooked lobster
1½ cups diced zucchini

Combine yogurt, chopped dill, lemon juice, and salt in medium serving bowl. Add lobster and zucchini; stir to combine. Cover and chill. Makes 6 servings.

SWEET AND SOUR MEATBALLS

Meatballs:

1 pound 2 ounces ground veal
1 tablespoon dehydrated onion flakes, reconstituted in 1 tablespoon water
2 teaspoons chopped fresh parsley

¼ teaspoon cinnamon
¼ teaspoon salt
Pepper to taste

Sweet and Sour Sauce:

¾ cup tomato sauce
2 tablespoons steak sauce
2 tablespoons red wine vinegar
Artificial sweetener to equal 1 teaspoon sugar

3 cloves
½ bay leaf

To Prepare Meatballs: Combine first 6 ingredients in medium bowl; mix well. Divide mixture evenly into 24 balls. In preheated nonstick skillet brown meatballs on all sides, cooking 5 to 7 minutes or until done.

To Prepare Sauce: Combine remaining ingredients in medium saucepan. Simmer 10 minutes. Remove cloves and bay leaf.

To Serve: Transfer meatballs to saucepan containing sauce. Simmer 5 minutes or until thoroughly heated. Serve immediately. Makes 6 servings.

LIME "SOUFFLÉ"

This dessert should be served on the same day that it is prepared.

1 cup orange juice
½ cup water
1 envelope lime-flavored low-calorie gelatin (4 servings)
Artificial sweetener to equal 8 teaspoons sugar

2 tablespoons lime juice
1 teaspoon grated lime rind
1 cup evaporated skimmed milk, chilled

Chill a mixing bowl and beaters. In medium saucepan combine orange juice and water; bring to a boil. Reduce heat and add gelatin. Stirring constantly, heat until gelatin is dissolved. Remove from heat; add sweetener, lime juice, and rind. Allow to cool. In chilled mixing bowl beat evaporated skimmed milk until very stiff. Immediately fold into cooled gelatin mixture. Divide evenly into six 4-ounce custard cups. Chill for at least 2 hours. Makes 6 servings.

April

April skies can be unpredictable, but we
can predict exciting culinary delights on
the horizon for this month! Traditional
holiday fare along with contemporary
party meals will balance your menu
planning and delight your guests.

SWING INTO SPRING LUNCHEON
FOR FOUR

Gazpacho
Asparagus Quiche
Carrot-Prune Salad
Strawberry-Cheese Parfait
Hot Coffee

Welcome spring with a dream of a luncheon that features "sparrow grass" and "honey underground"—the poetic names for asparagus and carrots that date back to olde England and Celtic lore. In this nutrition-conscious twentieth century, golden carrots and dark-hued prunes are skillfully combined into a healthy salad. Asparagus—still one of the world's prized vegetables—takes on a French accent when baked into a quiche. The Gazpacho from sunny Spain also makes good use of nutritious vegetables. Serve it chilled, as a culinary sign that winter is finally over. Include another sign-of-spring treat: a parfait made with juicy fresh strawberries. And let your table bloom with a variety of wildflowers. What a tasty way to swing into spring!

SUGGESTED SHOPPING LIST

Staples and Miscellaneous

Artificial sweetener
Brandy extract
Chopped chives
Dry mustard
Nutmeg
Salt
White pepper

Cider vinegar
Prepared mustard
Worcestershire sauce

Vegetable oil

Enriched white bread

Coffee

Eggs, 4
Part skim ricotta cheese, 1 16-ounce
container

Lemons, 2
Strawberries, 2 pints

Asparagus, 16 medium stalks
Carrots, 1 pound
Cucumbers, 2 medium
Garlic clove, 1

Green peppers, 2 medium
Tomatoes, 3 medium

Frozen orange juice concentrate,
1 6-fluid-ounce can

Evaporated skimmed milk, 2 13-fluid-
ounce cans

Prunes, medium, 1 16-ounce box

SUGGESTED EQUIPMENT LIST

Blender
Bowls (small, medium, large)
Can opener
Chef's knife
Cutting board
Egg beater
Grater
Kitchen knife

Measuring cups
Measuring spoons
Pie pan (9-inch)
Pot holder
Toaster
Vegetable peeler
Wooden spoon

GAZPACHO

*3 medium tomatoes, chopped,
    divided
1½ medium green peppers,
    seeded and chopped, divided
1½ medium cucumbers, pared
    and diced, divided
2 slices enriched white bread,
    torn into pieces*

*2 tablespoons cider vinegar
2 tablespoons vegetable oil
1 garlic clove
Salt and pepper to taste
½ cup cold water (optional)*

Chill 4 mugs. In small bowl combine 2 tablespoons each tomatoes, green peppers, and cucumbers; set aside. In blender container combine remaining ingredients except water. Process until desired consistency. Chill. Add water, if desired, to adjust consistency. Divide evenly into chilled mugs. Garnish each portion with an equal amount of reserved vegetables. Makes 4 servings.

ASPARAGUS QUICHE

*2 slices enriched white bread,
    toasted and made into crumbs
2 tablespoons water
16 cooked medium asparagus
    spears
1½ cups evaporated skimmed
    milk*

*4 eggs, beaten
1 teaspoon prepared mustard
1 teaspoon Worcestershire sauce
⅛ teaspoon nutmeg
Salt and white pepper to taste*

Press bread crumbs into bottom and sides of 9-inch pie pan or quiche dish. Sprinkle with water and bake at 350°F. for 10 minutes or until lightly golden; set aside. Cut 8 asparagus spears into ½-inch pieces; place in medium bowl. Add milk, eggs, mustard, Worcestershire, nutmeg, salt, and pepper; stir to combine. Pour into baked crust and arrange remaining asparagus spears on top. Bake at 350°F. for 40 minutes or until a knife, when inserted in center, comes out clean. Serve warm. Makes 4 servings

CARROT-PRUNE SALAD

4 cups grated carrots
12 medium prunes, pitted and diced
2 tablespoons vegetable oil

2 tablespoons lemon juice
1 tablespoon chopped chives
Dash dry mustard
Salt and white pepper to taste

Combine all ingredients in medium bowl; chill Makes 4 servings.

STRAWBERRY-CHEESE PARFAIT

1⅓ cups part skim ricotta cheese
2 tablespoons black coffee
1 tablespoon plus 1½ teaspoons lemon juice
1 tablespoon frozen orange juice concentrate

Artificial sweetener to equal 4 teaspoons sugar
½ teaspoon brandy extract
3½ cups strawberries, sliced

Combine all ingredients except strawberries in large bowl; beat until smooth and fluffy. Fold in strawberries. Spoon an equal amount into each of 4 parfait glasses. Chill. Makes 4 servings

PASSOVER SEDER FOR EIGHT

Golden Broth
Spring Green Salad
Lemony Vinaigrette in Lemon Cups
Roast Chicken
Matzo Farfel Casserole
Carrot Tsimmes
Beet Relish
Passover Fruit Compote
Beverage

Passover marks the season of renewal. Renew your own spirits with a traditional "festive meal" that celebrates the Israelites' freedom from bondage (while you *un*traditionally break the bonds of overweight)! Begin with Golden Broth, and since questions are in order at the Seder table, ask your guests if they ever heard of its most unusual ingredient—*petrouchka*! Parsley—the Seder symbol of spring's rebirth—adds life to a verdant salad and garnishes the ritual Roast Chicken and Beet Relish. Even Matzo Farfel and Carrot Tsimmes can appear on your streamlined menu. End with a fruit compote, which can be served either warmed or chilled. Of course, the entire menu observes the dietary dictates of Passover.

It was once the fashion to eat the Seder meal in a semi-reclining position to show that one was no longer a slave. *You'll* feel liberated, too, with these prepared-in-advance dishes that free you from kitchen bondage and leave you relaxed enough to feast on the beauty of the Seder ceremony.

SUGGESTED SHOPPING LIST

Staples and Miscellaneous

Garlic powder
Paprika
Pepper
Peppercorns
Salt
White pepper

Cider vinegar
Prepared horseradish

Vegetable oil

Matzo

Chicken carcasses, 5
Roasting chickens, 2 (4 to 4½ pounds each)

Asparagus stalks, 24 medium
Belgian endives, 8 medium
Carrots, 15 medium
Celery, 12 ribs
Dill, 1 bunch
Garlic cloves, 7
Mushrooms, 2 pounds
Onions, 2 medium
Parsley, 4 bunches

Petrouchka (root of Italian parsley), 1 medium
Watercress, 1 bunch

Apples, 2 small
Lemons, 5 small
Orange, 1 small
Pear, 1 small

Canned sliced beets, 2 16-ounce cans

Prunes, large, 1 12-ounce box

SUGGESTED EQUIPMENT LIST

Baking dish (1-quart)
Bowls (small and large)
Casserole with cover (1-quart)
Chef's knife
Cutting board
Food processor or food grinder
Kettle with cover (large)
Measuring cups
Measuring spoons

Nonstick skillet
Paring knife or grapefruit knife
Pot holder
Roasting pan and rack
Saucepans (large)
Scale
Serving dish (1½-quart)
Strainer
Wooden spoons

GOLDEN BROTH

5 chicken carcasses
7½ quarts water
5 medium carrots, sliced
5 celery ribs with leaves, sliced
15 parsley sprigs
15 dill sprigs

5 garlic cloves, crushed
15 peppercorns
3 small pieces petrouchka (root of Italian parsley)
Salt to taste

Combine all ingredients in large kettle. Bring to a boil; reduce heat. Cover and simmer for 2 to 2½ hours. Strain and discard solids. Refrigerate liquid until fat congeals on top; remove and discard congealed fat. Measure 1½ quarts broth;* pour into saucepan and heat. Divide evenly into 8 soup bowls. Makes 8 servings.

* Measure 1½ quarts broth for use in Matzo Farfel Casserole and Carrot Tsimmes (see recipes). Any remaining broth can be measured and frozen for use at another time.

SPRING GREEN SALAD

Serve with Lemony Vinaigrette in Lemon Cups (see recipe below).

8 medium Belgian endives
2 bunches parsley
1 bunch watercress

24 cooked medium asparagus
spears, chilled

Trim and discard root end from each endive; cut each in half lengthwise. Place in large saucepan; add boiling salted water to cover. Simmer 5 to 8 minutes; drain. Place under cold running water to cool; drain and refrigerate until chilled. Rinse parsley and watercress; remove and discard stems. Shake leaves to remove excess moisture. Make bed of parsley and watercress on serving platter. Arrange endive halves and asparagus over greens. Makes 8 servings.

LEMONY VINAIGRETTE IN LEMON CUPS

Serve with Spring Green Salad (see recipe above).

4 lemons
¼ cup vegetable oil

¼ cup water
Dash each salt and white pepper

Cut each lemon in half. Squeeze to extract juice, leaving rinds intact. Reserve juice. Using grapefruit or paring knife, remove pulp from rind halves; discard pulp. Level the bottom of each "cup" by cutting a very thin slice from each bottom so that "cups" stand upright. Set aside. In measuring cup combine ⅓ cup reserved lemon juice with oil, water, salt, and pepper; mix well. Divide evenly into prepared "lemon cups." Makes 8 servings.

ROAST CHICKEN

2 roasting chickens, 4 to 4½
pounds each
2 garlic cloves, cut

Salt and pepper to taste
Paprika and chopped fresh
parsley to garnish

Rub chickens inside and out with garlic; sprinkle with salt and pepper. Place chickens on rack in roasting pan; roast at 350°F. about 2 hours or until tender. Remove and discard skin. Carve and weigh eight 4-ounce portions. Sprinkle with paprika and parsley. Makes 8 servings.

MATZO FARFEL CASSEROLE

4 cups diced celery
3 cups Golden Broth (see recipe, page 123)
4 cups sliced mushrooms
1 cup chopped onions
4 matzo boards, broken into small pieces

2 tablespoons chopped fresh
parsley
Salt, pepper, and garlic powder
to taste

In large saucepan combine celery and broth; cook over medium heat until celery is tender and liquid is reduced by half. Brown mushrooms and onions in nonstick skillet; add to celery-broth mixture. Stir in matzo, parsley, and seasonings. Transfer to 1-quart baking pan. Bake at 350°F. for 15 to 20 minutes. Makes 8 servings.

CARROT TSIMMES

3 cups Golden Broth (see recipe, page 123)
4 cups finely diced carrots

8 large prunes, pitted and diced

Pour broth into saucepan. Add carrots and prunes. Cover and simmer for about 1 hour or until carrots are tender. Makes 8 servings.

BEET RELISH

3 cups drained canned sliced beets, reserve liquid
Cider vinegar

¼ cup prepared horseradish
Parsley sprigs to garnish

Place beets in large bowl; add vinegar to cover. Refrigerate overnight. Drain.* Put beets through food grinder or chop in food processor. Transfer to bowl; add horseradish, and, if desired, enough beet liquid to moisten. Stir to combine. Spoon into 1½-quart serving dish; chill. Garnish with parsley. Makes 8 servings.

* Don't discard the vinegar. Use in salad dressing recipes calling for cider vinegar. It will add an interesting and unique flavor.

PASSOVER FRUIT COMPOTE

2 small apples, pared, cored, and sliced
1 small orange, peeled and sliced

1 small pear, pared, cored, and sliced
1 lemon, sliced

Combine all ingredients in 1-quart casserole. Cover and bake at 350°F. about 45 minutes or until tender. Serve warm or chilled. Makes 8 servings.

EASTER BREAKFAST FOR SIX

Mixed Vegetable Juice
Springtime Omelet with Mushroom Sauce
Tarragon Cucumber Salad
Garlic Bread
Cinnamon Apricots à la Mode
Beverage

Greet a meaningful morning in a very special way by turning an often-routine meal into a party. Of course, you'll feature eggs—an edible Easter emblem—but you'll spruce them up into a Springtime Omelet. (An old superstition warns that refusing eggs on Easter will ruin a friendship, but you're not likely to get refusals with this dill-flavored delicacy!) Celebrate the wonders of fresh-blooming vegetables by sparking a holiday salad with a colorful blend of spring-green cucumbers and parsley with cherry-red tomatoes and crimson peppers, deliberately chosen for their color. No routine toast today but—as a taste treat—Italian or French bread, which you'll bravely flavor with garlic. Surprise everyone with an Easter "special" —spiced hot fruit served à la mode. What a good way to launch a joyous holiday (and still fit into your Easter outfit). For your centerpiece, arrange gaily decorated Easter eggs in a beribboned basket.

SUGGESTED SHOPPING LIST

Staples and Miscellaneous

Artificial sweetener
Cinnamon sticks
Cloves
Dehydrated parsley flakes
Garlic powder
Salt
Tarragon
Thyme
Vanilla extract
White pepper

Cider vinegar

Cornstarch
Flour
Nonstick cooking spray

Imitation (or diet) margarine
Vegetable oil

Enriched Italian or French bread

Additional Items

Eggs, 6
Skim milk, 1 cup

Lemon, 1

Carrots, 3 medium
Cherry tomatoes, 1 pint
Cucumbers, 5 medium
Dill, 1 bunch
Mushrooms, 1 pound
Onion, 1 medium
Parsley, 1 bunch
Red pepper, 1 medium
Zucchini, 3 medium

Vanilla-flavored dietary frozen dessert
1 quart

Canned apricots, no sugar added,
1 16-ounce can

Mixed vegetable juice, 2 12-fluid-
ounce cans

Dietetic root beer, 1 12-fluid-ounce
can

SUGGESTED EQUIPMENT LIST

Baking sheet
Bowls (medium)
Can opener
Chef's knife
Cutting board
Double boiler
Fork
Ice cream scoop
Measuring cups

Measuring spoons
Nonstick skillet (12-inch)
Plate (12-inch)
Pot holder
Rotary beater
Saucepan with cover (small)
Scale
Wooden spoon

MIXED VEGETABLE JUICE

Serve ½ cup chilled mixed vegetable juice to each person. Garnish each portion with a lemon wedge.

SPRINGTIME OMELET WITH MUSHROOM SAUCE

Omelet:

6 eggs
½ teaspoon thyme
¼ teaspoon garlic powder

3 cups cooked sliced zucchini
1½ cups grated carrots
Salt and white pepper to taste

Mushroom Sauce:

2 tablespoons imitation (or diet)
    margarine
2 cups sliced mushrooms
2 tablespoons flour

¼ teaspoon dill weed
1 cup skim milk
Salt and white pepper to taste

To Prepare Omelet: Combine eggs, thyme, and garlic powder in medium bowl; beat until frothy. Add zucchini, carrots, salt, and pepper; stir to combine. Pour into preheated 12-inch nonstick skillet that has been sprayed with nonstick cooking spray. Cook over medium heat until bottom is firm and top is still moist. Invert a 12-inch plate over skillet. Holding plate in place, turn skillet over; remove skillet. Slide omelet back into skillet, browned side up. Continue cooking until bottom is firm and browned.

To Prepare Mushroom Sauce: In top of double boiler, over boiling water, melt margarine. Add mushrooms; cook until mushrooms are tender. Stir in flour and dill weed. Stirring constantly, gradually add milk. Cook, stirring often, until sauce thickens. Season with salt and pepper.

To Serve: Transfer omelet to serving platter. Pour Mushroom Sauce over omelet. Makes 6 servings.

TARRAGON CUCUMBER SALAD

5 cups sliced, scored cucumbers
¾ cup thinly sliced onion
10 cherry tomatoes, cut into halves
1 medium red pepper, seeded and diced
¼ cup cider vinegar
2 tablespoons chopped fresh parsley

2 tablespoons water
1 tablespoon vegetable oil
Artificial sweetener to equal 2 teaspoons sugar
1 teaspoon tarragon
1 teaspoon salt
¼ teaspoon garlic powder

Combine all ingredients in medium bowl. Toss lightly. Chill at least 2 hours. Makes 6 servings.

GARLIC BREAD

6 slices enriched Italian or French bread, 2 ounces each
¼ cup imitation (or diet) margarine

1 tablespoon dehydrated parsley flakes
½ teaspoon garlic powder

Preheat broiler. Place bread on baking sheet. Spread each slice with 2 teaspoons margarine. Sprinkle parsley and garlic powder evenly over bread. Broil 3 to 4 inches from source of heat for 1 minute. Makes 6 servings.

CINNAMON APRICOTS À LA MODE

12 canned apricot halves with ¼ cup plus 2 tablespoons juice, no sugar added
½ cup dietetic root beer
¼ cinnamon stick
2 cloves

¼ teaspoon vanilla extract
1½ teaspoons cornstarch, dissolved in 2 teaspoons water
6 scoops vanilla-flavored dietary frozen dessert, 3 ounces each

In small saucepan combine apricot juice with remaining ingredients except apricot halves, cornstarch, and frozen dessert. Cover and cook over medium heat for 3 to 5 minutes. Stirring constantly, add dissolved cornstarch and cook until slightly thickened. Remove from heat. Add apricots and stir to coat. Chill at least 2 hours. Remove cinnamon stick and cloves. Place 1 scoop frozen dessert into each of 6 dessert dishes. Spoon ⅙ of apricot mixture over each portion of frozen dessert. Makes 6 servings.

AN ELEGANT EASTER DINNER FOR TWELVE

"Creamed" Zucchini Soup
Tomato Aspic
Boned Rolled Leg of Lamb
Parslied Parisienne Potatoes
Asparagus in Lemon "Butter" Sauce
Apricot-Yogurt Sherbet with Strawberry Sauce
Beverage

According to legend, twelve was the proper number of guests for a royal banquet. Here's a menu, fit for a king, that's intended for a dozen fortunate celebrants of spring's most joyous holiday. This basically simple but elegant meal is planned with a discreet eye for weight control as well. Highlighting your feast is a spring specialty—Leg of Lamb. Its delicate flavor needs a subtle-tasting accompaniment, such as Tomato Aspic—savored by gourmets for centuries. As banquet sophisticates know, it's fashionable to clear the palate with sherbet. Ours is flavored with two of the world's most highly prized fruits: apricots and strawberries. Appropriately enough, the apricot belongs to the lily family, the flower symbolic of Easter.

Accent this occasion with your finest linen and china, and use an Easter decor of purple and yellow. For a centerpiece, place a water lily in an exquisite container, or make a small arrangement of purple and yellow flowers in a low vase.

———————————◆•◆•◆———————————

SUGGESTED SHOPPING LIST
Staples and Miscellaneous

Almond extract
Artificial sweetener
Basil
Bay leaves
Chopped chives
Dehydrated onion flakes
Paprika
Peppercorns
Onion powder
Rosemary
Salt
White pepper

Unflavored gelatin

Imitation (or diet) margarine

Chicken Stock. 1½ quarts (see page 31

Additional Items

Boned and rolled and tied leg of lamb. 1 (4½ pounds)

Plain unflavored yogurt, 1 16-ounce container

Lemons, 5
Strawberries, 2 pints

Asparagus stalks, 72 medium
Celery, 8 ribs
Garlic cloves, 2
Lettuce or chicory, 1 head
Onion, 1 medium
Parsley, 1 bunch

Potatoes, 5 pounds
Zucchini, 6 medium (approximately 5 ounces each)

Canned apricot halves, no sugar added. 2 16-ounce cans

Canned tomatoes, 1 28-ounce can

Mixed vegetable juice, 1 32-fluid-ounce can

Evaporated skimmed milk, 2 13-fluid-ounce cans

SUGGESTED EQUIPMENT LIST

Asparagus steamer
Baking dish with cover (8 x 13 x 1 inches)
Blender
Bowl (medium)
Chef's knife
Cutting board
Electric mixer
Food mill
Measuring cups

Measuring spoons
Meat thermometer
Melon baller
Mold (6-cup)
Pot holder
Saucepans (medium and large)
Scale
String
Vegetable peeler
Wooden spoon

"CREAMED" ZUCCHINI SOUP

6 cups sliced zucchini
1½ quarts Chicken Stock (see page 31)
½ cup quartered onion

3 cups evaporated skimmed milk
2 teaspoons salt, or to taste
Chopped chives to garnish

Combine zucchini, stock, and onion in large saucepan. Bring to a boil; reduce heat. Simmer 10 minutes or until zucchini is tender. Set aside 12 slices of zucchini for garnish. In several batches, puree vegetable–stock mixture in blender container; return to saucepan. Add milk and salt; heat but *do not boil*. Divide evenly into 12 soup bowls. Garnish each portion with 1 reserved slice of zucchini and sprinkle with chives. Makes 12 servings.

TOMATO ASPIC

1 quart mixed vegetable juice
12 canned medium tomatoes
8 celery ribs with leaves, cut up
¼ cup lemon juice
3 tablespoons dehydrated onion flakes

2 teaspoons basil
1 teaspoon salt
1 teaspoon paprika
2 bay leaves
2 envelopes unflavored gelatin
Lettuce leaves or chicory

Combine first 9 ingredients in saucepan; simmer 30 minutes. Put through food mill and discard solids. Return liquid to saucepan. Sprinkle gelatin over liquid; allow to soften. Cook over low heat, stirring constantly, until gelatin is dissolved. Pour into 5- to 6-cup mold. Chill until set. Arrange lettuce leaves or chicory on serving platter. Unmold aspic; serve on lettuce. Makes 12 servings.

Variation: When gelatin mixture is about the consistency of unbeaten egg whites, fold in 1½ cups chopped celery, green peppers, grated carrots, or any combination of the above.

BONED ROLLED LEG OF LAMB

If desired, ask the butcher to crack the bones for use in making Lamb Stock (see page 31). The bones or stock can be frozen until needed.

¼ cup chopped fresh parsley
3 tablespoons lemon juice
2 garlic cloves
¾ teaspoon salt
½ teaspoon rosemary

15 peppercorns
4½ pounds boned, rolled, and tied leg of lamb
Parsley sprigs to garnish

Place first 6 ingredients in blender container; process for 15 to 20 seconds or until thoroughly combined. With tip of knife, cut small slits all over lamb roast. With fingers, spread parsley mixture over lamb and into the slits. Cover and refrigerate several hours, if possible. Place lamb on rack in roasting pan. Insert meat thermometer in thickest part of meat.

Roast at 325°F. for 25 to 30 minutes per pound, or until thermometer registers 140° F., for rare; 30 to 35 minutes per pound, or until thermometer registers 160°F., for medium; 40 to 45 minutes per pound, or until thermometer registers 170 to 180°F., for well-done. Let stand 15 minutes before slicing. Serve garnished with parsley sprigs. Makes 12 servings.

PARSLIED PARISIENNE POTATOES

5 pounds potatoes
½ cup imitation (or diet)
  margarine, melted
2 tablespoons chopped fresh
  parsley

Salt, white pepper, and onion
  powder to taste

Pare potatoes. With parisienne scoop (melon baller), make 3 pounds of potato balls.* Place in large saucepan with boiling salted water to cover (½ teaspoon salt for each quart of water). Cover and cook about 20 to 25 minutes or until tender. Drain potatoes. Toss with remaining ingredients. Place in 9 x 13-inch baking pan. Bake covered, at 325°F., for 20 to 30 minutes, tossing once. Makes 12 servings.

* Save remaining potatoes. They can be cooked, mashed, and frozen in 4-ounce portions to be used at another time.

ASPARAGUS IN LEMON "BUTTER" SAUCE

Steaming asparagus in an upright position is an ideal method of preparation, as the tips are more tender than the stalks and therefore require less cooking. If you are steaming asparagus in smaller quantities than called for in this recipe, you can place them upright in the bottom of a double boiler with lower ends in ½ cup boiling water. Cover with inverted double boiler top. Proceed with method as directed below.

72 medium asparagus stalks
¼ cup lemon juice
¼ cup imitation (or diet)
  margarine, melted

Salt and freshly ground pepper to
  taste

Snap off lower part of asparagus stalks, where they break easily.* Remove heavy scales with sharp knife; rinse spears well. Tie asparagus spears together with string. Pour about 2 inches water into bottom of large asparagus steamer; bring to a boil. Place asparagus upright in steamer insert. Set insert over boiling water. Cover and steam 12 minutes or until tender. If liquid evaporates, add more as needed. Transfer asparagus to heated shallow serving dish, removing string. Combine lemon juice and margarine in small bowl. Pour over hot asparagus. Sprinkle with salt and pepper. Makes 12 servings.

* Save the lower parts to be used in soup, if desired.

APRICOT-YOGURT SHERBET WITH STRAWBERRY SAUCE

24 canned apricot halves with
  ¾ cup juice, no sugar added
1 envelope unflavored gelatin
1 cup plain unflavored yogurt
Artificial sweetener to equal 4
  teaspoons sugar

Dash almond extract, or to taste
Strawberry Sauce (see following
  recipe)

Pour juice from apricots into saucepan. Sprinkle gelatin over juice and allow to soften. Heat, stirring constantly, until gelatin is dissolved. In blender container or food processor combine apricots, yogurt, sweetener, almond extract, and gelatin mixture; process until smooth. Pour mixture into medium bowl and place in freezer; freeze until almost solid. Remove from freezer and beat. Repeat freezing and beating procedure 2 more times. Sherbet can be refrigerated up to 1 hour before serving. Divide evenly into 12 sherbet glasses. Divide Strawberry Sauce into 12 equal portions. Top each serving sherbet with 1 portion sauce. Makes 12 servings.

Strawberry Sauce

6 cups strawberries, divided
Artificial sweetener to equal 6
  teaspoons sugar (optional)

Combine 3 cups strawberries, and sweetener if desired, in blender container; process until smooth. Slice remaining strawberries; fold into pureed mixture. Serve as directed in recipe for Apricot-Yogurt Sherbet (see preceding recipe).

FROM RUSSIA—WITH TASTE FOR EIGHT

Chilled Borscht
Caraway Beef "Stroganoff" with Noodles
Steamed Broccoli
Mixed Salad with Vinaigrette Dressing
Cherry-Apricot Pudding
Tea

How exciting to visit the Soviet Union—when the only passport needed is an invitation to your Russian dinner! Actually, the USSR is so vast and varied and has so many cuisines, you can treat your friends to a taste tour of the provinces. Introduce them to Borscht, that ethnic beet-and-sour-cream favorite, originally improvised by Russian peasants to make thrifty use of leftover vegetables. Borscht can be served either hot or chilled. We suggest the cold version, since winter snows have melted. We also suggest exchanging the sour cream for a "safer" Russian favorite: yogurt. The same substitution works deliciously in Caraway Beef "Stroganoff"—an international gourmet favorite, which originated in Siberia. Serve it with the customary accompaniment—noodles, a staple of the Ukraine where wheat is so abundant that the area gained fame as "the breadbasket of Europe." Russians love sweets (a trait they have in common with a good part of the world's population!), and in the Georgian region a traditional dessert is slices of fruit swimming in syrup. Our recipe deftly translates this into a fruit pudding that's amazingly permissible on a weight-loss program! Although you may not have a samovar, the tea urn symbolic of Russian hospitality, you can serve tea Russian style—in tall glasses—along with cheery toasts of *"na zdorovie"* (to your health). Since your "trip" is so inexpensive, you may wish to invest in balalaika records to provide appropriate background music.

SUGGESTED SHOPPING LIST

Staples and Miscellaneous

Artificial sweetener
Bay leaves
Caraway seeds
Dehydrated onion flakes
Garlic powder
Instant beef broth and seasoning mix
Paprika
Salt
Vanilla extract
White pepper

Browning sauce
Cider vinegar
Red wine vinegar or tarragon vinegar

Cornstarch
Nonstick cooking spray
Tea

Vegetable oil

Raisin bread

Beef stock, 1½ cups (see page 31)

Additional Items

Boneless beef, 3 pounds

Plain unflavored yogurt, 1 16-ounce
  container

Broccoli, 1 medium bunch
Iceberg lettuce, 1 small head
Mushrooms, 1 pound
Onion, 1 medium
Radishes, 1 bag
Romaine lettuce, 1 small head
Tomatoes, 4 medium

Canned apricots, no sugar added,
  2 16-ounce cans
Canned pitted cherries, no sugar
  added, 1 16-ounce can

Canned whole beets, 2 16-ounce cans

Enriched broad noodles, 1 16-ounce
  box

SUGGESTED EQUIPMENT LIST

Baking pan
Blender
Bowl (large)
Can opener
Chef's knife
Cutting board
Measuring cups

Measuring spoons
Pot holder
Saucepans (with covers)
Scale
Steamer insert and 2-quart saucepan
  or double boiler
Wooden spoon

CHILLED BORSCHT

3½ cups drained canned whole
   beets, chopped, reserve liquid
½ cup cider vinegar
¼ cup dehydrated onion flakes
Artificial sweetener to equal 4
   teaspoons sugar (optional)

3 packets instant beef broth and
   seasoning mix
½ cup plain unflavored yogurt

Add enough water to reserved beet liquid to equal 1½ quarts liquid. In saucepan combine liquid with remaining ingredients except yogurt. Cover and simmer for 20 minutes. Place ½ of borscht in blender container and process until smooth. Combine with remaining borscht; chill. Divide borscht evenly into 8 soup bowls. Top each portion with 1 tablespoon yogurt. Makes 8 servings.

CARAWAY BEEF "STROGANOFF" WITH NOODLES

3 cups sliced mushrooms
½ cup sliced onion
1 tablespoon paprika
1 teaspoon caraway seeds
1 bay leaf
⅛ teaspoon garlic powder
1½ cups Beef Stock (see page
   31)
¾ cup water

1 teaspoon browning sauce
3 tablespoons cornstarch,
   dissolved in 3 tablespoons
   water
2 pounds boned cooked beef, cut
   into thin strips
½ cup plain unflavored yogurt
4 cups cooked enriched broad
   noodles, hot

In saucepan combine mushrooms, onion, paprika, caraway seeds, bay leaf, and garlic powder. Cook about 5 minutes or until mushrooms are tender. Add stock, water, and browning sauce; bring to a boil. Stir in cornstarch; reduce heat and cook, stirring constantly, until sauce thickens. Remove bay leaf. Add beef; cook until beef is thoroughly heated. Remove from heat and fold in yogurt. Place hot noodles in large serving bowl. Top with "Stroganoff." Serve immediately. Makes 8 servings

STEAMED BROCCOLI

1 medium bunch broccoli,
   washed, stem ends trimmed

2 cups water

Stand broccoli, stems down, in steamer insert. Pour water into 2-quart pan. Set insert in pan and place over medium heat. When water begins to boil, cover pan and steam 6 to 8 minutes. Makes 8 servings.

Note: If steamer is unavailable, broccoli can be steamed in double boiler. Pour about 1 inch water into bottom half of double boiler. Stand broccoli in water. Place over medium heat. When water begins to boil, invert top half of double boiler over broccoli. Steam 6 to 8 minutes.

MIXED SALAD WITH VINAIGRETTE DRESSING

*1 medium head iceberg lettuce,
washed and torn into bite-size
pieces*
*1 small head romaine lettuce,
washed and torn into bite-size
pieces*

*4 medium tomatoes, each cut
into 8 wedges*
1 cup sliced radishes
*Vinaigrette Dressing (see page
30)*

Combine vegetables in large salad bowl; chill. When ready to serve, pour Vinaigrette Dressing over salad; toss to coat all vegetables. Makes 8 servings.

CHERRY-APRICOT PUDDING

8 slices raisin bread
*32 canned apricot halves with 1
cup juice, no sugar added*
*1 cup canned pitted cherries, no
sugar added*
*Artificial sweetener to equal 6
teaspoons sugar*

1 teaspoon vanilla extract
*2 tablespoons plus 2 teaspoons
cornstarch, dissolved in 3
tablespoons water*

Press 6 slices of bread into bottom and along sides of an 8 x 8 x 2-inch baking pan that has been sprayed with nonstick cooking spray. In saucepan combine remaining ingredients except bread and cornstarch. Bring to a boil. Reduce heat and stir in cornstarch. Cook, stirring constantly, until thickened. Pour fruit mixture into baking pan; top with remaining 2 slices bread. Cover and bake at 400°F. for 20 minutes. Chill. Invert onto serving dish. Makes 8 servings.

CONFIRMATION PARTY FOR TWELVE

Tomato Juice
Roast Veal with Paprikash Sauce
Barley Pilaf Forestière
Savory Green Beans
Spinach-Orange Salad
Lemon "Soufflé" with Blackberry Sauce
Beverage

Confirm your culinary skill with an elegant dinner party in honor of a confirmation or any other meaningful event you'd like to honor. Roast Veal makes a delicious entrée that is popular among gourmets. Since it's a delicate meat, veal is especially appropriate in the spring. The mild taste calls for a highly flavored sauce, such as our spicy Paprikash. Surprise guests with an unusual accompaniment—Barley Pilaf Forestière, instead of the more customary rice. The colorful duo of spinach and oranges is an imaginative combination for a piquant spring salad. A well-made soufflé is always impressive, and this one, which combines lemon and blackberry flavors, will delight eyes as well as palates. It's easier on your schedule than it looks, too, for the gelatin base helps the "soufflé" hold together so well it can even be made ahead of time. This high-style menu helps hold shapes for high styles!

SUGGESTED SHOPPING LIST

Staples and Miscellaneous

Artificial sweetener
Bay leaves
Garlic powder
Instant beef broth and seasoning mix
Instant chicken broth and seasoning
  mix
Marjoram
Nutmeg
Paprika
Peppercorns
Salt
Thyme
Vanilla extract
White pepper
Yellow food coloring

Browning sauce
Worcestershire sauce

Cornstarch
Unflavored gelatin

Imitation (or diet) margarine
Mayonnaise

Additional Items

Boned, rolled and tied veal roast,
  4½-pound

Lemons, 3
Oranges, 6 small

Carrots, 3 medium
Celery, 2 ribs
Green beans, 2 pounds
Onions, 2 medium
Spinach, 3 pounds

Frozen blackberries, no sugar added,
  1 16-ounce bag

Frozen orange juice concentrate,
  1 6-fluid-ounce can

Canned mushroom stems and pieces,
  2 8-ounce cans
Pimientos, 1 4-ounce jar
Tomato puree, 1 16-ounce can
Canned water chestnuts, 1 8-ounce can

Tomato juice, 4 12-fluid-ounce cans

Evaporated skimmed milk, 2 13-fluid-
  ounce cans

Barley, 1 16-ounce box

SUGGESTED EQUIPMENT LIST

Baking pan (9 x 13 inches)
Blender
Bowls (small, large)
Can opener
Chef's knife
Colander
Cutting board
Electric mixer
Measuring cups
Measuring spoons

Meat thermometer
Pepper mill
Pot holder
Rack
Roasting pan
Saucepans
Scale
Vegetable peeler
Wooden spoon

TOMATO JUICE

Serve ½ cup chilled tomato juice to each person. Garnish each portion with a lemon wedge.

ROAST VEAL WITH PAPRIKASH SAUCE

4½-pound boned, rolled, and
   tied veal roast
½ teaspoon garlic powder
Salt and freshly ground pepper
   to taste

Paprikash Sauce (see following
   recipe)

Preheat oven to 300°F. Place veal on rack in roasting pan; season with garlic powder, salt, and pepper. Insert meat thermometer in center of roast. Roast for about 40 minutes per pound (approximately 3 hours), or until thermometer registers 170°F. Divide Paprikash Sauce into 12 equal servings. Serve each portion of veal with 1 serving sauce. Makes 12 servings.

Paprikash Sauce

1 cup finely diced onions
1 cup finely diced carrots
1 cup finely diced celery
4 packets instant chicken broth
   and seasoning mix
2 teaspoons paprika
Artificial sweetener to equal 2
   teaspoons sugar (optional)

1 bay leaf
½ teaspoon each garlic powder,
   thyme, salt, and Worcestershire
   sauce
¼ teaspoon freshly ground
   pepper
1 quart water
2 cups tomato puree

In saucepan combine first 9 ingredients. Cook 3 to 5 minutes, stirring occasionally. Add water and tomato puree. Bring to a boil; reduce heat and simmer 25 minutes or until vegetables are tender. Remove from heat and remove bay leaf. Serve as directed in recipe for Roast Veal (see preceding recipe).

BARLEY PILAF FORESTIÈRE

1½ cups drained canned
   mushrooms, chopped
1 cup finely diced onions
¼ cup imitation (or diet)
   margarine
2 packets instant beef broth and
   seasoning mix

2 teaspoons Worcestershire
   sauce
1 teaspoon browning sauce
½ teaspoon marjoram
¼ teaspoon garlic powder
6 cups cooked barley

In 9 x 13-inch baking pan combine all ingredients except barley. Bake at 450°F. for 10 minutes. Remove from oven and stir in barley. Reduce oven temperature to 300°F. and continue baking for 25 minutes longer or until thoroughly heated. Makes 12 servings.

SAVORY GREEN BEANS

1 cup sliced, drained, canned
  water chestnuts
¼ cup diced pimientos
1 tablespoon plus 1 teaspoon
  cornstarch, dissolved in 1
  tablespoon water
2 packets instant chicken broth
  and seasoning mix

¼ teaspoon garlic powder
⅛ teaspoon nutmeg
1 cup water
6 cups cooked cut green beans
2 tablespoons imitation (or diet)
  margarine
Salt and white pepper to taste

In saucepan combine first 6 ingredients; add water and stir to combine.
Cook over medium heat, stirring constantly, until thickened. Add green
beans; continue to cook until thoroughly heated. Remove from heat; add
margarine and toss. Season with salt and pepper. Makes 12 servings.

SPINACH-ORANGE SALAD

½ cup mayonnaise
Artificial sweetener to equal 6
  teaspoons sugar
1½ teaspoons vanilla extract
1½ teaspoons lemon juice

12 cups spinach leaves, rinsed
  well
6 small oranges, peeled and
  sliced into rings

In small bowl combine mayonnaise, sweetener, vanilla, and lemon juice.
Place 1 cup spinach leaves on each of 12 salad plates. Divide orange slices
into 12 equal portions. Arrange 1 portion of orange slices over spinach, on
each plate. Top each serving of salad with an equal amount of dressing.
Makes 12 servings.

LEMON "SOUFFLÉ" WITH BLACKBERRY SAUCE

Lemon "Soufflé":

2 cups evaporated skimmed milk
Artificial sweetener to equal 20
  teaspoons sugar, divided
2 teaspoons vanilla extract,
  divided
1 cup water
½ cup lemon juice
¼ cup plus 2 tablespoons frozen
  orange juice concentrate

2 envelopes unflavored gelatin
1 tablespoon plus 1 teaspoon
  cornstarch
1 tablespoon plus 1 teaspoon
  grated lemon rind
6 drops yellow food coloring

Blackberry Sauce:

3 cups frozen blackberries, no
  sugar added, thawed

Artificial sweetener to equal 12
  teaspoons sugar
1 teaspoon vanilla extract

To Prepare "Soufflé": In large bowl combine milk, artificial sweetener to equal 8 teaspoons sugar, and 1 teaspoon vanilla. Chill. In saucepan combine next 7 ingredients, 1 teaspoon vanilla, and artificial sweetener to equal 12 teaspoons sugar. Stir to dissolve cornstarch. Let stand a few minutes to allow gelatin to soften. Heat, stirring constantly, until gelatin is dissolved. Refrigerate until mixture is cool and the consistency of syrup. Beat chilled milk mixture until stiff; fold in cooled gelatin mixture. Divide evenly into 12 dessert dishes. Chill

To Prepare Blackberry Sauce: Combine thawed berries, artificial sweetener, and vanilla in blender container; process until smooth. Chill.

To Serve: Divide sauce into 12 equal portions. Top each serving of Lemon "Soufflé" with 1 portion of sauce. Makes 12 servings

May

With springtime gardens bursting into
full bloom, our May menus are alive
with color and freshness to reflect this
season! The Spring Vegetable Bouquet,
Vegetable Salad Bar, and Baked Tomato
with Basil are all pleasing to the eye
and a pleasure to the palate! These along
with our other May specialties will
bring the beauty of the season to
your table.

A SIMPLE SPRING BUFFET FOR EIGHT

Spring Vegetable Bouquet □ Mustard-Vinaigrette Dressing
Roast Beef □ Mushroom Sauce
Lemon Potatoes
Honeydew and Pineapple in Melon Container
Coffee or Tea

Many an ancient culture greeted the spring season with a joyous feast. Welcome spring with a relaxed buffet that "stars" a wonderful array of fresh vegetables and fruits. Each dish can be prepared ahead of time, so that you can greet guests calmly, clad in your brightest spring attire. (Your guests can relax, too, knowing that your tempting table will help them stay in shape for revealing warm-weather fashions.) Remember that successful buffet hosting calls for utensils to keep hot foods from cooling off too soon. A hot tray and chafing dish are invaluable items. To keep cold foods at the right temperature, chill the serving platters first. The colorful Spring Vegetable Bouquet and luscious fruit dessert will brighten the buffet table. We suggest pastel shades for tablecloth and napkins—cloth, if you prefer, although paper is perfectly appropriate, especially if you're hosting in a garden. And, of course, use flowers everywhere!

———— ◆•◆ ————

SUGGESTED SHOPPING LIST

Staples and Miscellaneous

Anise extract (optional)	Capers
Instant beef broth and seasoning mix or bouillon cubes	Dijon mustard
	Wine vinegar
Instant chicken broth and seasoning mix	
	Coffee or tea
Peppercorns	Cornstarch
Salt	
Tarragon (optional)	Vegetable oil

Additional Items

Boned, rolled, and tied rib roast beef, 1 (3-pound)

Honeydew melon, 1 large (about 6¾ pounds)

Lemons, 2

Pineapple, 1 small, or canned pineapple chunks, no sugar added, 1 20-ounce can

Asparagus stalks, 24 medium

Carrots, 6 medium

Cauliflower, 2 medium heads

Cherry tomatoes, 3 pints

Garlic clove, 1

Dill, 1 bunch

Green beans, 1½ pounds

Iceberg lettuce, 1 head

Mint, 1 bunch (optional)

Mushrooms, 1 pound

Parsley, 1 bunch

Potatoes, 2 pounds

Scallions, 1 bunch

Watercress, 1 bunch

Frozen peas, 2 10-ounce packages, or fresh peas, 1 pound

Canned julienne beets, 2 16-ounce cans

SUGGESTED EQUIPMENT LIST

Can opener

Carving knife

Casserole (shallow) with cover

Chef's knife

Colander

Cutting board

Jar with tight-fitting cover

Large strainer

Measuring cups

Measuring spoons

Meat thermometer

Melon baller

Pepper mill

Pot holder

Roasting pan with rack

Saucepans with covers (medium and large)

Scale

Vegetable peeler

Wooden spoon

SPRING VEGETABLE BOUQUET

Serve with Mustard-Vinaigrette Dressing (see recipe, page 149).

Cook vegetables early in the day. Cook each vegetable separately. The easiest way is to partially fill large saucepan with boiling salted water (use 1 teaspoon salt for each quart of water). Place 1 type of vegetable in large strainer. Immerse strainer in boiling water and cook until vegetables are tender-crisp. Then hold strainer under cold running water in order to stop the cooking process and quickly cool vegetables. Drain well and refrigerate. Repeat procedure with each vegetable that is to be cooked. Keep varieties of vegetables separate. Minimum preparation and cooking times are noted for each vegetable.

Peas: Use 2 cups fresh or frozen peas. Cook 5 to 7 minutes.

Carrots: Pare 6 medium carrots, then slice thinly. Cook 4 to 5 minutes.

Green Beans: Snap or cut off tips of about 1½ pounds green beans, leaving remaining beans whole; measure 4 cups. Cook for 7 to 8 minutes.

Asparagus: Break off tough bottom portion of 24 medium asparagus stalks; trim away any tough scales. Wash thoroughly. Cook for 6 to 8 minutes.

Cauliflower: Use 4 cups cauliflower florets. Add juice from 1 medium lemon or 2 tablespoons lemon juice to water. Cook 4 to 6 minutes.

Beets: Use 1½ cups drained canned julienne beets. Form 2 large lettuce leaves into a cup; fill with beets. Sprinkle with ½ cup chopped scallions.

Cherry Tomatoes: Use 40 cherry tomatoes. Rinse and drain.

To Assemble: Do this 1 or 2 hours before your guests arrive. Place beets in center of large, round serving platter. Arrange remaining vegetables, except cherry tomatoes, around beets in separate groups. Arrange a row of 8 cherry tomatoes between each group of vegetables, radiating out from the center. Cover platter with plastic wrap and refrigerate. Just before serving, pour Mustard-Vinaigrette Dressing over vegetables. Garnish by sprinkling 1 teaspoon minced fresh parsley over the green beans, 1 teaspoon minced fresh mint leaves or tarragon over the peas and 1 teaspoon over the carrots, and 1 teaspoon rinsed and finely chopped capers over the asparagus. Makes 8 servings.

MUSTARD-VINAIGRETTE DRESSING

⅓ cup vegetable oil
3 tablespoons plus 1 teaspoon
   wine vinegar

2 teaspoons Dijon mustard
Salt and freshly ground pepper
   to taste

Combine all ingredients in jar with tight-fitting cover or in bowl. Cover and shake or mix well before serving. Use as directed in recipe for Spring Vegetable Bouquet.

ROAST BEEF

Serve with Mushroom Sauce (see recipe, page 150).

3-pound boned, rolled, and tied
   rib roast of beef
1 garlic clove, cut
Salt and freshly ground pepper
   to taste

Parsley sprigs and carrot curls
   to garnish (see page 13)

Rub beef with cut garlic clove. Sprinkle with salt and pepper. Insert meat thermometer so tip is in center of thickest part of roast. Place beef on rack in roasting pan. Roast at 325°F. until thermometer registers 140°F. for rare, 160°F. for medium, 170°F. for well-done, or about 30 to 45 minutes per pound, depending on desired degree of doneness. Remove from oven; allow roast to "rest" 15 minutes before carving. Garnish with parsley and carrot curls. Makes 8 servings.

MUSHROOM SAUCE

Serve with Roast Beef (see recipe, page 149).

2 cups sliced mushrooms
1½ cups beef bouillon, divided
1 tablespoon plus 1 teaspoon
   cornstarch, dissolved in ¼
   cup water

Salt and pepper to taste

Combine mushrooms and ¼ cup bouillon in medium saucepan. Cover; cook 3 to 5 minutes or until mushrooms are tender. Add remaining bouillon; then stir in cornstarch. Continue to stir and cook until thickened. Season with salt and pepper. Makes 8 servings.

LEMON POTATOES

To prevent raw potatoes from darkening, place them in a bowl with water to cover and refrigerate until ready to cook.

2 pounds pared potatoes, cut
   into ½-inch dice
3 tablespoons lemon juice
1 packet instant chicken broth
   and seasoning mix

1 tablespoon chopped fresh
   parsley or dill
1 teaspoon grated lemon rind

Place potatoes in saucepan with boiling salted water to cover. Return water to boil; reduce heat and simmer 12 to 15 minutes or until potatoes are tender. Drain; transfer potatoes to shallow casserole. Sprinkle with lemon juice and broth mix; toss gently. Cover and bake at 325°F. for 10 to 15 minutes or until piping hot. Remove cover and sprinkle with parsley or dill, and lemon rind. Makes 8 servings.

HONEYDEW AND PINEAPPLE IN MELON CONTAINER

This should be prepared several hours before your guests arrive. If a ripe pineapple is unavailable, use 2 cups canned pineapple chunks, no sugar added.

1 large honeydew melon, about
   6¾ pounds
1 small pineapple, pared, cored,
   and cubed

½ teaspoon anise extract
   (optional)
Mint sprigs to garnish (optional)

Remove thin slice from bottom of honeydew, being careful not to cut through to pulp. This will allow melon to stand upright. Cut slice off top of melon, about 6 inches in diameter, in zigzag fashion (refer to Orange Bowls, page 16). Using a parisienne scoop (melon baller), scoop out 4 cups melon balls; place in large bowl. Remove seeds, excess pulp, and liquid from melon; reserve pulp for another use. Set melon "container" aside. Combine pineapple with melon balls. Sprinkle with extract, if desired; toss to combine. Fill melon "container" with fruit mixture; garnish with mint sprigs if desired. Refrigerate until chilled. Makes 8 servings.

BRIDGE CLUB BUFFET FOR EIGHT

Vegetable Salad Bar
Chived Yogurt Dressing □ Ketchup Dressing
Buttermilk-Mustard Dressing
Noodle Pudding with Blueberry Topping
Fresh Fruit Cup
Coffee or Tea

Hold a winning hand by setting up a weight-guarding salad bar . . . an ace way of serving when several card games are going at the same time. Actually, this menu goes well with any kind of meeting when you want a luncheon that will sit well on the sidelines while you concentrate on the main business of the day. There is nothing as effortless as a do-it-yourself buffet, and these economical dishes can easily be multiplied for a larger crowd. Feature a nutritious arrangement of vegetables, garnished as imaginatively as you wish—perhaps in a way that highlights the meeting's theme. Invite guests to help themselves from the trio of zesty dressings. The Noodle Pudding with its mouth-watering topping will score extra points. To make your hosting easier, prepare everything ahead of time. Wrap the vegetables and fruits in individual plastic bags in the refrigerator. (Sprinkling lemon juice over the apple pieces will keep them from discoloring.) The eggs can be boiled and shelled in advance, but it's best to slice them just before serving. Maintain an everything-under-control tone by setting the scene in casual style, with paper plates and plastic forks and spoons. Note that nothing has to be cut, so no balancing acts are necessary. (Bet your guests vote for your being one smart "dummy"!)

SUGGESTED SHOPPING LIST
Staples and Miscellaneous

Artificial sweetener
Celery seed
Chopped chives
Dehydrated onion flakes
Garlic powder
Onion powder
Pepper
Salt
Vanilla extract

Ketchup
Prepared mustard
Wine vinegar
Worcestershire sauce

Coffee or tea
Cornstarch
Nonstick cooking spray

Margarine

Additional Items

Buttermilk, ¾ cup
Cottage cheese, 1 32-ounce container
Eggs, 8
Plain unflavored yogurt, 3 8-ounce
    containers

Apple, 1 small
Grapefruits, 2 medium
Lemon, 1
Oranges, 3 small
Strawberries, 1 pint

Carrots, 8 medium
Cauliflower, 1 head
Cherry tomatoes, 2 pints

Cucumbers, 4 medium
Green beans, 1¼ pounds
Mushrooms, 2 pounds
Parsley, 1 bunch
Zucchini, 4 medium (approximately
    5 ounces each)

Frozen blueberries, no sugar added,
    1 16-ounce bag

Evaporated skimmed milk, 1 13-fluid-
    ounce can

Enriched noodles, ½-inch wide,
    1 16-ounce box

SUGGESTED EQUIPMENT LIST

Bowls (small, large)
Casserole (2½-quart, shallow)
Chef's knife
Cutting board
Electric mixer
Measuring cups

Measuring spoons
Pot holder
Saucepans (medium)
Vegetable peeler
Wire whisk
Wooden spoon

VEGETABLE SALAD BAR

Serve with Chived Yogurt, Ketchup, and Buttermilk-Mustard Dressings
(see recipes, page 154).

Vegetables should be cooked just until tender-crisp and drained immediately.

    4 eggs, hard-cooked and chilled
    4 cups cooked green beans,
        chilled
    4 cups cooked carrot slices,
        chilled
    4 cups cooked cauliflower florets,
        chilled

    4 cups mushroom caps, blanched
        and chilled
    4 cups sliced zucchini, chilled
    40 cherry tomatoes, unhulled,
        chilled
    4 medium cucumbers, pared, cut
        into thin strips, and chilled

Slice each egg in half lengthwise. Arrange egg halves and each type of vegetable in a separate decorative container. Use new clay flowerpots or matching narrow wooden trays or clear glass bowls. Invite guests to help themselves to eggs, vegetables, and dressings. Makes 8 servings.

CHIVED YOGURT DRESSING

Serve with Vegetable Salad Bar (see recipe, page 153)

¾ cup plain unflavored yogurt
3 tablespoons chopped chives
3 tablespoons minced fresh
    parsley

¾ teaspoon onion powder
½ teaspoon garlic powder

In small bowl combine all ingredients. Chill for at least 4 hours. Makes 8 servings.

KETCHUP DRESSING

Serve with Vegetable Salad Bar (see recipe, page 153).

¾ cup evaporated skimmed milk
3 tablespoons ketchup
1 tablespoon plus 1½ teaspoons
    dehydrated onion flakes

1 tablespoon plus 1½ teaspoons
    wine vinegar
¾ teaspoon Worcestershire sauce
Salt and pepper to taste

In small bowl, using wire whisk, combine all ingredients. Chill for at least 2 hours. Makes 8 servings.

BUTTERMILK-MUSTARD DRESSING

Serve with Vegetable Salad Bar (see recipe, page 153)

¾ cup buttermilk
2 tablespoons prepared mustard

⅛ teaspoon celery seed.

In small bowl, using wire whisk, combine all ingredients. Chill for at least 2 hours. Makes 8 servings.

NOODLE PUDDING WITH BLUEBERRY TOPPING

Serve warm or chilled.

2⅔ cups cottage cheese
1 cup plain unflavored yogurt
4 eggs
Artificial sweetener to equal 16
    teaspoons sugar
2 tablespoons cornstarch

2 tablespoons margarine, melted
2 teaspoons vanilla extract
4 cups cooked enriched noodles,
    ½-inch wide
Blueberry Topping (see recipe,
    page 155)

In large mixing bowl combine first 7 ingredients. Beat with electric mixer on medium speed until smooth. Stir in noodles. Transfer to shallow 2½-quart casserole that has been sprayed with nonstick cooking spray. Bake at 350°F. for 45 minutes. Divide evenly into 8 serving dishes. Top each portion with ⅛ of the Blueberry Topping. Makes 8 servings.

Blueberry Topping

2 cups frozen blueberries, no
  sugar added, thawed
Artificial sweetener to equal 6
  teaspoons sugar

1 tablespoon plus 1 teaspoon
  cornstarch
1 tablespoon each lemon juice
  and water

Combine all ingredients in medium saucepan. Bring to a boil; reduce heat and, stirring constantly, simmer for 3 minutes or until mixture thickens. Use as directed in recipe for Noodle Pudding (see recipe, page 154).

FRESH FRUIT CUP

1½ cups fresh grapefruit
  sections
1½ cups fresh orange sections

1 cup fresh strawberries, cut
  into halves
1 small apple, cored and diced

In medium bowl combine all ingredients; toss gently. Divide evenly into eight 6-ounce dessert dishes. Makes 8 servings.

LET'S TOUR TURKEY FOR SIX

Domates Corbasi ("Creamed" Tomato Soup)
Broiled Lamb Steaks with Mint Sauce
"Creamed" Eggplant
Skewered Vegetables
Rice Pudding with Rose Water
Turkish Coffee

Invite friends to dine like sultans on the cuisine of one of the world's most ancient civilizations. Our Turkish-flavored menu, updated in modern, weight-controlling manner, features lamb—a national favorite. Vegetables grow in incredible colors and sizes in that fertile land, so we suggest a varied sampling served in Eastern style on skewers. Eggplant—a native Asian vegetable—is so popular that Turkish cooks have invented more than forty ways to prepare it! Since they do not consider a meal complete without rice, we've translated that into a pudding (the Turks also dote on desserts) and have given it exotic flavor with scented rose water. You need travel no farther than your local stores for all the ingredients except the rose water, which should be available in the nearest specialty store. Concoct our easy version of that famous thick brew known as Turkish Coffee, and serve it in the traditional fashion—in tiny cups on a metal tray. Your guests might find it fun to come garbed in gorgeously patterned Byzantine fashions. You may also want to emulate another Turkish tradition, that of beginning a meal with the toast *"Afiyet olsun"* ("Enjoy your meal"). Chances are, your guests will want to echo the delightful compliment one pays a superb cook: *"Elinize saglik"* ("I wish your hands good health").

SUGGESTED SHOPPING LIST
Staples and Miscellaneous

Allspice
Artificial sweetener
Cinnamon
Dried mint
Instant chicken broth and seasoning
  mix
Salt
Vanilla extract
White pepper

Rose water

Ground espresso coffee

Lamb steaks, 6, 8 ounces each	Onion, 1 large
	Parsley, 1 bunch
Plain unflavored yogurt, 1 16-ounce container	Red peppers, 2 medium
Skim milk, 3 cups	Frozen whole okra, 1 16-ounce bag
	Tomato puree, 1 28-ounce can
Lemons, 2	
	Evaporated skimmed milk, 1 13-fluid-ounce can
Bermuda onion, 1 small	
Cucumbers, 2 medium	
Eggplant, 1 large (about 2 pounds)	Enriched rice, 1 16-ounce box
Mushrooms, ½ pound	Prunes, large, 1 12-ounce box

SUGGESTED EQUIPMENT LIST

Baking pan	Measuring spoons
Bowls (small and medium)	Pot holder
Can opener	Roasting pan with rack
Casserole (1-quart)	Saucepan (large)
Chef's knife	Saucepan (small, shallow)
Cutting board	Scale
Fork	6-inch skewers, 6
Grater	Vegetable peeler
Measuring cups	Wooden spoons

DOMATES CORBASI ("CREAMED" TOMATO SOUP)

1 cup finely chopped onions
2 packets instant chicken broth and seasoning mix
3 cups tomato puree
3 cups water

1 tablespoon chopped fresh parsley
2 teaspoons salt
¼ teaspoon pepper
1 cup evaporated skimmed milk

In large saucepan combine onions and broth mix; cook, stirring frequently, until onions are tender. Add tomato puree, water, parsley, salt, and pepper; bring to a boil. Reduce heat; simmer for 40 minutes, stirring frequently. Transfer 1 cup of tomato soup to medium bowl. Gradually add milk to bowl, stirring constantly. Combine milk mixture with soup in saucepan, stirring constantly. Remove from heat and serve. Makes 6 servings.

BROILED LAMB STEAKS WITH MINT SAUCE

1 cup plain unflavored yogurt
1 cup grated, pared cucumber
6 large prunes, pitted and diced
3 tablespoons chopped Bermuda onion

½ teaspoon dried mint
Salt to taste
6 lamb steaks, 8 ounces each

Combine first 6 ingredients in small serving bowl; chill. Broil lamb steaks on a rack, turning once, until done to taste. Transfer steaks to serving platter. Serve each steak with ⅙ of the chilled sauce. Makes 6 servings.

"CREAMED" EGGPLANT

Serve with Skewered Vegetables (see recipe below) and lemon wedges.

1 large eggplant, about 2 pounds   *⅛ teaspoon allspice*
¼ cup evaporated skimmed milk   *Salt and pepper to taste*

With the prongs of fork, pierce eggplant skin in several places. Place in baking pan and broil 4 inches from source of heat, turning several times until skin is charred. Let eggplant cool; strip off charred skin. Place pulp in bowl; mash with fork. Add remaining ingredients; stir to combine. Transfer to 1-quart casserole. Bake at 350°F. for 20 minutes. Transfer eggplant mixture to small serving dish. Makes 6 servings.

To Serve: Place dish of "Creamed" Eggplant in center of large, round serving platter. Arrange skewers of vegetables, like spokes of a wheel, around eggplant. Garnish by interspersing lemon wedges between skewers.

SKEWERED VEGETABLES

Serve with "Creamed" Eggplant (see recipe above).

1 cup frozen whole okra   *1 medium cucumber, scored*
½ cup mushroom caps   *2 medium red peppers, seeded*
2 tablespoons lemon juice   *and cut into 24 equal pieces*

Cook frozen okra according to package directions. Set aside. Place mushrooms in saucepan with boiling water to cover; add lemon juice. Cook for 5 minutes; drain and reserve. Cut cucumber into 6 equal chunks. Divide each vegetable into 6 equal portions. Alternating ingredients, thread 1 portion of each vegetable onto a 6-inch skewer. Repeat with 5 more skewers and remaining vegetables. Serve as directed in recipe for "Creamed" Eggplant. Makes 6 servings.

RICE PUDDING WITH ROSE WATER

3 cups cooked enriched rice   *1 tablespoon vanilla extract*
3 cups skim milk   *1 teaspoon rose water*
Artificial sweetener to equal 8   *¼ teaspoon cinnamon*
teaspoons sugar

In saucepan combine all ingredients. Bring to a boil; reduce heat and simmer, stirring frequently, for 25 minutes or until milk is absorbed. Divide pudding evenly into six 8-ounce dessert dishes. Chill for at least 2 hours. Makes 6 servings.

TURKISH COFFEE

If you have a decorative Turkish coffee pot, use it of course. However, no special equipment is necessary. Our recipe uses a shallow saucepan.

*3 tablespoons ground espresso
  coffee
Artificial sweetener to equal 12
  teaspoons sugar*

*2 cups water
A few drops rose water (optional)*

In small, shallow saucepan combine espresso and sweetener; add water. Bring to a boil; remove from heat and let cool for 5 minutes. Repeat boiling process twice more. Drain the coffee from the grounds. Divide evenly into 6 demitasse cups. Place a drop of rose water into each cup, if desired. Serve immediately. Makes 6 servings.

MOTHER'S DAY TRAY FOR ONE

Scalloped Cantaloupe
Noodles and Cheese Surprise
Viennese Coffee or Chrysanthemum Tea

Some 300 years ago, it was the custom in England to visit one's parent on "Mothering Sunday" carrying a rather dangerous gift—fruitcake! Modern-day mothers appreciate loving offerings that are less weighty! Honor your own mother (or hint that your offspring might wish to "go-a-mothering") with our thoughtful breakfast-in-bed tray. The appealing menu looks as if it takes some effort but is actually quite simple to make, even for youngsters. Fruit festively scalloped and garnished with lime is complemented by a savory "Surprise" of noodles baked with cottage cheese. And what happier "waker-upper" could one ask for than our version of Viennese Coffee, or exotic Chrysanthemum Tea? Lovingly place a long-stemmed rose across the tray to add to a repast that tastefully says, "You're a very special mother" (and I'm helping you *look* special, too!).

———— •♦• ————

SUGGESTED SHOPPING LIST

Staples and Miscellaneous

Cinnamon	Coffee or Chrysanthemum tea
Nutmeg	
Pepper	Imitation (or diet) margarine

Additional Items

Cottage cheese, 1 8-ounce container	Enriched noodles, 1 16-ounce box
	Prunes, large, 1 12-ounce box
Cantaloupe, 1 small	
Lime, 1	Low-calorie whipped topping, 1 2½-ounce box

SUGGESTED EQUIPMENT LIST

Chef's knife	Measuring spoons
Coffee pot or tea kettle	Pot holder
Cutting board	Saucepan
Double boiler	Wooden spoon
Measuring cups	

SCALLOPED CANTALOUPE

1 small cantaloupe   *2 lime slices*

Cut cantalope in half crosswise in a zigzag fashion (refer to Orange
Bowls, page 16). Remove seeds. Reserve ½ cantaloupe for use at another
time. Serve ½ scalloped cantaloupe garnished with lime slices. Makes 1
serving.

NOODLES AND CHEESE SURPRISE

½ cup cooked enriched noodles   *1 teaspoon imitation (or diet)*
⅓ cup cottage cheese   *margarine*
1 large prune, pitted and   *Dash each nutmeg and pepper*
  diced

Combine all ingredients in top of double boiler, over boiling water. Cook,
stirring constantly, until thoroughly heated. Makes 1 serving.

VIENNESE COFFEE

Serve strong coffee in mug topped with 1½ tablespoons low-calorie
whipped topping. Sprinkle dash of cinnamon or nutmeg over whipped
topping.

CHRYSANTHEMUM TEA

This product is available in stores selling Chinese foods and in specialty
shops. Brew as you would any other tea.

A TASTE OF THE ORIENT FOR SIX

Chinese Lettuce Rolls
Barbecue Shrimp with Fluffy White Rice
Gingered Broccoli
Stir-Cooked Snow Peas
Orange-Cucumber Salad
Baked Pineapple Slices
Jasmine Tea

Sample the Orient without paying for it in pounds! For in this barbecue you can add flavor without fat via the use of lemon and that Asiatic staple, soy sauce. (In China, where the soybean grows, soy sauce is commonly used as a substitute for salt.) One of the great advantages of Chinese cookery is that it's fast. These delectable recipes take only moments to cook, and, in case of rain, they can be broiled indoors. Make sure every ingredient is ready ahead of time, however, since the preparation is more time-consuming than the actual cooking. Of course, your menu will include rice, but you'll surround it with a wealth of flavors, including ginger, one of the most widely used spices in Chinese cuisine. Here it lends a piquant taste to broccoli. And oranges, also native to the Orient, are included in the salad.

An imaginative decor will add to the scene. Ransack an Oriental crafts store for many-hued paper lanterns as well as chopsticks for the adventuresome. And how about a basket of rolled-up "fortunes" you can invent for each guest? (Sans the cookies, of course!)

SUGGESTED SHOPPING LIST

Staples and Miscellaneous

Artificial sweetener
Cinnamon
Dehydrated onion flakes
Garlic powder
Ginger
Instant beef broth and seasoning mix
Instant chicken broth and seasoning
   mix
Pepper
Salt
Sherry extract (optional)
Thyme

Soy sauce

Jasmine tea

Additional Items

Peeled and deveined shrimp, 2¼
   pounds

Buttermilk, ¾ cup

Lemons, 4
Pineapples, 2 small

Broccoli, 1 medium bunch
Cabbage, 1 small head
Celery, 1 rib
Cucumbers, 2 medium
Garlic cloves, 3
Ginger root, 1
Green peppers, 4 medium

Lettuce, 1 small head
Parsley, 1 bunch
Scallions, 9
Snow peas, 1 pound 2 ounces

Canned bamboo shoots, 1 8-ounce can
Canned bean sprouts, 2 16-ounce cans
Canned water chestnuts, 1 8-ounce can

Canned mandarin orange sections, no
   sugar added, 2 10½-ounce cans

Enriched white rice, 1 16-ounce box

SUGGESTED EQUIPMENT LIST

Bowls (small, medium)
Can opener
Casserole (shallow)
Chef's knife
Cutting board
Measuring cups
Measuring spoons
Nonstick baking pan (8 x 8 inches)
Paring knife

Pot holder
Saucepan with cover
Scale
12-inch skewers, 12
Strainer
Wide spatula
Wok (or nonstick skillet)
Wooden spoon

CHINESE LETTUCE ROLLS

2 garlic cloves, minced
½ teaspoon grated fresh ginger
  root
2 cups shredded cabbage
1 cup drained canned bean
  sprouts
½ cup diced celery
½ cup drained, canned sliced
  bamboo shoots
½ cup finely chopped scallions

½ cup sliced, drained, canned
  water chestnuts
1 packet instant chicken broth
  and seasoning mix
1 packet instant beef broth and
  seasoning mix
Artificial sweetener to equal 2
  teaspoons sugar (optional)
2 teaspoons soy sauce
6 large lettuce leaves

Heat wok or nonstick skillet. Add garlic and ginger root; stir-cook 10 seconds. Add vegetables; stir-cook 2 to 3 minutes. Sprinkle broth mixes, sweetener if desired, and soy sauce over vegetables. Continue stir-cooking about 2 or 3 minutes. Remove from heat. Divide mixture into 6 equal portions. Place 1 portion on each lettuce leaf. Form leaves into rolls, tucking in edges as you roll. Place rolls, seam side down, in shallow casserole. Cover and bake at 400°F. for 10 minutes or until heated. Makes 6 servings.

BARBECUE SHRIMP WITH FLUFFY WHITE RICE

2¼ pounds peeled and deveined
  shrimp
¼ cup soy sauce
¼ cup lemon juice
2 tablespoons chopped fresh
  parsley

Dash pepper
3 medium green peppers, seeded
  and cut into 1-inch pieces
3 cups Fluffy White Rice (see
  page 32)
Parsley sprigs to garnish

Combine first 5 ingredients in bowl. Cover and refrigerate about 30 minutes, turning occasionally. Remove shrimp from marinade. Divide shrimp and peppers into 12 equal portions of each. Thread 1 portion of each onto a 12-inch skewer, alternating shrimp and green pepper. Repeat with 11 more skewers and remaining shrimp and peppers. Broil about 4 inches from source of heat, or grill over hot coals, turning occasionally. Cook 5 to 10 minutes or until shrimp are pink and firm. Place rice on serving platter; top with skewers of Barbecue Shrimp. Garnish with parsley sprigs. Makes 6 servings.

GINGERED BROCCOLI

6 cups broccoli florets
3 tablespoons lemon juice
3 tablespoons water
3 tablespoons soy sauce
  tablespoon dehydrated onion
  flakes, reconstituted in 1
  tablespoon water

½ teaspoon sherry extract
  (optional)
½ teaspoon ginger
¼ teaspoon garlic powder
Salt to taste

Place broccoli in saucepan. Add about 1 inch of water; cover and cook about 4 minutes or until tender-crisp. Drain. In small bowl combine remaining ingredients and pour over broccoli; toss to combine. Continue to cook until liquid is heated. Makes 6 servings.

STIR-COOKED SNOW PEAS

1 garlic clove, minced
2 cups snow peas, tips and
    strings removed
1 packet instant chicken broth
    and seasoning mix

¼ cup water (optional)
Salt and pepper to taste

Heat wok or nonstick skillet. Stir-cook garlic for 10 seconds; add snow peas and broth mix. Stir-cook 1 to 2 minutes; add water to prevent sticking, if necessary. Season to taste with salt and pepper. Makes 6 servings.

ORANGE-CUCUMBER SALAD

1½ cups pared and thinly sliced
    cucumbers
¼ teaspoon salt
Dash pepper
1½ cups canned mandarin
    orange sections, no sugar
    added
1 cup drained canned bean
    sprouts, rinsed

½ cup chopped green pepper
2 tablespoons chopped fresh
    parsley
¾ cup buttermilk
¼ teaspoon thyme
Crisp greens

In small mixing bowl sprinkle cucumbers with salt and pepper; add orange sections, bean sprouts, green pepper, and parsley. In measuring cup combine buttermilk and thyme; pour over salad and toss lightly to coat. Cover and chill. Serve on bed of crisp greens. Makes 6 servings.

BAKED PINEAPPLE SLICES

1½ small pineapples, pared,
    cored, and cut into ½-inch
    slices
¼ cup water

Artificial sweetener to equal 4
    teaspoons sugar (optional)
1 tablespoon lemon juice
1 teaspoon cinnamon

Place pineapple slices in 8 x 8-inch nonstick baking pan; combine remaining ingredients in measuring cup; pour over pineapple. Bake at 400°F. for 10 to 15 minutes or until pineapple slices are tender. Makes 6 servings.

MEMORIAL DAY ON THE PATIO FOR FOUR

Spinach Salad with Yogurt Mayonnaise
Cheese Soufflé
Baked Tomato with Basil
Peach Chiffon Pie
Beverage

The calendar doesn't say it, but we all know that summer really begins with Memorial Day Weekend! So open the patio doors—outdoor dining time has arrived. And here's a no-fuss menu to launch the casual season. A soufflé is a refreshingly light dish for warm-weather spirits. It's festive for a holiday, without being as difficult to make as rumored. The trick is to get the egg whites the right consistency, and the key is to follow our specific directions *to the letter*. All the other dishes are deliciously simple too. The Baked Tomatoes are spiced with basil, a harmonious combination any time of the year. The nutritious Spinach Salad has a creamy, yogurt-based dressing, and yogurt blends with peaches too, for a fruit dessert that celebrates summer. A lighthearted (and lightening) meal that's also easy on a vacation-minded budget!

SUGGESTED SHOPPING LIST

Staples and Miscellaneous

Artificial sweetener	Worcestershire sauce
Basil	
Cayenne pepper	Unflavored gelatin
Cinnamon	
Dry mustard	Imitation (or diet) margarine
Garlic powder	Imitation mayonnaise
Salt	
Vanilla extract	Enriched white bread
White pepper	Raisin bread

Additional Items

Cheddar cheese, 4 ounces
Eggs, 4
Plain unflavored yogurt, 1 16-ounce
   container
Skim milk, 1 cup

Celery, 2 ribs
Mushrooms, ½ pound
Onion, 1 small
Spinach, 1 pound
Tomatoes, 4 medium, firm

Lemon, 1

Canned sliced peaches, no sugar
   added, 1 16-ounce can

SUGGESTED EQUIPMENT LIST

Baking sheet
Blender or food processor
Bowls (small, medium)
Can opener
Casserole (1½-quart)
Chef's knife
Colander
Custard cups
Cutting board

Measuring cups
Measuring spoons
Paring knife
Pie plate (8-inch)
Pot holder
Rotary beater or electric mixer
Saucepan
Scale
Wooden spoon

SPINACH SALAD WITH YOGURT MAYONNAISE

4 cups spinach leaves
1 cup finely chopped celery
1 cup sliced mushrooms

¼ cup diced onion
Yogurt Mayonnaise (see
*   following recipe)*

Wash spinach and drain in colander; place in large salad bowl. Add celery, mushrooms, and onion; toss to combine. Serve with Yogurt Mayonnaise. Makes 4 servings.

Yogurt Mayonnaise

½ cup plain unflavored yogurt
2 tablespoons imitation
*   mayonnaise*

1 teaspoon lemon juice
⅛ teaspoon garlic powder
Salt and white pepper to taste

Combine all ingredients in small bowl. Chill. Use as directed in recipe for Spinach Salad (see preceding recipe).

CHEESE SOUFFLÉ

4 ounces Cheddar cheese, finely
*   diced*
1 cup skim milk, scalded
2 slices enriched white bread,
*   made into crumbs*

2 eggs, separated
1 teaspoon dry mustard
1 teaspoon Worcestershire sauce
½ teaspoon salt
⅛ teaspoon cayenne pepper

Preheat oven to 375°F. In medium bowl combine cheese, milk, bread, egg yolks, and seasonings. In separate bowl beat egg whites until stiff but not dry. Gently fold whites into cheese-yolk mixture. Transfer to 1½-quart casserole; bake for 40 minutes or until a knife, when inserted in center, comes out clean. Makes 4 servings.

BAKED TOMATO WITH BASIL

4 firm medium tomatoes
2 teaspoons imitation (or diet)
  margarine, melted

¼ teaspoon basil
⅛ teaspoon garlic powder
Salt to taste

Cut off stem end of each tomato in zigzag fashion;* discard ends. Place each tomato in a custard cup. In small bowl combine remaining ingredients. Spoon an equal amount of margarine mixture onto each tomato "crown." Set custard cups on baking sheet; bake at 375°F. for 15 minutes. Makes 4 servings.

* Refer to Orange Bowls (see page 16) for method; insert knife ¼ of the way down.

PEACH CHIFFON PIE

Crust:

2 slices raisin bread, toasted and
  made into crumbs
2 tablespoons imitation (or diet)
  margarine

¼ teaspoon vanilla extract

Filling:

2 cups canned sliced peaches, no
  sugar added, drain and reserve
  juice
1 cup plain unflavored yogurt
2 eggs, separated

Artificial sweetener to equal 8
  teaspoons sugar
1 teaspoon lemon juice
⅛ teaspoon cinnamon
1 envelope unflavored gelatin

To Prepare Crust: Combine first 3 ingredients in medium bowl. Mix to a smooth paste, adding water a few drops at a time, if necessary. Press into 8-inch pie pan, using the back of a teaspoon which has been dipped in warm water. Bake at 350°F. for 15 minutes. Cool.

To Prepare Filling: Set aside 4 peach slices for garnish. Place remaining peaches, yogurt, egg yolks, sweetener, lemon juice, and cinnamon in blender container; process until smooth. In saucepan sprinkle gelatin over reserved peach juice; let stand a few minutes to soften. Add yogurt–peach mixture; cook over low heat, stirring constantly, until gelatin is dissolved. In medium bowl beat egg whites until stiff but not dry. Fold into yogurt–peach mixture.

To Serve: Spoon filling into cooled pie crust. Garnish with reserved peach slices; chill. Makes 4 servings.

June

As the warm weather reminds us that
summer is approaching, our June menus
remind us of the foods that are abundant
this month. The markets are filled with
plump strawberries, juicy melons, meaty
tomatoes, and crisp greens. Celebrate
your special June occasions with
these gifts of the season!

NO-COOKING SUPPER FOR TWO

Clam-Tomato Juice Cocktail
Ham, Asparagus, and Fruit Salad
Curry-Yogurt Dressing
Cabbage Slaw
Pumpernickel Bread with Chive Spread
Iced Coffee

A languid June day . . . no time to hang over a hot stove! So here's a no-cooking menu to help you keep your cool. That special person you're dining with will appreciate your unruffled way of coping, too. Even unexpected guests needn't raise your temperature, since these recipes can easily be increased by any number. You're also coping well with your budget, for the menu makes frugal use of leftovers. Spiking the Yogurt Dressing with curry will add gusto to your Fruit Salad, and using *canned* fruits saves the hassle of last-minute shopping. The Cabbage Slaw is an energy saver, too, because it can be made a day or two ahead and left to marinate in the refrigerator. Pumpernickel has a strong flavor that goes particularly well with the Chive Spread, but—if it makes things easier for you—cracked wheat or rye bread provide a savory alternative. As a leisure-time bonus, this summery repast sits well on paper plates. (It also sits well on bikini-bound figures!)

SUGGESTED SHOPPING LIST

Staples and Miscellaneous

Artificial sweetener
Celery seed
Chopped chives
Curry powder
Peppercorns

Cider vinegar
Dijon mustard
Soy sauce
Worcestershire sauce

Coffee

Imitation (or diet) margarine
Imitation mayonnaise

Pumpernickel bread

Ham, 6 ounces, cooked

Plain unflavored yogurt, 1 8-ounce container

Apple, 1 small
Lemon, 1

Asparagus stalks, 6 medium
Cabbage, 1 small head
Celery, 1 rib
Iceberg lettuce, 1 small head
Red onion, 1 small

Clam juice, 1 8-fluid-ounce bottle
Tomato juice, 1 12-fluid-ounce can

Canned mandarin orange sections, no sugar added, 1 10½-ounce can
Canned pineapple chunks, no sugar added, 1 8-ounce can

Pimientos, 1 4-ounce jar

SUGGESTED EQUIPMENT LIST

Baking sheet
Bowls (small, large)
Can opener
Chef's knife
Corer
Cutting board
1-pint jar with cover
Measuring cups

Measuring spoons
Pepper mill
Pot holder
Scale
Spreading knife
Vegetable peeler
Wooden spoon

CLAM-TOMATO JUICE COCKTAIL

1 cup tomato juice
½ cup clam juice
2 teaspoons Worcestershire sauce

1 teaspoon lemon juice
Freshly ground pepper to taste

Combine all ingredients in 1-pint jar with tight-fitting cover. Cover and chill. Shake well before serving. Makes 2 servings.

HAM, ASPARAGUS, AND FRUIT SALAD

Serve with Curry-Yogurt Dressing (see recipe, page 173).

6 ounces diced cooked ham
1 small apple, pared, cored, and diced
½ cup canned mandarin orange sections, no sugar added
½ cup canned pineapple chunks, no sugar added

½ cup diced celery
¼ cup diced red onion
2 cups shredded iceberg lettuce
6 cooked medium asparagus spears

In large bowl combine ham, apple, orange, pineapple, celery, and onion. Chill. Place lettuce in salad bowl; top with ham-fruit mixture. Arrange asparagus spears around edge of salad so that they radiate out. Makes 2 servings.

CURRY-YOGURT DRESSING

Serve with Ham, Asparagus, and Fruit Salad (see recipe, page 172)

½ cup plain unflavored yogurt
Artificial sweetener to equal 2
   teaspoons sugar

1 teaspoon curry powder
1 teaspoon soy sauce
½ teaspoon Dijon mustard

Combine all ingredients in small serving dish. Chill. Makes 2 servings

CABBAGE SLAW

2 tablespoons imitation
   mayonnaise
1 tablespoon chopped pimiento
1 tablespoon cider vinegar
Artificial sweetener to equal 2
   teaspoons sugar

1 teaspoon Dijon mustard
½ teaspoon celery seed
Salt and freshly ground pepper
   to taste
1½ cups shredded cabbage

In bowl combine all ingredients except cabbage. Add cabbage; toss to combine. Makes 2 servings.

PUMPERNICKEL BREAD WITH CHIVE SPREAD

1 tablespoon imitation (or diet)
   margarine
1 teaspoon chopped chives

⅛ teaspoon lemon juice
2 slices pumpernickel bread

In bowl combine margarine, chives, and lemon juice. Spread an equal amount on each slice of bread. Place on baking sheet, margarine side up; bake at 350°F. for 5 minutes. Cut each slice of bread into quarters. Makes 2 servings.

COUNTRY FRENCH DINNER FOR FOUR

Melon Wedge
Chicken Peasant-Style en Casserole
Spiced Green Beans and Rice Salad
Apple Scallop
Sparking Mineral Water with Lime Wedge

After a strenuous day in the fields, French farmers like to dine on hearty casseroles and tart apple desserts from their orchard-rich provinces. Of course, French cookery relies heavily on wine. To lighten the results, we winningly substituted wine vinegar. (Try this technique with beef and liver, too.) Since the French admire distinctive touches, combine Spiced Green Beans and Rice for an intriguingly unusual salad. Carry out the Continental motif by serving sparkling mineral water, refreshingly laced with lime. As a final touch, decorate your table with a centerpiece of casually arranged wildflowers. Your guests will appreciate not only the French-style meal but the recipes that help them stay in shape for French styles!

SUGGESTED SHOPPING LIST

Staples and Miscellaneous

Apple pie spice or cinnamon	Browning sauce
Artificial sweetener	Cider vinegar
Bay leaves	Red wine vinegar
Brandy extract	White vinegar
Dehydrated onion flakes	
Garlic powder	Cornstarch
Instant beef broth and seasoning mix	
Paprika	Vegetable oil
Peppercorns	
Pickling spice	
Salt	
Thyme	

Additional Items

Chicken, 1 (4- to 4½-pound), skinned and cut into pieces

Apples, 4 small
Lemon, 1
Lime, 1
Melon, 1 (honeydew, casaba, cranshaw, or similar melon)

Carrots, 2 medium
Garlic cloves, 2
Green beans, ½ pound

Mushrooms, 1 pound
Onion, 1 medium

Frozen pearl onions (small white), 1 20-ounce bag

Tomato sauce, 1 8-ounce can

Enriched white rice, 1 16-ounce box

Sparkling mineral water, 2 23-fluid-ounce bottles

SUGGESTED EQUIPMENT LIST

Bowls (small, large)
Broiling pan
Can opener
Casserole (4-quart, covered)
Casserole (small)
Chef's knife
Colander
Corer
Cutting board

Fork and spoon for tossing
Measuring cups
Measuring spoons
Pepper mill
Pot holder
Saucepans (medium, large)
Scale
Vegetable peeler
Wooden spoon

MELON WEDGE

Serve a 2-inch wedge of honeydew, casaba, cranshaw, or similar melon to each person. Garnish each portion with a lemon wedge.

CHICKEN PEASANT-STYLE EN CASSEROLE

4-to 4½-pound chicken, skinned and cut into pieces
Salt, pepper, garlic powder, and paprika to taste
2 cups mushrooms, quartered
1 cup thinly sliced carrots
¾ cup diced onion, 1-inch dice
½ cup tomato sauce
4 packets instant beef broth and seasoning mix
2 large garlic cloves, minced

1 teaspoon browning sauce
1 bay leaf
¼ teaspoon thyme
Freshly ground pepper to taste
2 cups water
2 tablespoons red wine vinegar
1 tablespoon plus 1 teaspoon cornstarch, dissolved in 2 tablespoons water
¾ cup cooked pearl onions

Season chicken with salt, pepper, garlic powder, and paprika. Broil, turning once, for 10 minutes on each side or until browned. In a large saucepan combine next 10 ingredients; cook 10 minutes. Add water and vinegar;

bring to a boil. Reduce heat; simmer 5 minutes. Stir in cornstarch; simmer 2 to 3 minutes longer or until sauce thickens. Remove chicken from bones. Weigh 1 pound meat and place in 4-quart casserole. Add sauce; top with pearl onions. Cover and bake at 350°F. for 45 minutes or until chicken is tender. Makes 4 servings.

SPICED GREEN BEANS AND RICE SALAD

¼ cup white vinegar
Artificial sweetener to equal 4 teaspoons sugar
1 teaspoon pickling spice
¼ teaspoon garlic powder, divided
3 cups water
2 cups cut green beans, 1-inch pieces

2 cups cooked enriched rice
1 tablespoon plus 1 teaspoon vegetable oil
1 tablespoon dehydrated onion flakes, reconstituted in 1 tablespoon water
2 teaspoons cider vinegar

In medium saucepan combine white vinegar, sweetener, pickling spice, and ⅛ teaspoon garlic powder; add water. Bring to a boil; add green beans. Reduce heat and simmer 15 minutes; drain. Transfer beans to large bowl; add rice. In small bowl combine oil, onion flakes, cider vinegar, and remaining ⅛ teaspoon garlic powder. Pour over bean–rice mixture; toss lightly. Makes 4 servings.

APPLE SCALLOP

4 small apples, pared, cored, and thinly sliced
¼ cup water
Artificial sweetener to equal 12 teaspoons sugar

¾ teaspoon brandy extract
½ teaspoon apple pie spice or cinnamon
Dash salt

Combine all ingredients in small casserole. Bake at 350°F. for 30 minutes or until apples are tender. Serve warm. Makes 4 servings.

WEDDING RECEPTION FOR TWELVE

Artichoke Hearts with Sauce Louis
Cock-a-Leekie Soup
Broiled Ham Steaks with Cumberland Sauce
Whipped Potatoes
Carrots and Zucchini en Casserole
Strawberry Sundae
Beverage

Here's a sweetheart of a menu, in which every dish proclaims "special occasion." In very French fashion, Artichoke Hearts with Sauce Louis sets an elegant tone right from the start. For a surprising contrast, follow it with Scotland's tangy treat, Cock-a-Leekie Soup. Ham Steaks are also a traditional banquet item. They're most savory when glazed, and our Cumberland Sauce adds this sweet coating in figure-saving style. Wedding festivities should be pretty, so provide visual appeal by serving the creamy Whipped Potatoes atop ruby-red slices of tomato, and by artfully combining gold and green in an attractive casserole of julienne carrots and zucchini. Of course, dessert should be very special, and our Strawberry Sundae is the pièce de résistance. ("Resistance" isn't needed, since this luscious concoction won't threaten anyone's slimming efforts!) This gourmet-style feast adroitly masks its behind-the-scenes preparation, for many of the dishes can be made ahead of time, while the potatoes can be popped into the oven at the last minute. Of course, you'll wed the menu to a table impeccably set with lacy linen, gleaming silver, elegant candlesticks, and an exquisite floral centerpiece.

SUGGESTED SHOPPING LIST

Staples and Miscellaneous

Artificial sweetener
Bay leaves
Chopped chives
Cinnamon stick
Cloves
Dehydrated onion flakes
Garlic powder
Instant chicken broth and seasoning
  mix
Nutmeg
Salt
Vanilla extract
White pepper

Browning sauce
Chili sauce
Prepared mustard
Worcestershire sauce

Cornstarch
Unflavored gelatin

Imitation (or diet) margarine
Imitation mayonnaise

Low-calorie grape jelly

Additional Items

Ham steaks, 6 (6 ounces each),
  cooked

Lemon, 1
Strawberries, 2 pints

Carrots, 12 medium
Green pepper, 1 medium
Leeks, 2 pounds
Chicory or lettuce, 1 head
Parsley, 1 bunch
Potatoes, 3 pounds

Tomatoes, 8 medium
Zucchini, 5 medium

Frozen artichoke hearts, 4 10-ounce
  packages
Vanilla-flavored dietary frozen dessert,
  ½ gallon

Evaporated skimmed milk, 2 13-fluid-
  ounce cans

Dietetic ginger ale, 1 28-fluid-ounce
  bottle

SUGGESTED EQUIPMENT LIST

Baking pan
Blender
Bowls (small)
Broiler pan and rack
Can opener
Casserole (4-quart)
Chef's knife
Cutting board

Electric mixer
Measuring cups
Measuring spoons
Pot holder
Saucepans (medium)
Scale
Vegetable peeler
Wooden spoon

ARTICHOKE HEARTS WITH SAUCE LOUIS

½ cup imitation mayonnaise
2 tablespoons plus 2 teaspoons
  chili sauce
1 tablespoon plus 1 teaspoon
  minced green pepper
1 teaspoon dehydrated onion
  flakes, reconstituted in 1
  teaspoon water

2 teaspoons water
¾ teaspoon lemon juice
¾ teaspoon Worcestershire
  sauce
Chicory or lettuce leaves
4 cups cooked artichoke hearts,
  chilled
Chopped fresh parsley to garnish

In small serving bowl combine first 7 ingredients; chill. Line serving dish
or platter with chicory. Set bowl of chilled dressing in center of dish; surround with artichoke hearts. Garnish sauce with chopped parsley. Makes
12 servings.

COCK-A-LEEKIE SOUP

Leeks must be carefully washed to remove all grit. Remove roots and
green leaves; use only the white portion.

2 cups leeks, white portion only
2¼ quarts water
12 packets instant chicken broth
  and seasoning mix

2 bay leaves
2 cups plus 2 tablespoons
  evaporated skimmed milk
2 teaspoons Worcestershire sauce

Cut leeks in half lengthwise; then cut crosswise into ⅛-inch slices. In saucepan combine leeks, water, broth mix, and bay leaves. Bring to a boil; reduce
heat and simmer until leeks are tender, about 20 minutes. Remove and discard bay leaves. Using slotted spoon, remove ¼ cup leeks and reserve. In
batches, purée remaining leek mixture in blender container. Return pureed
mixture to saucepan; stir in reserved leeks, evaporated skimmed milk, and
Worcestershire sauce. Heat but *do not boil*. Makes 12 servings.

BROILED HAM STEAKS WITH CUMBERLAND SAUCE

Ham Steaks:

6 boned, cooked ham steaks, 6
  ounces each, cut into halves

48 cloves

Cumberland Sauce:

3 cups dietetic ginger ale
¼ cup plus 2 tablespoons low-
  calorie grape jelly
2 tablespoons prepared mustard
Artificial sweetener to equal 4
  teaspoons sugar

½ cinnamon stick
½ teaspoon browning sauce
4 cloves
2 tablespoons plus 2 teaspoons
  cornstarch, dissolved in 2
  tablespoons water

Garnish:

Parsley sprigs

To Prepare Ham Steaks: Preheat broiler. Stud edges of each steak half with 4 cloves. Place on rack in broiler pan; broil 5 to 8 minutes.

To Prepare Cumberland Sauce: Combine remaining ingredients except cornstarch in medium saucepan. Bring to a boil; reduce heat and simmer 2 to 3 minutes. Remove and discard cinnamon stick and cloves. Add cornstarch; cook, stirring constantly, until sauce thickens.

To Serve: Transfer ham steaks to serving platter. Garnish with parsley sprigs and serve with Cumberland Sauce. Makes 12 servings.

WHIPPED POTATOES

3 pounds hot, cooked, pared potatoes, mashed
½ cup evaporated skimmed milk
½ cup imitation (or diet) margarine
2 tablespoons chopped chives
¾ teaspoon salt
⅛ teaspoon white pepper
Dash nutmeg
8 medium tomatoes, each cut into three slices

Combine potatoes with remaining ingredients except tomatoes in bowl of electric mixer; beat until fluffy. Divide mixture into 12 equal portions. Place tomato slices in baking pan; season each tomato slice with salt and pepper. Top each with 1 portion of potato mixture. Bake at 400°F. until thoroughly heated. Makes 12 servings.

CARROTS AND ZUCCHINI EN CASSEROLE

5 cups julienne zucchini, blanched
4 cups julienne carrots, blanched
½ cup imitation (or diet) margarine
4 packets instant chicken broth and seasoning mix
Artificial sweetener to equal 2 teaspoons sugar
¼ teaspoon garlic powder
Salt and white pepper to taste

Combine all ingredients in 4-quart casserole. Bake at 400°F., stirring occasionally, for 10 to 15 minutes or until thoroughly heated. Makes 12 servings.

STRAWBERRY SUNDAE

6 cups strawberries, sliced
(reserve 12 slices for garnish)
Artificial sweetener to equal 12
teaspoons sugar, or to taste
1 teaspoon vanilla extract

12 scoops vanilla-flavored dietary
frozen dessert, 3 ounces each
3 recipes Whipped Topping (see
page 30)

In bowl combine first 3 ingredients except reserved slices. Transfer 1½ cups strawberry mixture to blender container; process until smooth. Add to bowl containing sliced strawberries and stir to combine. Place 1 scoop frozen dessert into each of 12 dessert dishes. Spoon an equal amount of strawberry sauce over each serving of frozen dessert. Top each portion with an equal amount of Whipped Topping and garnish with 1 reserved strawberry slice. Makes 12 servings.

THE CHIC OF GREEK DINING FOR SIX

Greek-Style Salad Bar
Yogurt-Garlic Salad Dressing
Mixed Dolma (Stuffed Vegetables)
Skewered Fruits
Espresso

If you "take off your hat" to Greek fare, it should be a chef's hat. Back in the Middle Ages, Greek cooks, fleeing from slavery, hid in various European monasteries. Since the monks wanted them set apart, they ordered the cooks to wear high white hats, and today, that headgear is traditional chef's attire! The Greek cooks carried marvelous secrets under those hats, for Europe's oldest civilization not only produced a great culture but an outstanding cuisine. Indeed, the world's first cookbook was written by a Greek, and modern Greek cookbooks are marvels, too, for they capitalize on the abundance of fruits and vegetables that grow in brilliant profusion throughout that sunny land. In their restaurants a salad bar where diners select and season their own portions is invariably present. To duplicate this commendable Grecian habit, recreate a salad bar and encourage your guests to help themselves to a dressing that includes one of Greece's favorite foods: yogurt. Combine additional vegetables with beef for a traditional specialty, Mixed Dolma. ("Dolma" indicates a food that is stuffed.) Our version includes the exotic edible most associated with Grecian recipes: grape leaves. (You shouldn't have to travel farther than your neighborhood supermarket to find them since they're available in a jar.) On a refreshing bed of mint leaves, arrange skewered fruit subtly brushed with anise extract, like the liqueur customarily sipped in Greek *tavernas*. Add to the atmosphere with throbbing bouzouki music. . . . Your guests will take off their hats to *you*!

Staples and Miscellaneous

Allspice
Anise extract
Cinnamon
Dried mint
Garlic powder
Instant chicken broth and seasoning
   mix
Paprika
Pepper
Salt
Thyme

Prepared spicy brown mustard
Worcestershire sauce

Ground espresso coffee

Additional Items

Ground beef, 2¼ pounds

Plain unflavored yogurt, 1 16-ounce
   container

Banana, 1 medium
Cantaloupe, 1 small
Lemons, 2
Lime, 1
Navel orange, 1 small
Pineapple, 1 small
Strawberries, 1 pint

Cherry tomatoes, 2 pints
Chicory, 1 small head or Belgian
   endives, 2 medium
Cucumbers, 2 medium
Garlic cloves, 2

Green peppers, 6 medium
Iceberg or Boston lettuce, 1 small head
Mint or watercress, 1 bunch
Onion, 1 medium
Radishes, 1 bag
Red onion, 1 medium
Spinach, 1 pound
Zucchini, 3 medium (approximately
   5 ounces each)

Frozen peas, 1 10-ounce package

Canned artichoke hearts, 1 14-ounce
   can
Grape leaves, 1 16-ounce jar
Tomato paste, 1 16-ounce can

Enriched white rice, 1 16-ounce box

SUGGESTED EQUIPMENT LIST

Bowls (small, large)
Chef's knife
Colander
Cutting board
Measuring cups
Measuring spoons
Melon baller
Nonstick skillet (large)

Paper towels
Pastry brush
Pot holder
Saucepans and covers
Scale
9- or 10-inch skewers, 6
Wooden spoon

GREEK-STYLE SALAD BAR

Provide each guest with an individual salad bowl; then invite everyone to create and season his or her own salad. Serve each guest 3 tablespoons Yogurt–Garlic Dressing (see recipe below).

Seasonings and Condiments at the Table for Self-Service: salt, pepper, thyme, and lemon wedges

3 cups spinach leaves, rinsed well, drained, and chilled	1 cup sliced radishes
	30 cherry tomatoes
3 cups shredded lettuce (combination of any of the following: Boston, curly endive, chicory, and iceberg)	2 medium cucumbers, sliced
	¾ cup red onion rings
	¾ cup drained canned artichoke hearts, cut into quarters
1 cup watercress leaves	½ cup cooked peas

In large bowl combine spinach, lettuce, watercress, and radishes. Using 5 more bowls, place each remaining vegetable in a separate bowl.* Makes 6 servings.

* If preferred, vegetables may be arranged separately on a large serving platter.

YOGURT-GARLIC SALAD DRESSING

Serve with Greek-Style Salad Bar (see recipe above).

1 cup plus 2 tablespoons plain unflavored yogurt	½ teaspoon garlic powder
	½ teaspoon paprika
1 teaspoon Worcestershire sauce	⅛ teaspoon salt
1 teaspoon prepared spicy brown mustard	

In small bowl combine all ingredients; mix well. Chill. Makes 6 servings.

MIXED DOLMA (STUFFED VEGETABLES)

Vegetables:

6 medium green peppers	3 medium zucchini, about 5 ounces each
18 grape leaves, packed in brine	

Filling:

1 cup finely chopped onions	¼ cup tomato paste
2 packets instant chicken broth and seasoning mix	1 teaspoon dried mint
	½ teaspoon each cinnamon and allspice
2 garlic cloves, minced	Salt to taste
1½ pounds broiled ground beef, crumbled	3 cups cooked enriched rice

To Prepare Vegetables: Cut thin slice from stem end of each green pepper; reserve slices. Remove and discard seeds and membrane. Rinse each grape leaf individually. Pat dry with paper towel. Cut each zucchini in half lengthwise. Scoop out and discard pulp, leaving a firm shell.

To Prepare Filling: In large nonstick skillet combine onions, broth mix and garlic. Cook, stirring occasionally, until onions are tender. Add next 5 ingredients. Cook, stirring occasionally, for 5 minutes longer. Stir in rice and remove from heat.

To Prepare Dolma: Stuff each green pepper with an equal amount of filling; replace reserved pepper slices. Place an equal amount of filling in center of each grape leaf; fold sides of each leaf in and roll tightly from stem end toward the point of the leaf. Stuff each zucchini with an equal amount of filling. Place stuffed grape leaves in deep, wide saucepan. Top with peppers and zucchini. Add 1 quart water; cover pan and cook over medium heat for 1 hour.

To Serve: Arrange stuffed vegetables attractively on large serving platter Makes 6 servings—1 stuffed pepper, 3 stuffed grape leaves, and 1 stuffed zucchini half each.

SKEWERED FRUITS

½ small pineapple, pared and
  cut crosswise into 6 equal,
  half-moon-shaped slices
1 cup cantaloupe balls
1 cup strawberries
1 small navel orange, unpeeled,
  cut into 6 equal slices

½ medium banana, cut crosswise
  into 6 equal slices and
  sprinkled with lemon juice
1½ teaspoons anise extract
Mint leaves*
6 lime wedges

Divide each fruit into 6 equal portions. Thread 1 portion of each fruit onto 9- or 10-inch skewer, alternating ingredients and ending with pineapple slice. Repeat with 5 more skewers and remaining fruits. Brush each skewer of fruits with ¼ teaspoon extract. Arrange skewers, like spokes of a wheel, on bed of mint leaves. Garnish by interspersing lime wedges between skewers. Makes 6 servings.

* If mint leaves are unavailable, watercress may be substituted.

GRADUATION PARTY FOR EIGHT

Eggheads
Bologna "Crêpes"
Diploma Sandwiches
Mixed Fruit Gelatin
Chocolate Shake

Earn your diploma as an A-1 party host by creating a fun-style celebration. The "Eggheads" will earn you high marks for imagination! Although they look as if they call for great skill, they can be made quite easily by following our simple directions. Diploma sandwiches show a fun flair, too—and are handy finger foods. You'll score high grades in economy using bologna, an inexpensive meat popular with children of all ages. It's educational for youngsters—and oldsters!—to learn that "nutritious" can rhyme with "delicious," as it does in our slenderizing Mixed Fruit Gelatin dessert. "Shakes" are always a welcome treat, on or off the school scene, and ours is a swift blender treat. Give this menu gold stars for cooperation as well, since everything except the beverage can be made ahead of time, freeing you to trot off to the graduation ceremony. And isn't it additional cause for celebration to know that this little-cooking menu helps keep the kitchen cool on a warm June day?

Take your decorating cues from the special interests of your young guests. Tie the theme together with a gaily patterned paper cloth, napkins, and plates—perhaps a colorful barrage of balloons. It all adds up to an easy, economical, and very "class"-y party!

SUGGESTED SHOPPING LIST

Staples and Miscellaneous

Artificial sweetener
Chopped chives
Cinnamon
Vanilla extract

Nonfat dry milk powder
Unflavored gelatin

Dijon mustard

Imitation (or diet) margarine
Imitation mayonnaise

Enriched white bread

Additional Items

Bologna, ¾ pound

Eggs, 8

Asparagus stalks, 8 medium
Carrot, 1 medium
Celery, 1 rib
Mushrooms, ¼ pound
Red pepper, 1 medium

Frozen orange juice concentrate,
  1 6-fluid-ounce can

Applesauce, no sugar added, 1
  8-ounce jar
Canned fruit cocktail, no sugar added,
  2 16-ounce cans

Pimientos, 1 4-ounce jar

Prunes, large, 1 12-ounce box

Chocolate-flavored dietetic soda,
  1 28-fluid-ounce bottle

SUGGESTED EQUIPMENT LIST

Blender or food processor
Bowls (small, medium)
Can opener
Chef's knife
Cutting board
Measuring cups
Measuring spoons

Mold (1-quart)
Paring knife
Pot holder
Rolling pin
Saucepans (medium)
Toothpicks
Wooden spoon

EGGHEADS

  8 eggs, hard-cooked
  8 small mushroom caps
  16 pieces diced carrot, about
    ¼ inch each

  8 red pepper strips, about 1 inch
    each

Insert a toothpick in large end of each egg, allowing half of the toothpick to remain exposed. Place 1 mushroom cap over exposed half of each toothpick. In each egg, cut two ¼-inch slits for eyes and a 1-inch slit for the mouth. Press 1 carrot piece into each ¼-inch opening, and 1 red pepper strip into each 1-inch opening. Makes 8 servings.

BOLOGNA "CRÊPES"

  12 ounces sliced bologna
  Crusts from 8 slices enriched
    white bread, made into
    crumbs*
  ¼ cup finely diced celery
  ¼ cup imitation mayonnaise

  2 teaspoons Dijon mustard
  1 cup applesauce, no sugar added
  8 large prunes, pitted and
    diced
  ⅛ teaspoon cinnamon

* Bread slices are used in recipe for Diploma Sandwiches.

Reserve 8 slices of bologna. Chop remaining bologna; place into bowl. Add bread crumbs, celery, mayonnaise, and mustard; mix well. Divide mixture into 8 equal portions. Roll 1 bologna slice around each portion of chopped bologna mixture. Place onto serving platter, seam side down. Spoon applesauce over bologna "crêpes." Top with prunes and sprinkle with cinnamon. Makes 8 servings.

DIPLOMA SANDWICHES

*8 slices enriched white bread,
  crusts removed**
*2 tablespoons plus 2 teaspoons
  imitation (or diet) margarine*
*2 tablespoons plus 2 teaspoons
  imitation mayonnaise*

1 teaspoon chopped chives
*8 cooked medium asparagus
  spears*
Pimiento strips to garnish

Using a rolling pin, flatten each slice of bread. In small bowl combine margarine, mayonnaise, and chives. Divide mixture into 8 equal portions; spread 1 portion on each slice of flattened bread. Roll each slice of bread around 1 asparagus spear. Garnish with pimiento strips. Makes 8 servings.

* Crusts are used in recipe for Bologna "Crêpes."

MIXED FRUIT GELATIN

2 envelopes unflavored gelatin
2 cups orange juice
*2 cups canned fruit cocktail, no
  sugar added*

*Artificial sweetener to equal 16
  teaspoons sugar*

In medium saucepan sprinkle gelatin over orange juice; let stand a few minutes to soften. Cook over medium heat, stirring constantly, until gelatin is dissolved. Remove from heat; stir in fruit cocktail and sweetener. Pour into 1-quart mold. Allow to cool. Chill until firm. Unmold. Makes 8 servings.

CHOCOLATE SHAKE

Pour 1 cup chocolate-flavored dietetic soda into blender container. Add 2 tablespoons plus 2 teaspoons nonfat dry milk powder and ⅛ teaspoon vanilla extract; process to combine. Add 4 ice cubes, 1 at a time, processing after each addition. Divide evenly into two 8-ounce glasses. Repeat procedure 3 more times. Serve immediately. Makes 8 servings.

HIGH TEA IN THE GARDEN FOR SIX

Combination Vegetable Salad with Deviled Herb Salad Dressing

Cinnamon-Raisin Strips
Cottage Cheesecake
Hot Tea

A beautiful June day—and your garden's in full bloom. Take advantage of the setting by hosting a "High Tea," the gracious English way of socializing. (The difference between "Tea" and "High Tea" is that the latter is served later in the day and has a more elaborate menu.) The British recommend that any pastry served with tea be light, so as not to overpower the taste of their favorite beverage. Our Cottage Cheesecake not only blends well with tea, it's also light enough not to overpower the scale. With this, serve a summery salad appealingly arranged on leafy spinach and dainty Cinnamon–Raisin Strips. The English take proper brewing quite seriously, so we have served up some expert tea tips for you. Do venture a bit by sampling more exotic varieties than you may be accustomed to, and remember that tea should be served quite hot. Add to the scene by setting a classic English tea table, complete with a pretty cloth, a bowl of carefully arranged flowers, exquisite china and silver, and—of course—your most impressive tea service. (Borrow, if necessary.) Although silver looks elegant, the knowledgeable tea makers actually advise porcelain for both the pot and the cups, since it holds the heat better. No ordinary garden-variety party, this!

SUGGESTED SHOPPING LIST
Staples and Miscellaneous

Anise seed	Worcestershire sauce
Artificial sweetener	
Chopped chives	Tea
Cinnamon	
Cinnamon sticks	Imitation mayonnaise
Cloves	
Dehydrated orange or lemon peel	Cinnamon-raisin bread
Dry mustard	
Nutmeg	
Vanilla extract	
Whole allspice	

Additional Items

Cottage cheese, 2 16-ounce containers
Eggs, 6
Plain unflavored yogurt, 2 16-ounce
   containers
Skim milk, 1 quart

Lemons, 2

Asparagus stalks, 18 medium
Carrots, 2 medium

Cucumber, 1 medium
Green peppers, 3 medium
Mint, 1 bunch, or dried mint
Scallions, 1 bunch
Spinach, 2 pounds
Tomatoes, 6 medium

Canned hearts of palm, 2 14-ounce
   cans

SUGGESTED EQUIPMENT LIST

Baking sheet
Blender and/or food processor
Bowls (large)
Can opener
Chef's knife
Colander
Cutting board
Electric mixer
Fork
Grater

Kitchen spoon
Paring knife
Pie pan (9-inch)
Pot holder
Saucepans
Strainer
Tea kettle
Toaster
Vegetable peeler
Wooden spoons

COMBINATION VEGETABLE SALAD WITH DEVILED HERB SALAD DRESSING

> 3 medium green peppers
> Deviled Herb Salad Dressing (see
>   recipe, page 191)
> 6 cups spinach leaves, rinsed well
> 18 cooked medium asparagus
>   spears
> 3 medium tomatoes, each cut into
>   8 wedges
>
> 1½ cups sliced, drained canned
>   hearts of palm
> 1½ medium carrots, scraped and
>   cut into 12 sticks
> 1 medium cucumber, scored and
>   cut into 24 slices
> ½ cup sliced scallions

Cut each green pepper in half crosswise; remove and discard seeds. Fill each pepper half with ⅓ cup salad dressing. Line each of 6 individual salad plates with 1 cup spinach leaves. Place 1 filled pepper half in center of each plate. Surround each pepper half with 3 asparagus spears, 4 tomato wedges, ¼ cup hearts of palm slices, 2 carrot sticks, and 4 cucumber slices. Sprinkle each salad with 4 teaspoons scallions. Makes 6 servings.

Deviled Herb Salad Dressing

1 cup plain unflavored yogurt
3 eggs, hard-cooked
¼ cup imitation mayonnaise
1 tablespoon chopped chives

½ teaspoon dry mustard
½ teaspoon Worcestershire
  sauce

Combine all ingredients in blender container; process until smooth. Serve as directed in recipe for Combination Vegetable Salad (see recipe, page 190).

CINNAMON-RAISIN STRIPS

3 slices cinnamon-raisin bread, toasted

Cut each slice of toast into 4 equal strips. Place upright in small, napkin-lined basket. Makes 6 servings.

COTTAGE CHEESECAKE

Crust:

3 slices cinnamon-raisin bread,
  toasted and made into fine
  crumbs

3 tablespoons water
1 teaspoon cinnamon

Filling:

2 cups cottage cheese
1 cup plain unflavored yogurt
3 eggs
Artificial sweetener to equal 12
  teaspoons sugar

3 tablespoons cornstarch
2 tablespoons lemon juice
1 teaspoon grated lemon rind
1 teaspoon vanilla extract

To Prepare Crust: In mixing bowl combine bread crumbs, water, and cinnamon. Mix to a smooth paste; press into 9-inch pie pan, covering sides and bottom of pan with crumbs. Bake for 10 minutes at 350°F.

To Prepare Filling: Process cottage cheese in food processor or blender container until smooth. Transfer to large mixing bowl. Add yogurt; beat with electric mixer until smooth. Add eggs, 1 at a time, beating until smooth after each addition. Add remaining ingredients. Beat 2 minutes longer.

To Prepare Cheesecake: Pour filling into prepared crust. Place pie pan on baking sheet and bake at 350°F. for 1 hour. If cake browns too quickly, cover loosely with aluminum foil. Chill. Makes 6 servings.

HOT TEA

Choosing the Brand: Don't settle on the brands you've always used unless you've tried many different ones. Gourmet food departments and specialty shops offer exciting varieties and blends, exquisitely scented, full-bodied, and exotic.

Making Flavored and Scented Teas: Tea leaves can be mixed with any one or several of the following to produce an original tea blend:

Dehydrated orange or lemon peel Crushed fresh mint leaves or
Bits of cloves, pieces of cinnamon   crumbled dried mint
    stick, crushed whole allspice,
    grated nutmeg, anise seed

Fresh herbs should be steeped for approximately 10 minutes to extract flavor.

Brewing the Tea: Bring water to a boil in tea kettle. Meanwhile, warm teapot by filling it with hot water. Pour off water and place 2 tablespoons tea leaves or 6 teabags in teapot. Pour boiling water onto the leaves. Let stand 3 to 5 minutes. Serve immediately. If tea leaves have not settled, pour tea through a strainer. Makes 6 servings.

Making a Tea Concentrate: Pour only 1½ cups of boiling water over leaves or teabags in teapot. Let stand 3 to 5 minutes. Pour ¼ cup freshly brewed concentrate into each tea cup; then fill each cup with boiling water. Makes 6 servings.

The Tea Table: Set the table with the following:

Teacups, saucers, and silverware Decorative small dishes contain-
Fancy paper napkins   ing artificial sweetener and
Pitchers of skim milk   lemon wedges

July

Summertime is vacation time, so why not prepare one of our July menus and invite your guests to "come along for the ride"! We'll be visiting Hawaii, Japan . . . even the coastal states of the United States for a shore dinner! And for the Fourth of July, you'll find our specially selected dishes to be a Yankee Doodle Dandy!

FOR THE FOURTH OF JULY—RED, WHITE, AND BLUEBERRY FOR SIX

Tomato Ice
Crab Meat à la King
Confetti Vegetables
Rice Pudding with Blueberry Sauce
Lemonade

Earn four-star raves with a cool Fourth of July luncheon patriotically served up in red, white, and blue! Refresh wilting spirits with a colorful Tomato Ice, gustily seasoned with hot sauce. Offer it in novel style by molding lettuce leaves into cups. Since a chilled fish salad is always welcome on simmering summer days, add a light (and white) crab meat entrée. (Although our forefathers rebelled against a king, this "king" dish isn't likely to meet resistance!) Decorate the holiday with a collage of Confetti Vegetables that make prudent use of in-season produce. For a dessert that will send up sparklers, top creamy Rice Pudding (a year-round favorite) with fragrant blueberries—the native American fruit with which the Indians marked the beginning of summer. As any youngster who's ever set up a homespun beverage stand can tell you, lemonade is the all-American hot-weather hit, so add a cooling pitcherful.

Our country's birthday has been jubilantly celebrated since 1777. However, twentieth-century hosts can proclaim their own freedom by serving in casual style, with toss-away paper plates and napkins that colorfully carry out the Independence Day motif. (You'll also want to celebrate freedom from calorie-laden celebrations!)

SUGGESTED SHOPPING LIST

Staples and Miscellaneous

Artificial sweetener	Hot sauce
Chopped chives	Worcestershire sauce
Cinnamon	
Instant chicken broth and seasoning mix	Cornstarch
	Flour
Salt	
Vanilla extract	Imitation (or diet) margarine
White pepper	
	Enriched white bread

Additional Items

Frozen Alaskan king crab, 2 6-ounce
 packages

Eggs, 6
Skim milk, 3½ cups

Blueberries, 1 pint
Lemons, 9

Asparagus, 12 medium stalks
Carrots, 4 medium
Cauliflower, 1 small head
Green beans, ½ pound
Lettuce, 1 small head

Mint, 1 bunch
Mushrooms, ½ pound
Parsley, 1 bunch
Watercress, 1 bunch

Frozen peas, 2 10-ounce packages

Tomato puree, 1 16-ounce can

Tomato juice, 1 32-fluid-ounce jar

Evaporated skimmed milk, 1 13-fluid-
ounce can

Enriched white rice, 1 16-ounce box

SUGGESTED EQUIPMENT LIST

Blender
Bowls
Can opener
Chef's knife
Cutting board
Double boiler
Kitchen fork
Measuring cups
Measuring spoons

Metal spoon
Pitcher (large)
Pot holder
Saucepans
Scale
Toaster
Vegetable peeler
Wire whisk
Wooden spoon

TOMATO ICE

3 cups tomato juice
¼ cup tomato puree
¼ cup evaporated skimmed milk
2 tablespoons lemon juice

Hot sauce and salt to taste
6 large lettuce leaves, formed into
 cups

Chill 6 dessert bowls. In bowl, using wire whisk, combine all ingredients
except lettuce. Place in freezer; freeze to slushy consistency, beating often.
If mixture becomes solid, allow to defrost slightly before serving. Place 1
lettuce cup in each chilled bowl; spoon an equal amount of "ice" into each
lettuce cup. Makes 6 servings.

CRAB MEAT À LA KING

2 tablespoons imitation (or diet)
 margarine
2 tablespoons flour
1½ cups skim milk
12 ounces cooked crab meat,
 flaked
4 eggs, hard-cooked and chopped
2 teaspoons Worcestershire sauce

1½ teaspoons chopped chives
Dash hot sauce
Salt and white pepper to taste
6 slices enriched white bread,
 toasted and sliced diagonally to
 form 24 equal toast points
6 watercress sprigs

Melt margarine in top of a double boiler, over boiling water. Stir in flour and cook 5 minutes. Stirring constantly, add milk and cook until thickened and smooth. Fold in remaining ingredients except bread and watercress; cook 5 minutes or until heated throughout. Place an equal amount of crab meat mixture on each of 6 plates. Arrange 4 toast points around each portion of crab meat. Garnish each portion with a watercress sprig. Makes 6 servings.

CONFETTI VEGETABLES

2 cups peas
2 cups sliced carrots
1 cup sliced mushrooms
1 cup cut green beans
1 cup cauliflower florets
12 medium asparagus spears, cut into 1-inch pieces

2 packets instant chicken broth and seasoning mix
Salt and pepper to taste
1 tablespoon minced fresh parsley

In saucepan cook each vegetable separately in boiling salted water until tender. When ready to serve, combine cooked vegetables, broth mix, salt, and pepper in nonstick skillet; cook until thoroughly heated. If necessary, add a few tablespoons water to skillet to prevent sticking. Transfer vegetables to large serving bowl. Sprinkle with minced parsley. Makes 6 servings.

RICE PUDDING WITH BLUEBERRY SAUCE

Serve warm or chilled.

Pudding:

3 cups cooked enriched rice
2 cups skim milk
Artificial sweetener to equal 10 teaspoons sugar
1½ teaspoons vanilla extract

½ teaspoon cinnamon
1½ teaspoons cornstarch, dissolved in 2 teaspoons water
2 eggs, beaten

Blueberry Sauce:

1½ cups blueberries
Artificial sweetener to equal 4 teaspoons sugar

¼ teaspoon vanilla extract

To Prepare Pudding: Combine first 5 ingredients in top of double boiler, over boiling water. Cover and cook, stirring often, for 20 minutes. Stir in cornstarch. Stirring constantly, gradually add eggs to rice mixture. Cook until thickened.

To Prepare Sauce: Combine berries, sweetener, and extract in bowl. Transfer ¼ cup berry mixture to blender container; process until smooth. Return pureed berries to bowl; mix well.

To Serve: Divide pudding equally into 6 dessert glasses. Top each portion with ⅙ of the Blueberry Sauce. Makes 6 servings.

LEMONADE

¾ *cup lemon juice*
Artificial sweetener to equal 24
   teaspoons sugar
1½ quarts water

1½ lemons, cut into 9 slices
Ice cubes
6 mint sprigs

Combine lemon juice and sweetener in large pitcher Add water and 3 lemon slices; stir well. Partially fill six 12-ounce glasses with ice cubes. Pour an equal amount of lemonade into each glass. Garnish each serving with 1 lemon slice and a mint sprig. Makes 6 servings.

JAPANESE FEAST FOR TWO

Clam Broth with Carrot Flower Garnish
Beef and Tofu Sukiyaki
Sesame Rice
Sliced Cucumbers with Vinegar Dressing
Almond-Mandarin Gelatin
Japanese Tea

Someone special coming for dinner? Or perhaps you want to make your "in-house" partner *feel* special? Take a cue from the astute Japanese, who know that beautiful food can be mood-enhancing. This charming tête-à-tête dinner, though impressive in appearance, is disarmingly simple to prepare at home. Many of the ingredients can be prepared in advance, and all of them can be found in local stores. (Note that we've suggested you use shoyu, the Japanese soy sauce, which is lighter than the Chinese variety.) Remember, too, that you're aiming to appeal to *all* the senses, so take time to make the food look attractive by skillfully slicing the vegetables into pieces of uniform size. By following our simple directions you can create artful carrot "flowers" to float in the Clam Broth.

This imaginative repast deserves a romantic atmosphere. Clear off a low cocktail table and set it to perfection with dainty dishes and a simple arrangement of delicate flowers. Place two large cushions on the floor to sit on—in Japanese style—and "plant" a bonsai tree in the middle of the room. Don't forget that typically Oriental touch—a hot towel, neatly folded on a tray, to be used at the beginning of the meal. Dress for the occasion in a beautifully patterned kimono (and aren't you grateful for menus that help *you* look enchanting, too?).

P.S. This recipe for romance need not be limited to July

SUGGESTED SHOPPING LIST

Staples and Miscellaneous

Almond extract
Artificial sweetener
Garlic powder
Ginger
Instant beef broth and seasoning mix
  or bouillon cubes
Instant chicken broth and seasoning
  mix or bouillon cubes
Paprika
Pepper
Salt
Sesame seeds

Japanese shoyu (soy sauce)
Rice vinegar

Japanese tea
Unflavored gelatin

Sesame oil

Additional Items

Boneless rib steak, 6 ounces

Soybean curd (tofu), 8 ounces

Lemon, 1

Carrot, 1 medium
Celery, 1 rib
Cucumber, 1 medium
Lettuce, 1 small head
Onion, 1 small
Scallions, 3

Spinach, 1 pound
Tomato, 1 medium, firm

Canned mandarin orange sections, no
  sugar added, 1 10½-ounce can

Canned sliced bamboo shoots, 1
  8-ounce can

Canned sliced mushrooms, 1 8-ounce
  can

Clam juice, 1 8-fluid-ounce bottle

Enriched white rice, 1 16-ounce box

SUGGESTED EQUIPMENT LIST

Bowl (small)
Can opener
Chef's knife
Cutting board
Measuring cups
Measuring spoons
Nonstick skillet

Pot holder
Roasting pan and rack
Saucepans (small)
Scale
Vegetable peeler
Wooden spoon

CLAM BROTH WITH CARROT FLOWER GARNISH

¾ cup clam juice
¾ cup chicken bouillon
¼ teaspoon Japanese shoyu
  (soy sauce)

Carrot Flower Garnish (see
  following instructions)

In small saucepan combine clam juice, chicken bouillon, and shoyu. Simmer 5 minutes. Divide evenly into 2 small bowls. Garnish by floating carrot flower on each portion. Makes 2 servings.

Carrot Flower Garnish

2 center-cut carrot slices, each ⅛ inch thick

In saucepan blanch carrots in boiling salted water to cover. Cut six V notches along the edge of each carrot so that it resembles a daisy petal. Use as directed in recipe for Clam Broth (see preceding recipe).

BEEF AND TOFU SUKIYAKI

6 ounces boneless rib steak
Salt, pepper, garlic powder, and paprika to taste
½ cup sliced onion
¼ cup Japanese shoyu (soy sauce), divided
½ cup drained, canned sliced mushrooms
½ cup sliced celery
½ cup drained, canned sliced bamboo shoots

½ cup beef bouillon
¼ teaspoon garlic powder
2 cups torn spinach leaves
10 cherry tomatoes
8 ounces soybean curd (tofu), cut into ½-inch cubes*
¼ cup plus 2 tablespoons sliced scallions

Season steak with salt, pepper, garlic powder, and paprika. Broil on a rack until rare. Cut into very thin diagonal slices and reserve. In nonstick skillet combine onion and 1 tablespoon shoyu. Cook, stirring often, until onion is tender. Add mushrooms, celery, and bamboo shoots; cook 1 minute, stirring often. Add bouillon, remaining shoyu, and ¼ teaspoon garlic powder; cook for 5 minutes, stirring occasionally. Add spinach and cherry tomatoes. Cook for 2 minutes. Add reserved meat and tofu and cook 3 minutes longer or until thoroughly heated. Stir in scallions. Makes 2 servings.

* If tofu is not available, increase steak to 12 ounces and proceed as directed above.

SESAME RICE

1 cup freshly cooked, hot enriched rice
2 tablespoons thinly sliced scallion

2 teaspoons Japanese shoyu (soy sauce)
1 teaspoon sesame seeds, toasted
1 teaspoon sesame oil

Combine all ingredients in serving dish; stir well. Makes 2 servings.

SLICED CUCUMBERS WITH VINEGAR DRESSING

2 tablespoons rice vinegar
1 tablespoon Japanese shoyu
   (soy sauce)
Artificial sweetener to equal 1
   teaspoon sugar (optional)

¼ teaspoon ginger
⅛ teaspoon garlic powder
1 medium cucumber, pared,
   scored, and sliced
1 cup shredded lettuce

In small bowl combine vinegar, shoyu, sweetener if desired, ginger, and garlic powder. Add cucumbers; toss. Chill at least 2 hours, stirring once. Serve on bed of lettuce. Makes 2 servings.

ALMOND-MANDARIN GELATIN

½ envelope unflavored gelatin
¼ cup water
1 cup canned mandarin orange
   sections, no sugar added

Artificial sweetener to equal 4
   teaspoons sugar (optional)
1½ teaspoons almond extract
1 teaspoon lemon juice

In small saucepan sprinkle gelatin over water; let stand a few minutes to soften. Add remaining ingredients and cook, stirring constantly, for 5 minutes or until gelatin is dissolved. Divide evenly into two ¾-cup dessert dishes. Chill until firm. Makes 2 servings.

A SHORE DINNER FOR SIX

Clam Chowder
Lobster Tails with Garlic "Butter" Sauce
Corn on the Cob
Hearty Spinach and Mushroom Salad
Yogurt Green Goddess Dressing
Blueberry-Peach Parfait
Beverage

Stoke hearty outdoor appetites with a delicious seaside menu that can be prepared so swiftly you won't have to cut short your day in the sun. It's easy cooking, even in the most rustic seaside cottage. As a plus, if you're picnicking, these dishes are all portable! Make the Clam Chowder ahead of time and then *gently* reheat it (don't boil!) at the last minute. For a picnic, the Chowder—and the Garlic Sauce—transport easily in thermos jugs. Lobster Tails are an effortless but elegant summer treat. Along with that year-round favorite—Corn on the Cob—they can be cooked on the spot, either indoors or over a charcoal fire in the salty air. Spinach becomes an easy summer salad when mixed with a gourmet touch of mushrooms. Chill the salad ingredients ahead of time, then pack them in separate plastic bags to carry in an iced picnic box. Just before serving, mix the ingredients thoroughly in one plastic bag. The Yogurt Dressing will travel safely in a screw-top jar; just shake well before using. Parfait refreshingly rounds off a summer meal. For a picnic, however, you may find it simpler to substitute fresh fruit, artfully arranged on paper plates or in a wicker basket. This convertible menu will help you look your best in *any* setting.

SUGGESTED SHOPPING LIST

Staples and Miscellaneous

Almond extract
Artificial sweetener
Bay leaves
Chopped chives
Garlic powder
Instant chicken broth and seasoning
   mix
Peppercorns
Salt
Thyme
Vanilla extract
White pepper
Yellow food coloring (optional)

Hot sauce
Red wine vinegar
Worcestershire sauce

Unflavored gelatin

Margarine

Additional Items

Lobster tails, 6 6-ounce tails

Plain unflavored yogurt, 1 16-ounce
   container

Blueberries, 1 pint
Lemons, 3

Celery, 2 ribs
Corn-on-the-cob, 6 medium ears
Garlic cloves, 2
Green pepper, 1 medium
Mushrooms, 1 pound
Onion, 1 medium
Parsley, 1 bunch
Radishes, 1 bag
Spinach, 2 pounds

Zucchini, 1 medium (approximately
   5 ounces)

Canned sliced peaches, no sugar
   added, 2 16-ounce cans

Canned crushed tomatoes, 1 28-ounce
   can

Tomato puree, 1 16-ounce can

Canned anchovy fillets, 1 2-ounce can
Canned minced clams, 2 6½-ounce
   cans

Clam juice, 2 8-fluid-ounce jars

Evaporated skimmed milk, 1 13-fluid-
   ounce can

SUGGESTED EQUIPMENT LIST

Aluminum foil
Bowls (medium, large)
Broiling pan
Can opener
Chef's knife
Cutting board
Double boiler
Electric mixer
Measuring cups

Measuring spoons
Pan (large)
Paring knife
Pepper mill
Pot (large)
Pot holder
Saucepans (small, large)
Scale
Wooden spoon

CLAM CHOWDER

1 cup diced celery
½ cup diced onion
½ cup diced green pepper
1 garlic clove, minced
1 bay leaf
2 cups clam juice
2 cups water
1½ cups canned crushed
tomatoes

1 cup tomato puree
5¾ ounces drained canned
minced clams
2 packets instant chicken broth
and seasoning mix
¼ teaspoon thyme
Dash hot sauce
Salt and freshly ground pepper
to taste

Combine first 5 ingredients in large saucepan. Cook 3 to 5 minutes. Add remaining ingredients. Bring to a boil; reduce heat and simmer 35 to 40 minutes. Remove bay leaf before serving. Makes 6 servings.

LOBSTER TAILS WITH GARLIC "BUTTER" SAUCE

6 lobster tails, 6 ounces each (see
Note)
Garlic "Butter" Sauce (see
following recipe)

Lemon wedges, parsley sprigs,
and radish roses (see page 17)
to garnish

Cut through upper shell of each lobster tail lengthwise and press shell halves apart; pull meat up. Place lobster tails on grill or in broiling pan. Grill over hot coals or broil 6 to 8 minutes on each side or until done. Serve 1 lobster tail per portion. Serve each portion with ⅙ of the Garlic "Butter" Sauce, garnished with lemon wedge, parsley sprig, and radish rose. Makes 6 servings.

Note: A 6-ounce lobster tail will yield about 3 ounces cooked lobster meat.

Garlic "Butter" Sauce

¼ cup evaporated skimmed milk
¼ cup margarine
½ teaspoon garlic powder

1 drop yellow food coloring
(optional)
Salt and white pepper to taste

Combine all ingredients in top of double boiler, over boiling water. Heat, stirring occasionally, until margarine is melted. Serve as directed in recipe for Lobster Tails (see preceding recipe).

CORN ON THE COB

6 medium ears of corn, unhusked

Pull husks of corn down, without breaking them off at the end. Remove and discard silky threads. Close husks and place corn in large pan of cold water; let stand 5 minutes. Drain and wrap corn in aluminum foil. Cook on grill or directly on hot coals for 10 to 15 minutes, turning occasionally. An alternate method is to remove husks and put corn in pot of cold water. Bring water to a boil. Remove corn and serve. Makes 6 servings.

HEARTY SPINACH AND MUSHROOM SALAD

Serve with Yogurt Green Goddess Dressing (see recipe below).

6 cups spinach	1 cup sliced zucchini, blanched
2 cups sliced mushrooms	

Wash spinach well; remove and discard stems. Shake leaves to remove moisture; tear into bite-size pieces. In large bowl toss spinach with mushrooms and zucchini. Divide evenly into 6 salad bowls. Makes 6 servings.

YOGURT GREEN GODDESS DRESSING

Serve with Hearty Spinach and Mushroom Salad (see recipe above).

1 cup plain unflavored yogurt	1 garlic clove, minced
⅓ cup chopped fresh parsley	Few drops Worcestershire sauce
3 tablespoons chopped chives	Dash each salt, pepper, and
2 tablespoons lemon juice	thyme
2 tablespoons red wine vinegar	
¼ ounce drained canned anchovy fillets, minced	

Combine all ingredients in bowl; mix well. Cover and refrigerate until chilled. Makes 6 servings.

BLUEBERRY-PEACH PARFAIT

1½ teaspoons unflavored gelatin	Artificial sweetener to equal 4
¼ cup water	teaspoons sugar (optional)
¾ cup evaporated skimmed milk, chilled	1 tablespoon lemon juice
	½ teaspoon vanilla extract
2 cups canned sliced peaches, no sugar added	¼ teaspoon almond extract
	1 cup blueberries

In small saucepan sprinkle gelatin over water; let stand a few minutes to soften. Heat, stirring constantly, until gelatin is dissolved. Set aside. In mixing bowl, using electric mixer, whip milk until stiff. Add gelatin mixture and continue to beat until combined. Cover and refrigerate for 1 hour. Reserve 6 peach slices for garnish. In another bowl mash remaining peaches and add sweetener if desired, lemon juice, and extracts. Fold peach mixture and blueberries into gelatin mixture. Chill until ready to serve. Divide mixture evenly into 6 parfait glasses and garnish each portion with 1 reserved peach slice. Makes 6 servings.

SUMMER LUNCHEON SUPREME FOR FOUR

Chicken in Aspic
Mayonnaise Dressing in Lemon Cups
Hot Rolls or Toast Points
Golden Glow Salad
Plum Compote
Hot Coffee □ Iced Coffee

"Cool elegance" is the phrase that best describes this luncheon. It's perfect for that special occasion in the summertime when you don't want the oven heating up the house. Except for the bread and beverage all these dishes can be prepared in advance (perhaps in the comparative cool of evening). The well-chilled Chicken in Aspic is gourmet fare for hot-weather dining, and the Mayonnaise Dressing served in ingenious Lemon Cups adds just the right visual touch. Summer means "salad days"; ours takes a "Golden Glow" with a cool blend of carrots, oranges, and pineapple, enhanced by a favorite southern refresher—mint. The fruits for both the salad and the Plum Compote are *canned*, which means you can keep the ingredients on hand without worrying about warm-weather spoilage. Offer guests a choice of coffee served either iced or hot (which some people prefer even in July) to round out a trim and tasty repast that's sure to draw warm praise.

———— • • ————

SUGGESTED SHOPPING LIST

Staples and Miscellaneous

Artificial sweetener
Cinnamon sticks
Cloves
Dried mint
Garlic powder
Instant chicken broth and seasoning
    mix
Nutmeg
Onion powder
Vanilla extract

White vinegar

Coffee
Cornstarch

Imitation mayonnaise

Enriched white or whole grain 1-ounce
    rolls or bread

Additional Items

Chicken, 1 3-pound

Plain unflavored yogurt, 1 8-ounce container

Lemons, 5

Carrots, 6 medium
Celery, 4 ribs
Dill, 1 bunch

Lettuce, 1 head

Frozen peas, 1 10-ounce package

Canned mandarin orange sections, no sugar added, 2 10½-ounce cans
Canned pineapple slices, no sugar added, 1 8-ounce can
Canned plums, no sugar added, 1 16-ounce can

SUGGESTED EQUIPMENT LIST

Bowls (small and medium)
Can opener
Chef's knife
Cutting board
Grater
Measuring cups
Measuring spoons

Pot holder
Saucepans (small)
Scale
Teaspoon or paring knife
Toaster
Vegetable peeler
Wooden spoon

CHICKEN IN ASPIC

1 envelope unflavored gelatin
¼ cup cold water
¾ cup warm water
¼ cup white vinegar
2 packets instant chicken broth and seasoning mix
⅛ teaspoon dill weed

1 pound diced cooked chicken
½ cup drained canned peas
Mayonnaise Dressing in Lemon Cups (see recipe below)
Hot Rolls or Toast Points (see recipe, page 209)

In small saucepan soften gelatin in cold water. Add warm water, vinegar, broth mix, and dill. Simmer, stirring constantly, for 5 minutes or until gelatin is dissolved. Pour thin layer of gelatin mixture into 1-quart mold; refrigerate until firm. In bowl combine chicken and peas. Arrange chicken and pea mixture over gelatin layer in mold. Pour remaining gelatin mixture over chicken. Chill 3 hours or until set. Unmold onto serving platter. Arrange filled Lemon Cups around aspic. Intersperse rolls or toast points between Lemon Cups. Makes 4 servings.

MAYONNAISE DRESSING IN LEMON CUPS

Serve with Chicken in Aspic (see recipe above).

½ cup plain unflavored yogurt
¼ cup imitation mayonnaise
Artificial sweetener to equal 1 teaspoon sugar

¼ teaspoon garlic powder
¼ teaspoon onion powder
¼ teaspoon dill weed
4 Lemon Cups (see page 15)

In small bowl combine first 6 ingredients; mix well. Chill. Spoon an equal amount of dressing into each Lemon Cup. Serve as directed in recipe for Chicken in Aspic.

HOT ROLLS OR TOAST POINTS

Serve with Chicken in Aspic (see recipe, page 208).

Heat four 1-ounce enriched white or whole grain rolls

or

Toast 4 slices enriched white or whole grain bread. Cut bread diagonally into triangles.

Serve rolls or toast points as directed in recipe for Chicken in Aspic.

GOLDEN GLOW SALAD

2 cups shredded carrots
1 cup canned mandarin orange sections, no sugar added
4 canned pineapple slices with ¼ cup juice, no sugar added

2 tablespoons plus 2 teaspoons imitation mayonnaise
½ teaspoon dried mint
4 cups shredded lettuce

In medium bowl combine carrots, orange sections, pineapple juice, mayonnaise, and mint. Chill for 1 hour. Place on serving platter. Cut each pineapple slice in half; arrange around carrot mixture. Surround with lettuce. Makes 4 servings.

PLUM COMPOTE

8 canned plums with ½ cup juice, no sugar added
¼ cup water
Artificial sweetener to equal 2 teaspoons sugar
1 cinnamon stick

2 cloves
Dash nutmeg
2 teaspoons cornstarch, dissolved in 2 tablespoons water
½ teaspoon vanilla extract

In small saucepan combine plum juice, water, sweetener, cinnamon, cloves, and nutmeg. Bring to a boil. Reduce heat; simmer 10 minutes. Remove and discard cinnamon and cloves. Add cornstarch; cook, stirring constantly, until mixture thickens. Stir in vanilla. Place 2 plums in each of four ¾-cup dessert dishes. Pour an equal amount of syrup over each portion of plums. Chill. Makes 4 servings.

TOTE-A-LUNCH FOR ONE

Bloody Shame
Cucumber and Smoked Fish Canapés
Roast Beef Sandwich with Chive Spread
Blueberry Yogurt □ Fresh Fruit
Beverage

"Have food, will travel . . ." and here's a lunch that does—in first-class style. It's excellent fare to bring along whether you're flying "no frills," traveling in the car, taking lunch to work, or going anywhere when you'd like to tote a treat for yourself. If drinks are being served, you can get "high" with a heady Bloody Shame (a vodka-less Bloody Mary). Complement it with sophisticated Cucumber and Smoked Fish Canapés. Then devour a hearty Roast Beef Sandwich flavored in unusual manner with Chive Spread. Treat yourself to dessert too . . . a cooling blend of yogurt and fruit. (Don't forget to pack a plastic spoon!) Include fresh fruit, in case you get hungry later on. Every item will travel safely in an insulated bag (and help *you* travel weightlessly).

SUGGESTED SHOPPING LIST

Staples and Miscellaneous

Artificial sweetener
Chopped chives
Dill weed
Peppercorns
Salt

Prepared horseradish
Worcestershire sauce

Margarine

Additional Items

Roast beef, ⅛ pound
Smoked sturgeon or whitefish, ⅛ pound

Plain unflavored yogurt, 1 8-ounce container

Blueberries, 1 pint
Choice of fruit (1 small orange or 1 small apple or 1 medium peach or 1 small pear or 2 medium apricots

or 2 medium plums or 1 large tangerine)
Lemon, 1 (optional)

Cucumber, 1 medium
Dill pickles, 1 16-ounce jar

Tomato juice, 1 12-fluid-ounce can

Enriched white roll, 1 1-ounce

Aluminum foil
Can opener
Chef's knife
Colander
Container (with tight-fitting cover)
Cup (small)
Cutting board
Insulated tote bag
Jar (with tight-fitting cover)
Measuring cups

Measuring spoons
Paper towels
Pepper mill
Plastic wrap
Pot holder
Saucepan (small)
Spreading knife
Vegetable peeler
Waxed paper
Wooden spoon

BLOODY SHAME

1 cup tomato juice
¼ teaspoon prepared horseradish
¼ teaspoon Worcestershire sauce

Salt and freshly ground pepper to taste
3 to 4 ice cubes
Lemon wedge (optional)

Combine all ingredients except lemon in jar with tight-fitting cover; cover jar. Wrap lemon, if desired, in plastic wrap. Pack in insulated tote bag. Serve in tall glass with lemon wedge. Makes 1 serving.

CUCUMBER AND SMOKED FISH CANAPÉS

1 medium cucumber, pared and cut into 12 slices
Salt

1½ ounces smoked sturgeon or whitefish
Dill weed to taste

Place cucumber slices in colander; sprinkle with salt. Set aside for 20 minutes. Rinse and pat dry. Cut fish into 12 pieces. Place 1 piece on each cucumber slice; sprinkle each with dill weed. Stack, placing waxed paper between layers; wrap securely in aluminum foil. Chill. Pack in insulated tote bag. Makes 1 serving.

ROAST BEEF SANDWICH WITH CHIVE SPREAD

1 teaspoon margarine
½ teaspoon chopped chives
1 enriched white roll, 1 ounce, cut in half

2 ounces sliced roast beef
1 medium dill pickle, cut into spears

In small cup combine margarine and chives; spread on cut side of each roll half. Place beef on bottom half of roll; place top half of roll over beef. Wrap securely in foil or plastic wrap. Wrap pickle separately. Chill. Pack in insulated tote bag. Makes 1 serving.

BLUEBERRY YOGURT

½ cup blueberries   ½ cup plain unflavored yogurt
2 tablespoons water
Artificial sweetener to equal 2
   teaspoons sugar

In small saucepan combine berries and water. Cook, stirring occasionally, until berries are very soft and most of the liquid is evaporated. Stir in sweetener; cool. Combine berry mixture with yogurt in container with tight-fitting cover. Cover and chill. Pack in insulated tote bag. Makes 1 serving.

FRESH FRUIT

Choose 1 of the following fresh fruits: 1 small orange, 1 small apple, 1 medium peach, 1 small pear, 2 medium apricots, 2 medium plums, or 1 large tangerine. Wrap in aluminum foil or plastic wrap; chill. Pack in insulated tote bag. Makes 1 serving.

HOOLAULEA—A MIDSUMMER PARTY FOR EIGHT

Laulaus (Fish and Spinach Packages)
Banana "Poi"
Roast Pork
Brown Rice
Baked Pumpkin
Carrot and Zucchini Salad with Sesame Seed Dressing
Haole Pineapple and Watermelon
Beverage

For an unusual July jamboree, host a *hukilau* (that's a party, in Hawaiian). Our menu adapts native Hawiian dishes. Poi, traditionally made from the roots of the taro plant, was used on the Islands as a substitute for starch. It was eaten with the fingers and its consistency was described as "one-finger," "two-finger," or "three-finger." Our version slimmingly substitutes banana, tropically flavored with coconut extract. Fish as well as pork is a staple of luaus. As an interesting change, serve brown rice instead of white. Fruit—abundant on the Islands—harmonizes well with pork, so let dessert be Hawaii's most famed export—pineapple, and add splashes of color with watermelon.

Encourage guests to come in muumuus or bright cotton shirts and skirts—even grass ones. Your friends will adore the chance to dare a sarong! Cover the table with a brown and black tapa-patterned cloth. Make your garden tropical with an abundance of brilliant flowers and exotic indoor plants carried outside. Hang many-hued paper lanterns from the trees. Surprise guests with flower leis to grace their necks. Turn on rhythmic Hawaiian music . . . and enjoy your Havoli Ahaaina (happy feast)!

Staples and Miscellaneous

Artificial sweetener
Cinnamon
Coarse salt
Coconut extract
Curry powder
Ginger
Instant chicken broth and seasoning
  mix or bouillon cube
Nutmeg
Salt
Sesame seeds
White pepper

Cider vinegar
Liquid smoke
Soy sauce

Imitation (or diet) margarine
Vegetable oil

Additional Items

Pork loin roast (2 to 3 pounds),
  rolled and tied

Bananas, 4 medium, very ripe
Lemons, 2
Pineapple, 1 small
Watermelon, ¼

Carrots, 3 medium
Garlic clove, 1
Onion, 1 small
Scallions, 3
Spinach, ¼ pound

Watercress, 1 bunch
Zucchini, 2 medium (approximately
  5 ounces each)

Canned salmon, 1 15-ounce can

Grape leaves, 1 16-ounce jar
Canned pumpkin, 1 32-ounce can
Tomato puree, 1 16-ounce can

Evaporated skimmed milk, 1 13-fluid-
  ounce can

Brown rice, 1 16-ounce box

SUGGESTED EQUIPMENT LIST

Aluminum foil
Bowls (small, medium)
Can opener
Casserole (7 x 5½ x 3 inches)
Chef's knife
Colander
Cutting board
Heavy saucepan with cover (medium)
Heavy heatproof plate
Jar with cover for salad dressing

Measuring cups
Measuring spoons
Meat thermometer
Melon baller
Paring knife
Pot holder
Roasting pan and rack
Scale
Wooden spoon

LAULAUS (FISH AND SPINACH PACKAGES)

*8 ounces drained canned salmon,
  flaked
½ cup chopped spinach
¼ cup thinly sliced scallions
2 teaspoons lemon juice*

*8 grape leaves, packed in brine
½ cup tomato puree
½ cup water
½ teaspoon curry powder
⅛ teaspoon pepper*

In small bowl combine salmon, spinach, scallions, and lemon juice. Gently place grape leaves in colander and rinse under cold running water, separating leaves. Dry gently. Place leaves, 1 at a time, on flat surface. Divide salmon mixture into 8 equal portions. Place 1 portion in center of each leaf. Roll each leaf tightly, from stem end toward the point of the leaf, tucking in the sides. Arrange stuffed leaves in heavy saucepan. In measuring cup combine tomato puree, water, curry powder, and pepper; pour over stuffed leaves. Place a heavy, heatproof plate, slightly smaller in diameter than the saucepan, over leaves to prevent them from opening. Cover saucepan and cook over low heat for 30 minutes. To serve, divide liquid in saucepan into 8 equal portions. Serve 1 portion over each stuffed grape leaf. Makes 8 servings.

BANANA "POI"

4 very ripe, medium bananas, unpeeled
½ cup evaporated skimmed milk

1 tablespoon plus 1½ teaspoons lemon juice
¼ teaspoon coconut extract

Cut each banana in half lengthwise. Remove fruit, reserving skins intact. Place fruit in bowl; mash, then beat to a smooth paste. Stir in milk, lemon juice, and coconut extract. Divide mixture into 8 equal portions. Spoon 1 portion into each reserved skin. Serve immediately. Makes 8 servings.

ROAST PORK

2- to 3-pound boned, rolled, and tied pork loin roast
½ teaspoon coarse salt

½ teaspoon soy sauce
½ teaspoon liquid smoke

Place pork on piece of aluminum foil that is large enough to enclose pork. Sprinkle pork with salt and soy sauce; rub in liquid smoke. Wrap foil around pork, folding edges together to seal tightly. Place in bowl. Refrigerate overnight or at least 3 hours. Remove meat from foil and place on rack in roasting pan; insert meat thermometer. Roast at 325°F. for 1 to 1½ hours or until thermometer registers 170°F. Weigh 3 ounces per portion. Makes about 8 servings.

BROWN RICE

Serve ½ cup hot, cooked brown rice per portion. For recipe, see page 32.

BAKED PUMPKIN

½ cup chopped onion
1 tablespoon plus 1 teaspoon
  imitation (or diet) margarine
Artificial sweetener to equal 4
  teaspoons sugar

½ teaspoon cinnamon
¼ teaspoon nutmeg
⅛ teaspoon salt
2¼ cups canned pumpkin
¼ cup chicken bouillon

Place onions, margarine, sweetener, cinnamon, nutmeg, and salt in 7 × 5½ × 3-inch casserole. Bake at 450°F., stirring occasionally, for 10 minutes or until onions are tender. Remove from oven; reduce oven temperature to 350°F. Stir pumpkin and bouillon into onion mixture. Bake for 20 minutes. Makes 8 servings.

CARROT AND ZUCCHINI SALAD WITH SESAME SEED DRESSING

2 cups julienne zucchini
1 cup julienne carrots
Sesame Seed Dressing (see
  following recipe)

2 cups watercress leaves

Combine zucchini and carrots in salad bowl. Add dressing; toss. Cover; refrigerate overnight or at least 3 hours. Remove crushed garlic. Serve on bed of watercress leaves. Makes 8 servings.

Sesame Seed Dressing

3 tablespoons cider vinegar
2 tablespoons plus 2 teaspoons
  vegetable oil
1 tablespoon soy sauce

1 tablespoon water
2 teaspoons sesame seeds, toasted
1 garlic clove, crushed

Combine all ingredients in jar with tight-fitting cover; cover and shake well. Use as directed in recipe for Carrot and Zucchini Salad (see preceding recipe).

HAOLE PINEAPPLE AND WATERMELON

1 small pineapple

4 cups watermelon balls

Cut pineapple into 8 equal wedges, cutting through crown to stem end. Cut off and discard fiberous core from each wedge. Place wedges on cutting board, rind side down. Using paring knife, cut away rind from each wedge, leaving pulp and rind intact. Place wedges of pulp on cutting board. Cutting downward, divide each wedge into 6 slices. Replace sliced wedges on reserved rinds. To serve, place each wedge on an individual dessert plate; surround each with ½ cup watermelon balls. Serve well chilled. Makes 8 servings.

August

Trying not to let the hot weather get
you down? Our August menus are filled
with ideas to help you beat the heat!
Have a poolside party and invite your
guests to wear their favorite swimming
attire. Or turn your summertime
barbecue into a meal with Middle
Eastern splendor! With menus such
as these, you'll surely stay
"cool as a cucumber"!

A TASTE OF ITALY FOR FOUR

Antipasto with Roasted Peppers
Anchovy-Garlic Dressing
Pasta Primavera
Macedonia di Frutta
Espresso

If your friends think Italian food just means pasta, let them guess again. Better still, invite them to sample Italy via our easy summertime menu. Italian meals traditionally begin with an inviting antipasto (the Italian word for hors d'oeuvres, which quite literally translates into "before the pasta"). Our menu adaptations take economic advantage of seasonal vegetables, including the roasted peppers the Italians adore. For a savory dressing, blend a trio of favorites: anchovy strips, oregano (what Italian dish is complete without this popular seasoning?), and—of course—garlic. Even pasta isn't prosaic in this Latin land, for it's served in every conceivable shape. Our Pasta Primavera gains excitement by using a variety of unusual forms. (No creativity is needed, since pasta comes packaged in various shapes.) Anyone who has wandered through Italian neighborhoods is familiar with their richly colorful fruit stands. Taking that nutritious cue, serve a Macedonia di Frutta (fruit mixture), an attractive hot-weather dessert. Relax over espresso—the native Mediterranean coffee that has become one of our most popular after-dinner beverages. It's customarily served in small cups. Set your scene using the Italian national colors: cool green, white, and vibrant red. What a tasty way to tour a food-and-fun-loving land (while proving that pasta doesn't have to translate into poundage)!

SUGGESTED SHOPPING LIST

Staples and Miscellaneous

Basil	Red wine vinegar
Capers	
Oregano	Ground espresso coffee
Pepper	
Salt	Vegetable oil

Additional Items

Apple, 1 small
Lemon, 1
Peaches, 2 medium
Pineapple, 1 small

Broccoli, 1 small bunch
Carrots, 2 medium
Celery hearts, 1 18-ounce bag
Eggplant, 1 small
Garlic cloves, 3
Lettuce, 1 small head
Mushrooms, ½ pound
Onion, 1 medium
Parsley, 1 bunch
Red or green peppers, 4 medium
Scallions, 6
Tomatoes, 2 medium

Zucchini, 1 medium (approximately 5 ounces)

Frozen orange juice concentrate, 1 6-fluid-ounce can

Frozen artichoke hearts, 1 10-ounce package

Anchovies, 3 2-ounce cans
Sardines, 2 3¾-ounce cans
Tuna, 1 13-ounce can

Canned crushed tomatoes, 1 28-ounce can

Enriched macaroni, 3 16-ounce boxes, assorted shapes

SUGGESTED EQUIPMENT LIST

Baking sheet
Blender
Bowl (medium)
Can opener
Chef's knife
Cutting board
Glass dish (1-quart)

Measuring cups
Measuring spoons
Paring knife
Pot holder
Saucepan and cover (large)
Scale
Wooden spoons

ANTIPASTO WITH ROASTED PEPPERS

Serve with Anchovy-Garlic Dressing (see recipe, page 221).

Lettuce leaves
2 cups celery hearts, cut into wedges
8 ounces drained canned tuna, chunked
Roasted Peppers (see following recipe)
½ cup cooked artichoke hearts
4 ounces drained canned sardines
2 medium tomatoes, each cut into 8 wedges
½ cup scallions
2 teaspoons drained capers
1 lemon, quartered

Cover large serving tray with lettuce leaves. Arrange remaining ingredients on platter. Cover and refrigerate until ready to serve. Makes 4 servings.

Roasted Peppers

Wash and dry 4 medium red or green peppers. Place peppers on baking sheet and broil 4 inches from source of heat, turning occasionally, about

15 minutes or until all sides are black and charred. Transfer peppers to medium bowl. Cover bowl; allow peppers to cool. Remove and discard charred skin. Cut peppers into 2-inch strips, removing seeds. Use as directed in recipe for Antipasto (see recipe, page 220).

ANCHOVY-GARLIC DRESSING

Serve with Antipasto (see recipe, page 220).

4 ounces drained canned anchovies	1 garlic clove
¼ cup red wine vinegar	¼ teaspoon oregano
2 tablespoons plus 2 teaspoons vegetable oil	

Combine all ingredients in blender container and process until smooth. Makes 4 servings.

PASTA PRIMAVERA

A change from the more prosaic pasta dishes.

1 cup diced onions	1 cup broccoli florets
1 cup sliced mushrooms	2 teaspoons basil
2 garlic cloves, minced	2 teaspoons chopped fresh parsley
2 cups canned crushed tomatoes	Salt and pepper to taste
1 cup cubed, pared eggplant	2⅔ cups cooked enriched macaroni*
1 cup sliced zucchini	
1 cup thinly sliced carrots	

In large saucepan combine onions, mushrooms, and garlic; cook, stirring occasionally, for 5 to 7 minutes. Add remaining ingredients except macaroni. Cover and simmer 40 minutes or until vegetables are tender. Stir in macaroni and cook 10 minutes longer. Makes 4 servings.

* Use an assortment of shapes, all about 1 to 2 inches in length. It's the variation of shape that makes this dish unusual.

MACEDONIA DI FRUTTA

1 small apple, cored and sliced	½ small pineapple, pared, cored, and diced
2 medium peaches, pitted and diced	½ cup orange juice

Layer apple slices in 1-quart glass dish. Arrange peaches and pineapple over apple. Pour juice over fruit; cover and refrigerate at least 2 hours. Makes 4 servings.

POOLSIDE SPLASH—A HAMBURGER PARTY FOR EIGHT

Herbed Salad with Vinaigrette Dressing
Hamburgers in Pita Pockets
Vegetable Buffet □ Fruit Buffet
Thousand Island Dip □ Deviled Dip
Iced Tea

Make a splash by serving a tempting poolside buffet. What better main course than hamburgers, *relished* (pun intended!) at casual parties from coast to coast. Keep your cool by shaping the patties ahead of time. You can either broil them indoors or outside on the grill in traditional barbecue fashion. What's *not* traditional is the innovative way of tucking each burger into a handy pita "pocket"! Invite guests to dip into a tantalizing array of seasonings and condiments. Add color with rainbow arrangements of chilled raw vegetables and fresh fruits. Invitingly grouped on trays, they can double as buffet centerpieces. Add to the informality with gay paper plates and napkins and plastic tumblers. (*Never* use glass near a pool!) It all adds up to easy hosting that keeps you in the slim swim.

———◆•◆———

SUGGESTED SHOPPING LIST
Staples and Miscellaneous

Artificial sweetener
Dehydrated onion flakes
Garlic powder
Peppercorns
Poppy seeds
Salt
Sesame seeds
White pepper

Chili sauce
Hot sauce
Ketchup
Prepared horseradish
Prepared mustards (assortment)
Soy sauce
Steak sauce
Wine vinegar or tarragon vinegar
Worcestershire sauce

Tea

Imitation mayonnaise
Vegetable oil

Pita breads, 2 ounces each

Ground beef, 3 pounds

Plain unflavored yogurt, 1 16-ounce container

Banana, 1 medium
Lemons, 2
Lime, 1
Oranges, 2 small
Pineapples, 1 small
Strawberries, 2 pints

Basil, 1 bunch, or dried basil
Carrots, 8 medium
Cauliflower, 1 head
Chervil, 1 bunch, or dried chervil
Cucumbers, 2 medium
Green beans, 1 pound
Green peppers, 2 medium

Lettuce (choice of iceberg, Boston, romaine, or chicory), 2 heads
Mint, 1 bunch
Mushrooms, 1 pound
Parsley, 2 bunches, or dehydrated parsley flakes
Radishes, 1 bag
Red cabbage, 1 head
Rosemary, 1 bunch, or dried rosemary
Scallions, 2 bunches
Spinach, 1 pound
Tomatoes, 2 medium

Canned artichoke hearts, 2 16-ounce cans
Canned beets, 1 16-ounce can
Dill pickles or sour pickles, 1 16-ounce jar

Prunes, large, 1 12-ounce box

SUGGESTED EQUIPMENT LIST

Bowls (small and large)
Broiling pan and rack
Can opener
Chef's knife
Colander
Cutting board
Measuring cups
Measuring spoons

Pepper mill
Pot holder
Salad bowl (large)
Saucepan
Serving tray
Vegetable peeler
Waxed paper
Wooden spoon

HERBED SALAD WITH VINAIGRETTE DRESSING

8 cups torn lettuce leaves, bite-size pieces (iceberg, Boston, romaine, chicory, or any combination)
4 cups torn spinach leaves, bite-size pieces
2 cups shredded red cabbage

½ cup chopped fresh herbs or 2 tablespoons dried (basil, rosemary, chervil, parsley, etc., or any combination)
Vinaigrette Dressing (see page 30)

Keep cleaned greens and cabbage wrapped and chilled until ready to use. When ready to serve, toss all ingredients except dressing, together in large salad bowl. Pour dressing over salad; toss again to coat all vegetables. Makes 8 servings.

HAMBURGERS IN PITA POCKETS

3 pounds ground beef
¼ cup chopped fresh parsley
  (optional)
Garlic powder, salt, and pepper
  to taste

8 pita breads, 2 ounces each,
  warmed
Seasoning and Condiment Tray
  (see below)

In large bowl combine beef, parsley if desired, garlic powder, salt, and pepper. Divide into 16 equal portions; shape each portion into a patty. Place on tray with waxed paper between layers; cover and refrigerate. When ready to use, grill patties over hot coals or broil on rack in broiling pan, turning once, until done to taste. Cut each pita bread into 2 half circles. Each half will have a pocket. Serve each hamburger in 1 pita pocket. Invite guests to help themselves from the Seasoning and Condiment Tray. Makes 8 servings.

Seasoning and Condiment Tray

A wide variety of seasonings and condiments go well with hamburgers. Here are a few suggestions:

1 tablespoon plus 1 teaspoon
  poppy seeds or toasted sesame
  seeds
¼ cup ketchup
¼ cup chili sauce
8 medium dill or sour pickles,
  cut into spears
Soy sauce

Worcestershire sauce
Hot sauce
Assorted prepared mustards
Garlic powder
Salt or seasoned salt
Pepper mill filled with
  peppercorns

Arrange seasonings and condiments on tray so that your guests can choose their favorites. Be sure to have the necessary serving utensils available. Serve with Hamburgers in Pita Pockets (see preceding recipe).

VEGETABLE BUFFET

Serve with Deviled and Thousand Island Dips (see recipes, page 225).

2 cups green beans
2 cups cauliflower florets
2 cups mushrooms
2 cups carrot curls (see page 13)
1 cup sliced radishes
2 medium tomatoes, each cut into
  8 wedges
2 medium cucumbers, pared and
  sliced

2 medium green peppers, seeded
  and cut into strips
2 cups drained canned artichoke
  hearts
1 cup scallions
1 cup drained canned beets
Lemon wedges to garnish

Snip off and discard ends of green beans. Place beans in saucepan with boiling salted water; cook 3 minutes or until beans are tender-crisp. Drain beans; place in colander under cool running water. Wrap each type of vegetable separately in plastic wrap. One or two hours before serving, arrange vegetables on serving platter. Garnish with lemon wedges. Chill. Makes 8 servings.

FRUIT BUFFET

Serve with Deviled and Thousand Island Dips (see recipes below).

*1 small pineapple, pared and cut
into bite-size pieces, chilled*
2 cups strawberries, chilled
*2 small oranges, peeled and
sectioned, chilled*

8 large prunes
1 medium banana, sliced
*Lemon and lime wedges and
fresh mint leaves to garnish*

Arrange fruit on serving platter. Garnish with lemon and lime wedges and mint leaves. Makes 8 servings.

THOUSAND ISLAND DIP

Serve with Vegetable and Fruit Buffets (see recipes, page 224 and above).

½ cup imitation mayonnaise
*1 tablespoon plus 1 teaspoon
chopped dill pickle*
1 tablespoon chili sauce
1 tablespoon ketchup
1 teaspoon lemon juice

*½ teaspoon dehydrated onion
flakes*
½ teaspoon prepared horseradish
Dash salt
*Dash artificial sweetener
(optional)*

In bowl combine all ingredients; mix well. Cover and chill. When ready to serve, transfer to serving bowl. Makes 8 servings.

DEVILED DIP

Serve with Vegetable and Fruit Buffets (see recipes, page 224 and above).

1 cup plain unflavored yogurt
*1 tablespoon dehydrated onion
flakes*

1 tablespoon prepared mustard
2 teaspoons steak sauce
Salt and hot sauce to taste

In bowl combine all ingredients; mix well. Cover and chill. When ready to serve, transfer mixture to serving bowl. Makes 8 servings.

CONTINENTAL BREAKFAST FOR FOUR

Freshly Squeezed Orange Juice
Banana Muffins
Café au Lait

Add the flavor of travel to an at-home morning with our version of the internationally famed Continental Breakfast. Traveling dieters are only too familiar with the hurdle of that meal, which traditionally features a sweet roll and coffee. In our nourishing translation, the Banana Muffins sweetly hide protein-supplying eggs. Fresh Orange Juice is a healthy way to start the day. For a further taste treat, serve coffee in very French fashion—*au lait*. An off-beat breakfast that helps you stay on course.

SUGGESTED SHOPPING LIST

Staples and Miscellaneous

Artificial sweetener
Vanilla extract

Imitation (or diet) margarine

Raisin bread

Baking powder
Coffee
Flour
Nonfat dry milk powder
Nonstick cooking spray

Additional Items

Eggs, 4
Skim milk, 1 cup

Bananas, 2 medium
Oranges, 4 small

SUGGESTED EQUIPMENT LIST

Blender or food processor
Bowls (medium)
Cake tester
Chef's knife
Cutting board
Fork
Masher

Measuring cups
Measuring spoons
Muffin cups, 8
Pot holder
Saucepans (small)
Wooden spoon

FRESHLY SQUEEZED ORANGE JUICE

Serve ½ cup chilled freshly squeezed orange juice per person.

BANANA MUFFINS

4 slices raisin bread, made into crumbs
⅔ cup nonfat dry milk powder
Artificial sweetener to equal 16 teaspoons sugar
¼ cup flour

1 teaspoon baking powder
¼ cup imitation (or diet) margarine, melted
4 eggs, beaten
2 medium bananas, mashed
1 teaspoon vanilla extract

Preheat oven to 375°F. In medium bowl combine bread crumbs, dry milk, sweetener, flour, and baking powder; add margarine; mix with fork until crumbly. Stir in remaining ingredients; mix well. Divide mixture evenly into 8 muffin cups that have been sprayed with nonstick cooking spray. Bake for 15 minutes or until a cake tester, inserted in center of muffin, comes out clean. Makes 4 servings.

CAFÉ AU LAIT

In small saucepan heat 1 cup skim milk; *do not boil*. Pour ¼ cup heated milk into each of 4 large coffee cups. Fill each cup with ½ cup hot coffee. Makes 4 servings.

BARBECUE WITH A MIDEAST FLAVOR
FOR FOUR

Yogurt-Cucumber Soup
Chicken Livers Shish Kebab
Bulgur Pilaf
Iman Bayildi (Stuffed Eggplant)
Persian Passion
Spiced Iced Coffee

Waft your guests to an exotic scene, not with magic—but with menu; for our Mideast flavoring transforms a routine barbecue into a culinary event. Pilaf is the national dish of Turkey, and eggplant originated in India. Now enormously popular throughout the Balkans, it's known in Albania by the rhythmic name of *Iman Bayildi*. Yogurt has been an Eastern favorite for more than a century, perhaps because it's rumored to promote longevity! And long-lived will be the accolades you'll receive for making liver so palatable in Turkish Shish Kebab style. Grill the livers close to the coals for swifter cooking, which enhances the taste. Bewitch ordinary summer fruit into chilled Persian Passion, exotically scented with rose water. To wind up on a spicy note, serve coffee flavored with bitters.

Colorful paper decorations dangling from the trees and Eastern music piping through the speakers will help transform an ordinary backyard into a magical Eden. (And there's nothing you're "forbidden" to eat!!)

SUGGESTED SHOPPING LIST

Staples and Miscellaneous

Artificial sweetener
Cinnamon sticks
Dry mustard
Marjoram
Mint
Peppercorns
Salt
Savory

Instant coffee
Nonstick cooking spray
Unflavored gelatin

Margarine
Vegetable oil

Chicken Stock, 1½ cups (see page 31)

Aromatic bitters
Cider vinegar
Ketchup
Rose water
Soy sauce
Steak sauce

Additional Items

Chicken livers, 1½ pounds

Plain unflavored yogurt, 3 8-ounce
    containers
Skim milk, ½ cup

Cantaloupe, 1 small
Lemons, 8 medium
Peaches, 2 medium

Cucumbers, 2 medium
Dill, 1 bunch
Eggplants, 4 small
Garlic cloves, 4
Ginger root, 1 small

Mushrooms, ½ pound
Onions, 3 medium
Parsley, 1 bunch
Tomatoes, 2 medium

Canned pineapple chunks, no sugar
    added, 1 8-ounce can

Tomato puree, 1 16-ounce can

Evaporated skimmed milk, 1 13-fluid-
    ounce can

Dry cracked wheat (Bulgur) 1
    16-ounce box

SUGGESTED EQUIPMENT LIST

Bowls (medium and large)
Can opener
Casserole (1-quart)
Casserole (shallow)
Chef's knife
Cutting board
Electric mixer
Measuring cups
Measuring spoons
Melon baller

Paring knife
Pepper mill
Pot holder
Rack
Saucepan
Scale
12-inch skewers, 12 (or 4 12-inch
    skewers and 4 sherbet glasses)
Vegetable peeler
Wooden spoons

YOGURT-CUCUMBER SOUP

Use chilled bowls for this soup

2 medium cucumbers
½ garlic clove, minced
½ teaspoon salt
2 cups plus 2 tablespoons plain
   unflavored yogurt

½ cup skim milk
1½ teaspoons chopped fresh dill
   or ½ teaspoon dill weed
Freshly ground pepper to taste

Chill a soup tureen. Pare, seed, and dice 3½ cucumbers. Score and cut remaining cucumber half into 4 equal slices and set aside. In medium bowl combine garlic and salt to make a paste. Add yogurt and milk; stir to combine. Stir in diced cucumbers and dill; cover and refrigerate until chilled. Transfer to chilled tureen. Sprinkle with pepper and garnish with reserved cucumber slices. Makes 4 servings.

CHICKEN LIVERS SHISH KEBAB

½ cup canned pineapple chunks,
   no sugar added, drain and
   reserve juice
½ cup water
¼ cup ketchup
¼ cup tomato puree
2 tablespoons soy sauce
1 teaspoon steak sauce
1 teaspoon cider vinegar

1 small garlic clove, minced
¼ teaspoon dry mustard
⅛ teaspoon minced fresh ginger
   root
1½ pounds chicken livers
1 cup mushroom caps
Bulgur Pilaf (see recipe, page
   231)
Parsley sprigs to garnish

In large bowl combine reserved pineapple juice with next 9 ingredients. Add livers; cover and refrigerate overnight. Remove livers from marinade and reserve marinade for sauce. Divide each of the following into 4 equal portions: livers, pineapple chunks, and mushrooms. Alternating ingredients, thread 1 portion of each onto a 12-inch skewer. Repeat with remaining portions and 3 more skewers. Place over hot coals on rack that has been sprayed with nonstick cooking spray. Cook, turning occasionally, approximately 12 minutes or until livers are firm. Cooking time will depend on the distance of the food from the heat. Place reserved marinade in small saucepan; heat. Transfer pilaf to serving platter. Top with skewers. Pour heated sauce over kebabs and garnish platter with parsley sprigs. Makes 4 servings.

BULGUR PILAF

Serve with Chicken Livers Shish Kebab (see recipe, page 230)

1½ cups Chicken Stock (see page
  31), divided
¼ cup diced onion
4 ounces uncooked cracked
  wheat (Bulgur)
1 garlic clove, minced

⅛ teaspoon marjoram
⅛ teaspoon savory
Salt and pepper to taste
1 tablespoon plus 1 teaspoon
  margarine

In flameproof 2-cup baking pan combine ¼ cup stock with onion; bring
to a boil. Cook, stirring occasionally, until onion is tender. Add cracked
wheat, garlic, marjoram, savory, salt, and pepper; stir to combine. Add remaining stock; remove from heat. Stir in margarine. Bake at 350°F. for
½ hour or until all liquid is absorbed. Serve hot, as directed in recipe for
Chicken Livers Shish Kebab.

IMAN BAYILDI (STUFFED EGGPLANT)

4 small eggplants, about 8 ounces
  each, stems removed
1¾ cups thinly sliced onions
2 medium tomatoes, peeled and
  chopped
2 tablespoons chopped fresh
  parsley

1 teaspoon dried mint
1 garlic clove, minced
½ teaspoon salt
¼ teaspoon pepper
¼ cup plus 2 tablespoons water
1 tablespoon plus 1 teaspoon
  vegetable oil

Using a vegetable peeler, remove a ½-inch-wide strip of skin lengthwise
from 1 eggplant. Repeat at ½-inch intervals, giving eggplant a striped
effect. Repeat with remaining eggplants. Place eggplants in large bowl with
salted water to cover; let stand at least ½ hour. In saucepan cook onions
in small amount of water until soft. Stir in tomatoes, parsley, mint, garlic,
salt, and pepper; remove from heat immediately. Drain eggplants and pat
dry. Cut thin slice from base of each eggplant so that it will stand upright.
With eggplant standing, make 2 vertical, intersecting cuts through top almost to the base, dividing eggplant into quarters. *Do not cut through base.*
Repeat with remaining eggplants. Carefully open each eggplant and stuff
with ¼ of onion mixture. Arrange eggplants, standing upright, in shallow
casserole. Select size of casserole so that eggplants will completely fill it
with little room to spare. Add water; bake at 350°F. for 1 hour. Serve
at room temperature or refrigerate overnight and serve chilled. Just before
serving, spoon 1 teaspoon oil into each eggplant. Makes 4 servings.

PERSIAN PASSION

2 cups cantaloupe balls
2 medium peaches, peeled,
   pitted, and cut into quarters
1 tablespoon plus 1½ teaspoons
   lemon juice

1 tablespoon plus 1½ teaspoons
   rose water

Combine all ingredients in medium bowl. Toss to coat all fruit. Refrigerate for at least 2 hours, tossing occasionally. Thread ½ cup melon balls and 2 peach quarters onto each of four 12-inch skewers, beginning and ending with peaches. Place over hot coals on rack that has been sprayed with nonstick cooking spray; heat. Makes 4 servings.

Alternate Method: Chill 4 sherbet glasses. In bowl combine cantaloupe, peaches, and lemon juice. Cover and refrigerate until chilled. Add rose water; stir to combine. Divide fruit mixture evenly into chilled glasses.

SPICED ICED COFFEE

2 tablespoons instant coffee
½ cinnamon stick
3 cups hot water
Dash aromatic bitters
Artificial sweetener to equal 4
   teaspoons sugar, or to taste

Crushed ice
Whipped Topping (see page 30)
1 teaspoon grated lemon rind

Combine instant coffee and cinnamon stick in 1-quart measure; add hot water and bitters. Sweeten to taste; cool. Partially fill 4 glasses with ice. Pour cooled mixture into glasses, discarding cinnamon stick. Top each portion with 1 serving Whipped Topping and ¼ teaspoon grated lemon rind. Makes 4 servings.

A VERY CHIC SUMMER BUFFET FOR EIGHT

Jellied "Consommé"
Oven-Poached Salmon Steaks
Watercress Sauce
Cucumber Cups
Vegetable Salad
Dinner Rolls
Orange "Crème" in Orange Cups
Beverage

When heads of state dine at the White House, the menu is pure elegance. This was certainly true when the president of food-conscious France—and his wife—were hosted at a state banquet several years ago. That elaborate dinner provided food for thought for Weight Watchers chefs, who were inspired to create this trimmed-down version.

Note that the salmon steaks (an expensive delicacy quite popular in France) are poached in the oven, rather than the customary top-of-the-stove. Our ingenious method makes it possible to cook all eight helpings at once, and oven timing is also easier to control. The vegetable salad lends a distinctive touch, because it's served in an interesting manner—first cooked, then chilled. The balancing act of textures (cold vegetables, poached steaks) and carefully contrasting colors display gourmet know-how. So does the choice of cucumbers, a traditional accompaniment of salmon, while the orange cups make an elite presentation of the dessert. Here's a "capital" meal that you can serve in capital style.

SUGGESTED SHOPPING LIST

Staples and Miscellaneous

Almond extract
Artificial sweetener (optional)
Garlic powder
Pepper
Peppercorns
Salt
Sherry extract (optional)
Vanilla extract
White pepper

Hot sauce
Vinegar (any kind)
Worcestershire sauce

Unflavored gelatin

Imitation mayonnaise

Enriched white or whole grain dinner rolls, 1 ounce each

Chicken Stock, 1½ quarts (see page 31)

Additional Items

Lobster meat, 4 ounces cooked or frozen lobster tails, ½ pound
Salmon steaks, 8, 6½ ounces each

Plain unflavored yogurt, 1 16-ounce container

Lemons, 4
Oranges, 4 small

Carrots, 7 medium
Celery, 1 rib
Cherry tomatoes, 1 pint

Cucumbers, 6 medium
Onion, 1 medium
Parsley, 1 bunch
Watercress, 1 bunch

Frozen orange juice concentrate, 1 6-fluid-ounce can

Frozen peas, 2 10-ounce packages

Evaporated skimmed milk, 2 13-fluid-ounce cans

SUGGESTED EQUIPMENT LIST

Baking sheet
Blender
Bowls (medium and large)
Can opener
Chef's knife
Cutting board
Electric mixer
Grapefruit knife
Kitchen spoon
Measuring cups
Measuring spoons

Melon baller or teaspoon
Pot holder
Roasting pan (large)
Saucepans and covers (small and medium)
Scale
Sharp knife or kitchen shears
Slotted spatula
Vegetable peeler
Wooden spoons

JELLIED "CONSOMMÉ"

3 envelopes unflavored gelatin
1½ quarts Chicken Stock (see
  page 31), divided
1 tablespoon plus 1½ teaspoons
  lemon juice

1½ teaspoons sherry extract
  (optional)
Salt and pepper to taste
Chopped fresh parsley to garnish

In saucepan sprinkle gelatin over ¾ cup stock; allow to soften. Place over low heat; cook, stirring constantly, until gelatin is dissolved. Stir in lemon juice, extract if desired, and remaining stock. Season to taste. Cover and refrigerate until firm. Chill 8 soup bowls. Divide "consommé" evenly into chilled bowls; garnish with chopped parsley. Makes 8 servings.

OVEN-POACHED SALMON STEAKS

Serve with Watercress Sauce (see recipe below) and lemon wedges.

1 cup diced onions
½ cup diced carrot
½ cup diced celery
3 tablespoons lemon juice
1 tablespoon vinegar (any kind)
2 teaspoons salt
6 peppercorns

1 parsley sprig
2½ cups water
8 salmon steaks, 6½ ounces each
4 ounces sliced, cooked lobster
Cucumber Cups (see recipe, page
  236)
Dill sprigs to garnish

Preheat oven to 375°F. In saucepan combine first 8 ingredients; add water. Bring to a boil. Arrange salmon steaks in 1 layer, in large roasting pan. Pour liquid and vegetables over salmon. If necessary, add additional boiling water to cover fish. Bake for 5 to 7 minutes. Turn oven off; let fish stand in oven with door open for 15 to 20 minutes. Remove fish with slotted spatula and place on serving platter. If desired, reserve court bouillon (liquid and vegetables) for use in other recipes. Place ½ ounce of sliced lobster on each salmon steak. Arrange Cucumber Cups around edge of platter. Garnish platter with dill sprigs. Makes 8 servings.

WATERCRESS SAUCE

Serve with Oven-Poached Salmon Steaks (see recipe above).

1 cup watercress leaves
3 tablespoons water
1 teaspoon lemon juice

1 teaspoon Worcestershire sauce
½ cup imitation mayonnaise

Place watercress, water, lemon juice, and Worcestershire sauce in blender container; process until smooth. Transfer to bowl; stir in mayonnaise. Chill. Makes 8 servings.

CUCUMBER CUPS

Serve with Oven-Poached Salmon Steaks (see recipe, page 235).

6 medium cucumbers
1 cup plain unflavored yogurt
Artificial sweetener to equal 2
    teaspoons sugar (optional)

1 teaspoon salt, or to taste
½ teaspoon hot sauce, or to
    taste

Pare and cut 2 cucumbers in half lengthwise. Remove and discard seeds. Dice cucumber halves and place in bowl. Add yogurt, sweetener if desired, salt, and hot sauce. Stir well and set aside. Score and cut remaining cucumbers in 1¾-inch-thick slices. Using a parisienne scoop (melon baller) or teaspoon, scoop out center of each slice, leaving the bottom and sides about ¼ inch thick. Fill each "cucumber cup" with an equal amount of cucumber-yogurt mixture. Chill. Serve as directed in recipe for Oven-Poached Salmon Steaks.

VEGETABLE SALAD

2½ cups cooked peas
2 cups cooked diced carrots
2 cups cooked diced celery
16 cherry tomatoes

½ cup imitation mayonnaise
½ teaspoon salt, or to taste
⅛ teaspoon garlic powder
Dash white pepper, or to taste

In bowl combine all ingredients; toss to coat all vegetables with dressing. Cover and chill at least 2 hours. Makes 8 servings.

DINNER ROLLS

Serve one 1-ounce enriched white or whole grain dinner roll, warmed in the oven, to each person.

ORANGE "CRÈME" IN ORANGE CUPS

4 small oranges
2 cups orange juice
Artificial sweetener to equal 3
    teaspoons sugar (optional)
2 teaspoons lemon juice
1½ teaspoons almond extract

1 teaspoon vanilla extract
1 envelope unflavored gelatin
1 cup water
2 cups evaporated skimmed milk,
    chilled

Chill mixing bowl and beaters. Cut each orange in half. With grapefruit knife carefully cut around each orange section to loosen fruit. Remove fruit from shells; finely chop fruit and set aside. Scrape shells clean with a spoon. If desired, notch or scallop edges of shells with sharp knife or kitchen shears. Set "orange cups" aside. In large bowl combine chopped oranges, orange juice, sweetener if desired, lemon juice, and extracts. In small saucepan sprinkle gelatin over water; allow to soften. Place over low heat and cook, stirring constantly, until gelatin is dissolved. Stir into orange mixture; refrigerate until syrupy. In chilled bowl beat milk with electric mixer until peaks form. Fold into orange mixture; chill 1 hour. Spoon an equal amount of Orange "Crème" into each "orange cup." Makes 8 servings.

A SUMMER SUNDAY PICNIC FOR FOUR

Chilled Zucchini Soup
Lemon-Lime Chicken Legs
Ziti Salad
Whole Italian Green Beans
Berries in Strawberry-Yogurt Dip
Iced Coffee

Half the fun of summer is being able to picnic—and here's a carry-along menu that enhances the August scene. All these flavorful foods travel well in an insulated picnic box. Chilled Zucchini Soup, an unusual starter, can easily be served in disposable cups. (Slicing the zucchini from the *flower* end will avert bitterness.) Paper plates and plastic forks are standard picnic items, although the Lemon-Lime Chicken Legs need no other "utensils" than eager fingers! Nutrition-aware people always include vegetables —here cleverly combined into a salad with a pasta favorite, ziti. Berries in Strawberry-Yogurt Dip sweetly beats anything the ice cream vendor can offer. See? Fun doesn't have to be fattening!

SUGGESTED SHOPPING LIST

Staples and Miscellaneous

Ginger	Wine vinegar
Nutmeg	Worcestershire sauce
Onion salt	
Pepper	Imitation mayonnaise
Peppercorns	
Salt	Coffee
	Chicken stock, 3 cups (see page 31)

Additional Items

Chicken legs, 4, 8 ounces each	Lemon, 1
	Lime, 1
Plain unflavored yogurt, 1 16-ounce container	Raspberries, 1 pint
	Strawberries, 2 pints

(continued)

Celery, 1 rib
Garlic cloves, 2
Green pepper, 1 medium
Italian green beans, 1 pound
Onions, 2 medium
Parsley, 1 bunch
Tomatoes, 3 medium
Zucchini, 1¼ pounds (about 4
  medium)

Pimientos, 1 4-ounce jar

Evaporated skimmed milk, 1 13-fluid-
  ounce can

Enriched ziti, 1 16-ounce box

SUGGESTED EQUIPMENT LIST

Baking pan (shallow)
Blender
Bowls (large)
Chef's knife
Containers with covers (medium and
  large)
Cutting board
Grater
Insulated bag
Measuring cups

Measuring spoons
Pepper mill
Plastic wrap
Pot holder
Saucepans with covers (medium)
Scale
Strainer
Thermal jar
Vegetable peeler
Wooden spoons

CHILLED ZUCCHINI SOUP

Serve in mugs or disposable cups.

*1¼ pounds zucchini, about 4
  medium
3 cups Chicken Stock (see page
  31)
½ cup diced onion*

*Salt to taste
⅛ teaspoon nutmeg
½ cup evaporated skimmed milk
Freshly ground pepper to taste*

Remove and finely dice the skin of 1 zucchini; reserve skin for garnish.
Slice all zucchini. In saucepan combine sliced zucchini, stock, onion, and
salt. Bring to a boil; reduce heat, cover, and simmer 20 minutes or until
vegetables are tender. Sprinkle with nutmeg; cool slightly. In 2 batches,
puree mixture in blender container and transfer to large bowl; stir in milk.
Refrigerate until well chilled. Pack in thermal jar. Before serving, stir to
combine and garnish with reserved zucchini skin and freshly ground pepper. Makes 4 servings.

LEMON-LIME CHICKEN LEGS

*¼ cup lemon juice
¼ cup water
1 tablespoon grated lemon rind
2 teaspoons chopped fresh
  parsley
½ teaspoon onion salt*

*⅛ teaspoon ginger
1 garlic clove, minced
Dash pepper
4 skinned chicken legs, 8 ounces
  each
4 lime slices*

In shallow baking pan combine all ingredients except chicken and lime slices. Add chicken legs and toss to coat. Cover and refrigerate for 3 hours, tossing occasionally. Bake at 400°F. for 10 to 12 minutes. Reduce heat to 325°F. and continue baking for 30 to 40 minutes or until chicken is done. Transfer chicken to container with tight-fitting cover; cover and chill. Wrap lime slices in plastic wrap or aluminum foil; chill. Pack chicken and lime in insulated bag. Serve each chicken leg with a lime slice. Makes 4 servings.

ZITI SALAD

2⅔ cups cooked enriched ziti
1½ cups diced tomatoes
¼ cup finely chopped green pepper
¼ cup finely chopped celery
¼ cup imitation mayonnaise
2 tablespoons finely chopped onion

1 tablespoon chopped fresh parsley
1 tablespoon diced pimiento
1 tablespoon wine vinegar
1 teaspoon Worcestershire sauce
1 small garlic clove, minced
½ teaspoon salt

Combine all ingredients in large container with tight-fitting cover. Cover and refrigerate until well chilled. Pack in insulated bag. Before serving, toss well. Makes 4 servings.

WHOLE ITALIAN GREEN BEANS

4 cups trimmed Italian green beans

Salt to taste

Place beans in large saucepan with boiling salted water. Return water to a boil; reduce heat and simmer until beans are tender-crisp, about 5 to 7 minutes. Immediately drain and place under cold running water to cool. Drain beans; place in plastic bag and refrigerate until chilled. Pack in insulated bag. When ready to serve, sprinkle with salt. Makes 4 servings.

BERRIES IN STRAWBERRY-YOGURT DIP

3 cups strawberries, sliced, divided

1 cup plain unflavored yogurt
1 cup raspberries

In large bowl mash 1 cup strawberries. Add yogurt and stir to combine. Fold in remaining berries and chill. Divide evenly into 4 individual containers with tight-fitting covers. Cover and pack in insulated bag. Makes 4 servings.

September

As the summer draws to a close, welcome
the beauty of autumn in international
style. Create a German ambience with an
Oktoberfest, complete with oompah music!
Or pass out the sombreros while enjoying
our adaptation of a national dish of Mexico!
In any language, these menus will
translate into meals that are sure to please!

LABOR DAY MENU WITHOUT MUCH LABOR FOR FOUR

Chilled Senegalese Soup
Baked Scrod with Mushrooms
Potatoes O'Brien
Parslied Tomato Slices
Hearts of Artichoke Salad with Croutons
Peach Cobbler
Beverage

Labor Day was created back in the 1880s as a way of recognizing America's working class. And you'll earn culinary recognition when you serve this meal that's practically labor-less, yet scores with a holiday flavor. Senegalese Soup says "special" to begin with, and, since it's still summer, a chilled soup is a real September palate-pleaser. Fish is another good warm-weather dish. For the best taste, it should be cooked to just the right degree of flakiness. Our Baked Scrod with Mushrooms takes only a brief 12 to 15 minutes, so time it carefully. It's customary to serve potatoes with fish, but isn't it incredible to find Potatoes O'Brien included in a weight-loss program? They bake at the same temperature as the fish, so you can conserve energy (your own, included) by cooking them at the same time. Thriftily gather in the best of your tomato crop—or harvest ripe ones from the market—for a cheery no-cooking accompaniment. Hearts of artichoke take salad out of the workaday class, especially when crunchily paired with croutons. Top off a job well done with a Peach Cobbler that "works" sweetly. When you read the recipe directions, you'll be delighted to see how energy-saving—and form-saving—this menu is.

———————◆•◆———————

SUGGESTED SHOPPING LIST

Staples and Miscellaneous

Allspice
Anise extract
Artificial sweetener
Chopped chives
Cinnamon
Curry powder
Dehydrated onion flakes
Dry mustard
Garlic powder
Instant chicken broth and seasoning
   mix or bouillon cubes
Paprika
Peppercorns
Salt
Vanilla extract
White pepper

Tarragon vinegar

Cornstarch
Nonfat dry milk powder

Imitation (or diet) margarine
Vegetable oil

Raisin bread
Whole wheat bread

Additional Items

Scrod fillets, 4 (6 ounces each)

Lemons, 2
Lime, 1

Beefsteak tomatoes, 4 small
Bibb lettuce, 2 heads
Garlic clove, 1
Green pepper, 1 medium
Mushrooms, ½ pound
Onion, 1 small
Parsley, 1 bunch
Radishes, 1 bag

Applesauce, no sugar added,
   1 8-ounce jar
Canned sliced peaches, no sugar
   added, 2 16-ounce cans

Canned artichoke hearts, 1 16-ounce
   can
Canned potatoes, 1 28-ounce can
Pimientos, 1 4-ounce jar

Evaporated skimmed milk, 1 13-fluid-
   ounce can

SUGGESTED EQUIPMENT LIST

Baking pan
Baking pan (1½-quart)
Baking sheet
Blender or food processor
Bowls (small and medium)
Butter knife
Can opener
Casserole (1-quart, shallow)
Chef's knife
Colander

Cutting board
Fork
Measuring cups
Measuring spoons
Pepper mill
Pot holder
Saucepan (medium)
Scale
Wooden spoon

CHILLED SENEGALESE SOUP

3 cups chicken bouillon
½ cup applesauce, no sugar added
1 teaspoon dehydrated onion flakes

1 teaspoon curry powder
⅛ teaspoon anise extract
Dash white pepper
½ cup evaporated skimmed milk
2 teaspoons chopped chives

Chill 4 soup cups. In medium saucepan combine all ingredients except milk and chives. Bring to a boil; reduce heat and simmer, stirring occasionally, for 15 minutes. Remove from heat. Stir in milk. Chill for at least 2 hours. Divide evenly into chilled cups. Sprinkle ½ teaspoon chives over each portion. Makes 4 servings.

BAKED SCROD WITH MUSHROOMS

4 scrod fillets, 6 ounces each
1 garlic clove, minced
Salt and freshly ground pepper to taste
1 tablespoon finely chopped fresh parsley

4 thin lemon slices
1 cup thickly sliced mushrooms
2 tablespoons lemon juice

Fold each fillet in thirds and place, seam side down, in baking pan. Sprinkle with garlic, salt, and pepper. Sprinkle parsley evenly over fish. Top with lemon slices. Sprinkle mushrooms with lemon juice and arrange around fish. Bake at 400°F. for 12 to 15 minutes or until fish flakes easily at the touch of a fork. Makes 4 servings.

POTATOES O'BRIEN

1 pound drained canned potatoes, cut into ½-inch cubes
⅓ cup finely minced onion
½ cup diced green pepper

2 tablespoons minced pimiento
2 tablespoon imitation (or diet) margarine
½ teaspoon paprika
Salt and white pepper to taste

Combine all ingredients in 1-quart casserole. Bake at 400°F. for 30 minutes, stirring occasionally. Makes 4 servings.

PARSLIED TOMATO SLICES

Buy farm-fresh, beefy, ripe tomatoes; the best you can find. Or, better yet, use home-grown!

4 small beefsteak tomatoes
1 tablespoon chopped fresh parsley

½ teaspoon allspice
Salt and freshly ground pepper to taste

Cut tomatoes into thick slices. Sprinkle evenly with parsley, allspice, salt, and pepper. Makes 4 servings.

HEARTS OF ARTICHOKE SALAD WITH CROUTONS

4 cups torn Bibb lettuce, bite-size
  pieces
1⅔ cups drained canned
  artichoke hearts
¼ cup sliced radishes
2 tablespoons vegetable oil

1 tablespoon lime juice
1 tablespoon tarragon vinegar
⅛ teaspoon dry mustard
Salt and freshly ground pepper
  to taste
Croutons (see following recipe)

Combine lettuce, artichoke hearts, and radishes in salad bowl. Mix next 5 ingredients in small bowl. Pour over salad; toss well to coat all vegetables. Sprinkle with Croutons. Makes 4 servings.

Croutons

2 slices whole wheat bread
2 teaspoons imitation (or diet)
  margarine

Salt, freshly ground pepper, and
  garlic powder to taste

Spread each slice of bread with 1 teaspoon margarine; sprinkle with salt, pepper, and garlic powder. Cut each slice into 6 equal fingers; then cut each finger into 6 equal pieces. Place on baking sheet, margarine side up. Bake at 400°F. for about 5 minutes or until crisp and golden. Serve as directed in recipe for Hearts of Artichoke Salad (see preceding recipe).

PEACH COBBLER

2 cups canned sliced peaches, no
  sugar added
Artificial sweetener to equal 6
  teaspoons sugar, divided
1 teaspoon cornstarch
½ teaspoon vanilla extract
½ teaspoon cinnamon

2 slices raisin bread, made into
  crumbs
⅓ cup nonfat dry milk powder
1 tablespoon plus 1 teaspoon
  imitation (or diet) margarine,
  melted

In medium bowl combine peaches, sweetener to equal 4 teaspoons sugar, cornstarch, vanilla, and cinnamon. Transfer to 1½-quart baking pan. In small bowl combine bread crumbs, dry milk, margarine, and sweetener to equal 2 teaspoons sugar; mix to a crumbly consistency. Top peaches evenly with crumb mixture. Bake at 400°F. for 25 minutes or until topping is browned. Makes 4 servings.

FRUGAL AND FUN CHILI PARTY
FOR TWELVE

Tomato Juice with Lime Wedge
Chili Con Carne
Garlic Tortillas
Orange Blossom Salad
Citrus Cooler

Want to toss a party without throwing your budget for a loss? Serve a welcome batch of that sizzling Spanish stew, Chili Con Carne. The popular dish thriftily stretches meat without sacrificing tastiness. The rest of the menu is low on the expense ledger, too. Add more spice to the evening with tortillas (the delicious Mexican substitute for bread) flavored with garlic. Your salad cuts corners, as well, with a healthy mixture of seasonal fruits and vegetables. The milky-orange dressing lends a sweet balance to the sharper-tasting ingredients. A drink goes a long way when it's a dietetic soda-based Citrus Cooler that makes "spirited" use of rum extract. Improvise a tablecloth out of your brightest remnant, use earthenware pottery or paper dishes, and prove that a fun fiesta doesn't have to cost much in dollars (or *pounds*)!

———————————— ◆ ◆◆◆ ————————————

SUGGESTED SHOPPING LIST

Staples and Miscellaneous

Bay leaves	Aromatic bitters
Chili powder	Hot sauce
Cumin	
Garlic powder	Unsweetened cocoa
Oregano	
Peppercorns	Margarine
Rum extract	
Salt (optional)	Tortillas, 6 inches each

Ground beef, 2¼ pounds

Limes, 3
Mango, 1 small
Oranges, 4 small
Papaya, 1 medium

Cauliflower, 2 medium heads
Celery, 3 ribs
Garlic cloves, 3
Green peppers, 7 medium
Onions, 6 large
Spinach, 2 pounds

Frozen orange juice concentrate,
 1 12-fluid-ounce can

Canned kidney beans, 4 16-ounce cans
Canned tomatoes, 1 28-ounce can
Tomato puree, 1 28-ounce can

Tomato juice, 2 32-fluid-ounce cans

Evaporated skimmed milk, 1 13-fluid-
 ounce can

Lemon-lime-flavored dietetic soda,
 4 28-fluid-ounce bottles

SUGGESTED EQUIPMENT LIST

Baking sheet
Blender
Bowls (small)
Can opener
Chef's knife
Cutting board
Measuring cups

Measuring spoons
Pepper mill
Pot holder
Saucepans (large)
Scale
Vegetable peeler
Wire whisk

TOMATO JUICE WITH LIME WEDGE

Serve each guest ½ cup chilled tomato juice garnished with lime wedge.
Provide hot sauce, salt, and pepper mill so that guests can season juice to
taste.

CHILI CON CARNE

2¼ pounds ground beef
6 cups diced onions, divided
1½ cups diced celery
1½ cups diced green peppers
3 garlic cloves, minced
3 tablespoons water (optional)
1 tablespoon plus 1½ teaspoons
 unsweetened cocoa
1 tablespoon plus 1½ teaspoons
 chili powder

1 teaspoon oregano
¾ teaspoon salt (optional)
¾ teaspoon cumin
2 bay leaves
2¼ pounds drained canned
 kidney beans
2 cups chopped canned tomatoes
2 cups tomato puree

In large saucepan cook beef in boiling salted water to cover. When meat
has lost its red color, drain and discard liquid. Break up any large pieces
of beef; set aside. In large saucepan combine 4½ cups onions, the celery,

green peppers, and garlic. Cook 2 to 3 minutes, adding water, if necessary, to prevent vegetables from sticking. Add cocoa, chili powder, oregano, salt, if desired, cumin, and bay leaves; stir to combine. Cook 2 to 3 minutes longer. Add cooked beef, kidney beans, tomatoes and puree. Simmer, stirring often, for 20 to 30 minutes. Remove bay leaves. Divide evenly into 12 bowls. Serve each portion topped with 2 tablespoons diced onions. Makes 12 servings.

GARLIC TORTILLAS

¼ cup margarine, melted
¼ teaspoon garlic powder

¼ teaspoon oregano
24 tortillas, 6 inches each

Preheat oven to 325°F. Combine margarine, garlic powder, and oregano in measuring cup. Spread each tortilla with an equal amount of margarine mixture. Place 6 tortillas on baking sheet. Bake for 2 minutes. Repeat with remaining tortillas. Makes 12 servings.

ORANGE BLOSSOM SALAD

5 cups small cauliflower florets
2 cups diced green peppers
4 small oranges, peeled and
    sectioned
1 medium papaya, pared, seeded,
    and diced
1 small mango, pared, pitted, and
    diced

¾ cup evaporated skimmed milk
½ cup frozen orange juice
    concentrate, thawed
5 cups torn spinach leaves,
    rinsed well

Combine first 5 ingredients in salad bowl. In small bowl combine milk with orange juice concentrate, beating with wire whisk until smooth. Pour dressing over salad; toss to combine. Chill. When ready to serve, arrange spinach on serving platter; top with chilled salad. Makes 12 servings.

CITRUS COOLER

3 quarts chilled lemon-lime-
    flavored dietetic soda, divided
¼ cup plus 2 tablespoons frozen
    orange juice concentrate,
    divided

1½ teaspoons rum extract,
    divided
⅛ teaspoon aromatic bitters
    divided (optional)
48 ice cubes

Pour 2 cups soda into blender container; add 1 tablespoon orange juice concentrate, ¼ teaspoon extract, and dash bitters if desired; process 15 seconds. Add 8 ice cubes, 1 at a time, processing 30 seconds after each addition. Divide evenly into 2 tall glasses. Repeat 5 more times. Makes 12 servings.

LA COMIDA MEXICANA FOR SIX

(a Mexican Main Meal)

"Sangrita" (Spicy Tomato-Orange Cocktail)
Guajolote Molé Poblano (Turkey with Molé Sauce)
Cauliflower Salad with Tomato Dressing
Mango "Ice Cream"
Café de Olla

Travel south of the border without leaving your dining room, via this zestily flavored *Comida Mexicana* (Mexican meal). You don't have to cross the border of your weight-loss plan to enjoy it, either! The word for Mexican menus is H-O-T, so bravely blend in your most peppery seasonings—coriander, chili, jalapeños, hot sauce, garlic—for a pungent evening! The star item—Guajolote Molé Poblano (turkey with molé sauce)—is our adaptation of Mexico's national dish. It's an appropriate combination, for turkeys were first glimpsed in the New World, and cocoa, which lends a rich, dark color to the sauce, was introduced to Spanish conquerors by the clever Aztec Indians. Cool off palates with an icy dessert that blends in tropical mangoes, rated by gourmets one of the world's most lusciously flavored fruits.

Mexicans also love to feast on rich colors, so create a bright ambience. Toss your most flamboyant cloth on the table, along with colorful burlap napkins and earthenware dishes. Enhance the setting with any typical Mexican ornaments you may be fortunate enough to own, borrow, or imitate—papier-mâché figures or gaily painted wooden or clay animals. Set one at each place or combine them in the center where they'll be at home with a potted cactus. Let a mariachi band strum excitingly from your stereo. Your *amigos* will shout *"olé"* for your good-neighbor hosting!

Staples and Miscellaneous

<table>
<tr><td>Artificial sweetener</td><td>Cider vinegar</td></tr>
<tr><td>Chili powder</td><td>Hot sauce</td></tr>
<tr><td>Cinnamon</td><td>Ketchup</td></tr>
<tr><td>Coriander</td><td></td></tr>
<tr><td>Garlic powder</td><td>Instant coffee</td></tr>
<tr><td>Instant chicken broth and seasoning mix</td><td>Unsweetened cocoa</td></tr>
<tr><td>Onion powder</td><td>Vegetable oil</td></tr>
<tr><td>Salt</td><td></td></tr>
<tr><td>White pepper</td><td></td></tr>
</table>

Additional Items

<table>
<tr><td>Boned turkey breasts, 2¼ pounds</td><td>Frozen artichoke hearts, 2 10-ounce packages</td></tr>
<tr><td>Lemon, 1</td><td>Frozen orange juice concentrate, 1 6-fluid-ounce can</td></tr>
<tr><td>Mangoes, 3 small</td><td></td></tr>
<tr><td></td><td>Jalapeño peppers, 1 4-ounce jar</td></tr>
<tr><td>Carrots, 4 large</td><td>Tomato puree, 1 16-ounce can</td></tr>
<tr><td>Cauliflower, 1 head</td><td></td></tr>
<tr><td>Garlic clove, 1</td><td>Tomato juice, 1 32-fluid-ounce jar</td></tr>
<tr><td>Green beans, ½ pound</td><td>Evaporated skimmed milk, 2 13-fluid-ounce cans</td></tr>
<tr><td>Onion, 1 large</td><td></td></tr>
<tr><td>Red onions, 2 medium</td><td></td></tr>
<tr><td>Zucchini, 2 medium (approximately 5 ounces each)</td><td>Enriched white rice, 1 16-ounce box</td></tr>
<tr><td></td><td>Prunes, medium, 1 16-ounce box</td></tr>
</table>

SUGGESTED EQUIPMENT LIST

<table>
<tr><td>Baking pan (large)</td><td>Measuring cups</td></tr>
<tr><td>Blender or food processor</td><td>Measuring spoons</td></tr>
<tr><td>Bowls (large)</td><td>Nonstick skillet</td></tr>
<tr><td>Can opener</td><td>Pitcher (large)</td></tr>
<tr><td>Casserole (5-quart)</td><td>Pot holder</td></tr>
<tr><td>Chef's knife</td><td>Saucepans</td></tr>
<tr><td>Coffee pot (6-cup size)</td><td>Scale</td></tr>
<tr><td>Cutting board</td><td>Vegetable peeler</td></tr>
<tr><td>Jar with cover</td><td>Wooden spoon</td></tr>
</table>

"SANGRITA" (SPICY TOMATO-ORANGE COCKTAIL)

3 cups tomato juice　　　　　*½ teaspoon hot sauce, or to taste*
2 cups orange juice　　　　　*Ice cubes*

Combine juices and hot sauce in large pitcher. Partially fill 6 glasses with ice cubes. Pour an equal amount of "Sangrita" into each glass. Makes 6 servings.

GUAJOLOTE MOLÉ POBLANO (TURKEY WITH MOLÉ SAUCE)

This dish is made with a truly favorite Mexican sauce.

2¼ pounds skinned and boned
   turkey breasts
1 garlic clove, minced
1 teaspoon minced jalapeño
   pepper
1 packet instant chicken broth
   and seasoning mix
1½ cups tomato puree

1 cup water
3 medium prunes, pitted and
   diced
1 tablespoon unsweetened cocoa
½ teaspoon coriander
¼ teaspoon chili powder
¼ teaspoon salt
3 cups cooked enriched rice

Place turkey breasts in large baking pan. Bake at 325°F. for 1¼ to 1½ hours or until tender. Remove from oven; let stand 20 minutes, then slice. Meanwhile, in nonstick skillet combine garlic, jalapeño pepper, and broth mix. Cook until garlic is browned. Add next 7 ingredients; simmer 30 minutes. Place rice in 5-quart casserole. Top with sliced turkey; pour sauce over turkey and rice. Bake at 350°F. for 30 minutes or until heated. Makes 6 servings.

CAULIFLOWER SALAD WITH TOMATO DRESSING

2 cups cooked cauliflower florets
2 cups cooked julienne carrots
2 cups cooked julienne zucchini
2 cups cooked green beans

1½ cups cooked artichoke hearts
1½ cups red onion rings
Tomato Dressing (see following
   recipe)

Combine vegetables in large bowl; add Tomato Dressing and toss to coat vegetables. Chill. Makes 6 servings.

Tomato Dressing

¼ cup vegetable oil
3 tablespoons cider vinegar
2 tablespoons ketchup

⅛ teaspoon garlic powder
⅛ teaspoon onion powder
Salt and white pepper to taste

Combine all ingredients in small screwtop jar. Cover and shake well. Serve as directed with Cauliflower Salad (see preceding recipe)

MANGO "ICE CREAM"

3 small mangoes, pared, pitted,
   and cubed
1 cup evaporated skimmed milk
Artificial sweetener to equal 24
   teaspoons sugar

½ cup orange juice
2 tablespoons lemon juice

Puree mangoes in food processor or blender container. Transfer to bowl. Add remaining ingredients; stir to combine. Place bowl in freezer; freeze for 4 hours, stirring occasionally. Divide evenly into 6 dessert dishes. Makes 6 servings.

CAFÉ DE OLLA

To create a truly Mexican ambience, serve this in small earthenware mugs.

2 tablespoons instant coffee
¼ teaspoon cinnamon
1 quart boiling water

2 cups evaporated skimmed milk, heated

Place coffee and cinnamon in decorative 6-cup coffee pot. Add boiling water; stir. Add evaporated skimmed milk. Serve immediately. Makes 6 servings.

SCANDINAVIAN WEDDING BREAKFAST FOR EIGHT

Sparkling Orange
Gravad Lax (Marinated Salmon)
Mustard-Dill Sauce
Cucumber and Tomato Salad with Lemon-Basil Dressing
Coffee or Tea

The greatest social occasion in rural Scandinavian villages is a wedding, but in order for it to be a social success the feasting must go on for at least three days! You can score a social success in *one* day by hosting a memorable Scandinavian Wedding Breakfast. To give it a lavish look, introduce the wedding party to an unusual food—Gravad Lax—the Scandinavian specialty of raw salmon marinated in dill. Since it needs to marinate for at least two days, this is no rush breakfast, and your guests will appreciate the extra effort you went to. Serve the Gravad Lax in *smorrebrod* style—the famous Danish open sandwich—on the hearty pumpernickel bread so popular in northern lands. Cucumbers, which harmonize beautifully with salmon, and tomatoes add color and texture. Toast the orange blossom day with Sparkling Orange. (Like the other recipes, it will help everyone stay slender for the big event.) The Scandinavians believe in feasting on the beauty of the table, too, so bring out your finest tableware to enhance the V.I.P. (Very Important Party).

———— ••• ————

SUGGESTED SHOPPING LIST

Staples and Miscellaneous

Artificial sweetener	Dijon mustard
Basil	Rice vinegar
Coarse salt	
Garlic powder	Coffee or tea
White peppercorns	
	Vegetable oil
	Pumpernickel bread

Additional Items

Salmon, 1 center-cut piece, 1¼ to 1½ pounds

Lemon, 1
Limes, 2

Cucumbers, 2 medium
Dill, 1 large bunch (about 1 cup)
Tomatoes, 2 medium

Frozen orange juice concentrate, 1 12-fluid-ounce can

Sparkling mineral water, 1 23-fluid-ounce bottle

SUGGESTED EQUIPMENT LIST

Baster or metal spoon
Bowls (small)
Can opener
Chef's knife
Cutting board
Heavy item as weight (3 to 5 pounds)
Measuring cups
Measuring spoons
Paper towels
Pitcher
Plate

Pot holder
Scale
Shallow dish
Shallow enamel, glass, or stainless-steel container
Slicing knife
Table knife
Vegetable peeler
Waxed paper
Wire whisk
Wooden spoon

SPARKLING ORANGE

3 cups sparkling mineral water, chilled
1 cup frozen orange juice concentrate, thawed

Ice cubes
4 lime slices, cut into halves

Combine mineral water and concentrate in pitcher. Add ice cubes; stir. Divide evenly into 8 champagne glasses. Garnish each with ½ lime slice. Serve immediately. Makes 8 servings.

GRAVAD LAX (MARINATED SALMON)

1 center-cut piece fresh salmon, 1¼ to 1½ pounds
2 tablespoons coarse salt
Artificial sweetener to equal 4 teaspoons sugar
½ teaspoon coarsely crushed white peppercorns

1 cup fresh dill, rinsed, stems removed
8 slices pumpernickel bread
Mustard-Dill Sauce (see recipe, page 256)

Cut fish along back into 2 fillets, carefully removing backbone. Wipe fillets with damp towel. Combine salt, sweetener, and crushed peppercorns. Rub ⅓ of salt mixture into fillets. Reserve several dill sprigs for garnish. Layer ⅓ of remaining dill over bottom of shallow enamel, glass, or stainless steel container that is about the size of salmon fillets. Place 1 fillet, skin side down, on dill. Sprinkle with ½ of remaining salt mixture; add ½ of remaining dill sprigs. Place remaining fillet, skin side up, on top of dill, "sandwich fashion." Sprinkle with remaining salt mixture and dill. Lay sheet of waxed paper over fish; place plate on top of paper. Place heavy book or item of comparable weight (3 to 5 pounds) on plate. Refrigerate for at least 48 hours, turning the "sandwich" every 12 hours and basting with liquid that accumulates. Separate halves a little to baste salmon inside. When ready to serve, scrape fish to remove seasonings and dill. Place on cutting board, skin side down. Thinly slice fish on the diagonal, cutting away from skin. Divide Mustard-Dill Sauce into 8 equal portions. Serve 2 ounces Gravad Lax on 1 slice pumpernickel bread; garnish with dill sprig and serve with 1 portion Mustard-Dill Sauce. Makes 8 servings.

Note: Gravad Lax will keep unsliced up to 2 weeks in the refrigerator.

MUSTARD-DILL SAUCE

Serve with Gravad Lax (see recipe, page 255).

¼ cup Dijon mustard	½ teaspoon chopped fresh dill
2 tablespoons vegetable oil	⅛ teaspoon garlic powder
2 tablespoons rice vinegar	

In small bowl combine all ingredients. Stir with wire whisk until smooth. Serve as directed in recipe for Gravad Lax.

CUCUMBER AND TOMATO SALAD
WITH LEMON-BASIL DRESSING

2 medium cucumbers, pared, scored, and cut into ¼-inch slices	2 tablespoons vegetable oil
	2 tablespoons lemon juice
	1 teaspoon basil
2 medium tomatoes, thinly sliced and cut into halves	

Place cucumber and tomato slices in shallow dish. In small bowl combine oil, lemon juice, and basil; mix well. Pour over cucumbers and tomatoes and mix lightly to combine. Divide salad evenly into 8 individual salad bowls. Makes 8 servings.

OKTOBERFEST FOR EIGHT

Cucumber Salad
Franks 'n' Dip
Cold-Cut Tree
Kartoffelsalat
Caraway-Kraut Relish
Mustard Beets in Cabbage Bowl
Apple Crumble
Dietetic Root Beer

One of the most joyous autumnal celebrations is Germany's famed Okto-berfest. It actually begins in mid-September and continues for sixteen riot-ous days of dining, wining, and carousing. The Ocktoberfest originated in the nineteenth century as a wedding celebration, and history records that the awesome menu included hundreds of thousands of chickens and sausages, as well as several tons of oxen!

You can improvise a trimmed-down Oktoberfest by serving German fare in fair-figure style. Of course, your menu should feature Frankfurt's famed "namesake"—the *frankfurter*. Sauerkraut and a cabbage bowl add to the Germanic flavor, as does a regional favorite, *Kartoffelsalat* (potato salad). For an imaginative—and edible—centerpiece, create a Cold-Cut Tree. Since apples are a prime harvest in that fruitful land, top off your feast with a luscious apple dessert.

The image of the beer-drinking—and rotund—German is outdated, for this weight-conscious country is now a leading producer of dietetic pro-ducts. So, appropriately, keep spirits high with dietetic root beer as you whirl to danceable German tunes on the stereo.

SUGGESTED SHOPPING LIST

Staples and Miscellaneous

Artificial sweetener
Caraway seeds
Chopped chives
Cinnamon
Garlic powder
Instant chicken broth and seasoning
   mix
Peppercorns
Salt
White pepper

Chili sauce
Cider vinegar
Ketchup
Prepared horseradish
Prepared mustard

Imitation (or diet) margarine
Mayonnaise
Vegetable oil

Raisin bread

Low-calorie jelly, any flavor

Additional Items

Cooked boneless ham, 6 ounces
Cooked boneless turkey, ½ pound
Frankfurters, 6 ounces
Roast beef, ½ pound

Plain unflavored yogurt, 1 8-ounce
   container

Apples, 8 small
Lemons, 4

Carrot, 1 medium
Celery, 1 rib
Cherry tomatoes, 2 pints
Cucumbers, 4 medium

Dill, 1 bunch
Green cabbage, 1 head (about 2½
   pounds)
Lettuce, 1 head
Onion, 1 large
Parsley, 1 bunch
Potatoes, 2 pounds
Radishes, 1 bag
Scallions, 1 bunch

Canned sauerkraut, 3 16-ounce cans
Canned sliced beets, 2 16-ounce cans

Dietetic root beer, 2 28-fluid-ounce
   bottles

SUGGESTED EQUIPMENT LIST

Aluminum foil
Baking dish (large, shallow)
Bowls (medium)
Can opener
Casseroles, 2 (1½-quart)
Chef's knife
Cutting board
Damp cloth
Fork
Grater

Measuring cups
Measuring spoons
Pepper mill
Polystyrene foam cone (12 inches
   high, 4 inches at base)
Pot holder
Saucepans (small)
Toothpicks
Vegetable peeler
Wooden spoons

CUCUMBER SALAD

4 medium cucumbers, pared and
  scored
¼ cup cider vinegar
2 tablespoons plus 2 teaspoons
  mayonnaise
2 tablespoons chopped fresh dill
2 tablespoons water

2 teaspoons chopped chives
1 teaspoon salt
⅛ teaspoon garlic powder
Lettuce leaves
Parsley sprigs and radish roses to
  garnish (see page 17)

Cut cucumbers in half lengthwise; remove and discard seeds. Slice cucumbers and place in medium bowl. Add remaining ingredients except lettuce, parsley, and radishes. Cover and refrigerate overnight, or at least 8 hours. Line serving bowl with lettuce leaves; fill with cucumber mixture. Garnish with parsley sprigs and radish roses. Makes 8 servings.

FRANKS 'N' DIP

⅓ cup ketchup
⅓ cup chili sauce
2 teaspoons prepared horseradish
2 teaspoons low-calorie jelly, any
  flavor

6 ounces frankfurters, cut into 24
  equal pieces

In small saucepan combine ketchup, chili sauce, horseradish, and jelly. Add frankfurters; stir to coat. Cook over medium heat, stirring occasionally, until frankfurters and sauce are heated throughout. Transfer to chafing dish. Serve with toothpicks. Makes 8 servings.

COLD-CUT TREE

To create this attractive centerpiece, in addition to the foods listed below, you will need 1 polystyrene foam cone about 12 inches high and 4 inches across the bottom, a roll of aluminum foil, and a box of wooden toothpicks.

8 ounces sliced cooked turkey
8 ounces sliced roast beef
6 ounces sliced cooked ham
32 cherry tomatoes

Parsley sprigs, chicory, radish
  roses, and carrot curls to
  garnish (refer to section on
  garnishing, page 13)

Cover foam cone with aluminum foil. Roll each slice of meat tightly and cut in half. Starting at the base of the "tree" and working upward, arrange rolled meat and tomatoes on cone, securing with toothpicks. Fill empty spaces with parsley sprigs. Line serving platter with chicory; place "tree" on platter. Garnish base of "tree" with radish roses and carrot curls. Makes 8 servings.

Serving Variation: Instead of creating Cold-Cut Tree, you can arrange sliced meats and cherry tomatoes on chicory-lined serving platter. Garnish platter with parsley sprigs, radish roses, and carrot curls.

KARTOFFELSALAT

2 pounds pared potatoes
½ cup diced celery
½ cup shredded carrots
½ cup sliced scallions, reserve 1
   tablespoon for garnish
¼ cup cider vinegar

2 packets instant chicken broth
   and seasoning mix
Salt and white pepper to taste
2 tablespoons plus 2 teaspoons
   imitation (or diet) margarine
1 teaspoon chopped fresh parsley

In saucepan cook potatoes in boiling salted water to cover until tender. While potatoes are cooking, combine celery, carrots, all but 1 tablespoon scallions, vinegar, and broth mix in small saucepan. Cook 3 to 5 minutes, stirring frequently. Remove from heat; set aside. When potatoes are tender, drain; cool slightly. Cut potatoes into ¼-inch-thick slices. Season with salt and white pepper. Layer potatoes and vegetables in 1½-quart casserole, ending with potatoes. Dot evenly with margarine. Bake at 375°F. for 30 to 40 minutes or until golden brown. Sprinkle with remaining 1 tablespoon scallions and parsley just before serving. Makes 8 servings.

CARAWAY-KRAUT RELISH

6 cups drained canned
   sauerkraut, rinsed
½ cup finely diced onion
3 tablespoons cider vinegar
Artificial sweetener to equal 4
   teaspoons sugar

2 teaspoons caraway seeds
1 tablespoon plus 1 teaspoon
   vegetable oil

In 1½- to 2-quart casserole combine all ingredients except oil. Cover and bake at 350°F. for 45 minutes. Cool to room temperature. Add oil; toss to combine. Refrigerate overnight or at least 3 hours. Makes 8 servings.

MUSTARD BEETS IN CABBAGE BOWL

½ cup plain unflavored yogurt
1 tablespoon prepared mustard
1 tablespoon cider vinegar
Freshly ground pepper to taste
2½ cups drained canned sliced
   beets

½ cup thinly sliced onion
Cabbage Bowl (see following
   instructions)

In medium bowl combine yogurt, mustard, vinegar, and pepper. Add beets and onion; toss to combine. Cover and refrigerate overnight or at least 3 hours. Serve in Cabbage Bowl. Makes 8 servings.

To Prepare Cabbage Bowl: Remove a few slices from bottom of a green cabbage that weighs approximately 2½ pounds. This will enable it to stand upright. Using a paring knife, cut into cabbage through top, about 1 inch from outer wall. Continue cutting around cabbage to form a circle. Remove cabbage leaves from center of circle, leaving cabbage bowl with about 1-inch-thick bottom. Cover with a damp cloth until ready to use.

APPLE CRUMBLE

8 small apples, pared, cored, and sliced
¼ cup lemon juice
2 teaspoons cinnamon, divided

8 slices raisin bread, toasted and made into crumbs
2 tablespoons plus 2 teaspoons imitation (or diet) margarine

Arrange apple slices in bottom of large, shallow baking pan. Sprinkle with lemon juice, then ½ teaspoon cinnamon. In medium bowl combine remaining 1½ teaspoons cinnamon with remaining ingredients. Mixture should be crumbly. Sprinkle crumb mixture over apples. Bake at 375°F. for 35 minutes or until apples are tender when tested with a toothpick. Serve warm or chilled. Makes 8 servings.

DIETETIC ROOT BEER

To each guest, serve 1½ cups dietetic root beer, icy cold, in frosted mugs or beer steins.

THALI—A TRAY BUFFET INDIAN-STYLE FOR SIX

Dal (Split Pea Soup)
Keema (Hamburger Mogul Style)
Saffron Rice Pilaf
Green Beans with Mustard Sauce
Curried Eggplant
Mint and Onion Chutney
Baked Bananas
Gajar Ka Halva (Carrot Pudding)
Yogurt or Buttermilk
Hot Tea

"Curry" favor with your friends by inviting them to a *thali*. In this typical Indian buffet, each person receives a round metal platter with small cups set on it, so that portions can be kept separate. You can easily improvise a *thali* by using individual trays for each diner—or by setting out a fascinating array of Indian dishes, buffet style. The most publicized Indian dish is curry, but few Westerners realize it's not necessarily hot. Indian curries actually have three degrees of hotness, and some of these dishes are surprisingly mild. Nor is curry one seasoning (as the packaged curry powder would suggest); instead, it is a combination of herbs and spices that vary according to each cook's preference. Many Indian families proudly hand down their curry recipes from one generation to another, as carefully guarded secrets. We've incorporated some of the most typical ingredients into a menu that's not-so-secretly geared to weight control. Chutney, pepper, and golden saffron are widely used, as are ginger and its relative, cardamom (called "grains of Paradise" because of its heavenly aroma). Cumin is found in nearly every curry recipe, but use it sparingly because it's said to stimulate the appetite! The slightly sweet taste of turmeric flavors Dal (a traditional split pea soup). We've Americanized our menu by adding hamburgers, but they're made with an Eastern staple—lamb—royally seasoned in "Mogul Style." The real menu surprise is carrots for dessert—a popular custom in India. No surprise is yogurt, found on almost every Eastern menu. As a pleasant variation, you might try buttermilk. Indian diners like to eat from trays, either at a table or sitting crosslegged on the floor. Whichever custom you'd like to imitate, set the scene with a batik cloth and napkins. Encourage the ladies to come beautifully costumed in saris . . . And prove that when East meets West, the result can be a culinary treat.

———————◆◆◆———————

SUGGESTED SHOPPING LIST
Staples and Miscellaneous

Artificial sweetener
Cayenne pepper
Cinnamon
Crushed red pepper
Cumin seed
Curry powder
Dehydrated onion flakes
Dry mustard
Garlic powder
Ginger
Ground cardamom
Ground coriander
Pepper
Saffron
Salt
Turmeric

Flour
Tea

Imitation (or diet) margarine

Chicken Stock, 3¼ cups plus
tablespoons (see page 31)

Additional Items

Ground lamb, 1 pound 2 ounces

Plain unflavored yogurt, 3 16-ounce
containers (or 1 8-ounce container
and 1 quart buttermilk)
Skim milk, 1 cup

Bananas, 3 medium, firm
Lemons, 3
Lime, 1

Carrots, 8 medium
Eggplant, 1 large
Green beans, 1 pound
Mint, 2 bunches
Onion, 1 large

Evaporated skimmed milk, 1 13-fluid-
ounce can

Enriched white rice, 1 16-ounce box

Prunes, large, 1 12-ounce box

Split peas, 2 16-ounce packages

SUGGESTED EQUIPMENT LIST

Baking pan and rack
Blender
Bowls (small, medium)
Can opener
Casserole (shallow, 1-quart)
Chef's knife
Colander
Cup (small)
Cutting board
Double boiler

Measuring cups
Measuring spoons
Nonstick baking sheet
Pastry brush
Pot (large)
Pot holder
Saucepan
Scale
Vegetable peeler
Wooden spoons

DAL (SPLIT PEA SOUP)

3¼ cups plus 2 tablespoons
   Chicken Stock (see page 31)
1 pound 2 ounces cooked dried
   split peas

¾ teaspoon salt
Dash each turmeric and pepper
6 lemon wedges

Combine all ingredients except lemon wedges in large pot. Bring to a boil; reduce heat and simmer 10 minutes, stirring occasionally. Puree mixture, no more than 2 cups at a time, in blender container. Return mixture to pot. Reheat, adding a little hot water to adjust consistency if necessary. Divide evenly into 6 soup bowls. Garnish each portion with a lemon wedge. Makes 6 servings.

KEEMA (HAMBURGER MOGUL STYLE)

1 pound 2 ounces ground lamb
¾ teaspoon salt
¾ teaspoon ginger
¼ teaspoon crushed red pepper,
   or to taste
¼ teaspoon garlic powder

¼ teaspoon cumin seed
Dash each ground cardamom,
   ground coriander, and pepper
1 lime, cut into 6 equal wedges
Mint sprigs to garnish

Combine all ingredients in medium bowl; mix well. Divide mixture into 6 equal portions. Shape each portion into a patty. Place on rack in baking pan. Bake at 375°F. for 20 minutes. Serve with lime wedges and garnished with mint sprigs. Makes 6 servings.

SAFFRON RICE PILAF

2 teaspoons dehydrated onion
   flakes
¼ teaspoon saffron

2 tablespoons hot water
3 cups cooked enriched rice, hot

In small cup combine onion flakes and saffron; add water. Let stand 15 minutes. Place rice in bowl. Stir saffron mixture into rice. Transfer to serving platter. Makes 6 servings.

GREEN BEANS WITH MUSTARD SAUCE

¼ cup plain unflavored yogurt
½ teaspoon dry mustard
⅛ teaspoon garlic powder

3 cups cooked whole green beans,
   hot

In small bowl combine yogurt, mustard, and garlic powder; mix well. Place green beans on serving plate. Spoon yogurt mixture over beans. Makes 6 servings.

CURRIED EGGPLANT

4 cups diced, pared eggplant
½ cup diced onion, ½-inch dice
2 tablespoons imitation (or diet)
   margarine
2 tablespoons flour

1 teaspoon curry powder
1 cup skim milk
6 large prunes, pitted and
   diced

Combine eggplant and onion in saucepan with boiling salted water to cover; cook for 10 minutes or until tender. Drain and set aside. Melt margarine in top of double boiler, over boiling water. Add flour and curry powder; stir to combine. Gradually stir in milk; cook, stirring occasionally, until mixture thickens. Add prunes and vegetables. Cook until well heated. Makes 6 servings.

MINT AND ONION CHUTNEY

2 cups finely chopped fresh
   mint leaves
½ cup chopped onion
3 tablespoons lemon juice

Artificial sweetener to equal 2
   teaspoons sugar
⅛ teaspoon cayenne pepper

Combine all ingredients in blender container. Process for 15 seconds. Place in small bowl. Chill for at least 2 hours. Makes 6 servings.

BAKED BANANAS

3 firm medium bananas
1 teaspoon lemon juice

⅛ teaspoon cinnamon

Cut bananas in half lengthwise. Brush bananas with lemon juice. Place on nonstick baking sheet. Sprinkle with cinnamon. Bake at 375°F. for 10 minutes. Makes 6 servings.

GAJAR KA HALVA (CARROT PUDDING)

Serve as a dessert with yogurt or buttermilk.

¼ cup imitation (or diet)
   margarine
3 cups grated carrots
2 tablespoons flour
⅛ teaspoon cinnamon

1½ cups evaporated skimmed
   milk
Artificial sweetener to equal 6
   teaspoons sugar

Melt margarine in top of double boiler, over boiling water. Add carrots; cook until tender. Add flour; stir to combine. Stir in cinnamon. Gradually stir in milk; cook, stirring constantly, until mixture thickens. Add sweetener. Transfer mixture to shallow 1-quart casserole. Bake at 350°F. for 50 minutes. Allow to cool. Chill for at least 4 hours. Makes 6 servings.

Yogurt or Buttermilk

Serve ½ cup plain unflavored yogurt or ¾ cup buttermilk to each person.

October

During October, the world changes from vibrant greens to rich browns, reds, and yellows. We honor this miracle of nature with a Fall Foliage Feast that dresses your table with a wealth of warm colors. We've even included a Jack O'Lantern Fruit Salad for Halloween! And with our special Columbus Day menu, we think you, too, will discover a "new world"!

CIAO ON COLUMBUS DAY FOR FOUR

Mussel Soup
Seafood Salad
Parsley-Rice Salad with Mustard Dressing
Minted Melon Balls or Grapefruit Cup
Beverage

Discover how exciting seafood can be in our eclectic Columbus Day feast. The famed explorer hailed from Italy, lived in Portugal, was financed by Spain, set sail for Asia—and discovered America! So our menu is appropriately drawn from all corners of the globe. We launch our luncheon with an Italian favorite: Mussel Soup. The Seafood Salad combines three of the Iberian Peninsula's favorite hauls—and what a world of eye appeal in the accompanying vegetables. Our platter cleverly presents an arrangement in the colors of Columbus's native land—the Italian green, white, and red! Sailing with the salad is a lively rice dish (a touch of the Orient) and a pungent mustard dressing. For an adventure in taste, cool your palate with a chilled fruit mixture—garnished by mint sprigs that bring hints of verandas in the Old South of the United States.

And for your decor, how about a sea-green tablecloth and a centerpiece of three gaily decorated toy boats? (They can even hold some "safe" nibbles!)

SUGGESTED SHOPPING LIST

Staples and Miscellaneous

Garlic powder	Flour
Marjoram	Prepared mustard
Paprika	
Salt	Margarine
White pepper	Vegetable oil

Frozen Alaskan king crab, 4-ounce package, or frozen lobster tails, 6 ounces
Peeled and deveined baby shrimp, ¼ pound
Scallops, ¼ pound
Unshucked mussels, 30 to 35

Skim milk, ½ cup

Cantaloupe, 1 small
and
Honeydew melon, 1 medium
OR
Pink grapefruit, 1 medium
and
White grapefruit, 1 medium
Lemon, 1

Carrots, 3 medium
Celery, 2 ribs
Cherry tomatoes, 1 pint
Cucumber, 1 medium
Garlic cloves, 2
Green beans, ½ pound
Green pepper, 1 medium
Mint, 1 bunch
Mushrooms, ½ pound
Onion, 1 medium
Parsley, 1 bunch
Scallions, 3
Tomato, 1 medium

Evaporated skimmed milk, 1 13-fluid-ounce can
Pimientos, 1 4-ounce jar
Enriched white rice, 1 16-ounce box

SUGGESTED EQUIPMENT LIST

Blender
Bowls (medium)
Can opener
Chef's knife
Cutting board
Double boiler
Measuring cups
Measuring spoons
Melon baller or grapefruit knife
Paper towels

Pot holder
Saucepan (medium)
Saucepan with cover (large)
Scale
Slotted spoons
Strainer
Vegetable brush
Vegetable peeler
Wooden spoons

MUSSEL SOUP

30 to 35 mussels in the shell
2 garlic cloves, cut
1 cup sliced mushrooms
¾ cup diced carrots

½ cup diced onion
1 medium tomato, diced
2 teaspoons marjoram

Scrub mussels; remove beards and particles that cling to shell. Place mussels and garlic in large saucepan with about 1½ inches water. Bring to a boil; reduce heat. Cover and simmer 4 to 6 minutes, or until shells open; discard any mussels that do not open. Remove mussels from shells; weigh 8 ounces and set aside. Strain and reserve liquid. In medium saucepan combine vegetables and marjoram; cook, stirring occasionally, for 7 minutes, adding a few tablespoons water, if necessary, to prevent sticking. Add enough water to reserved liquid so that total liquid equals 2½ cups; add to vegetable mixture. Bring to a boil; reduce heat and simmer until vegetables are tender. In blender container combine ½ cup vegetable mixture with 2 ounces mussels; process until smooth. Chop remaining mussels. Add pureed mixture and chopped mussels to saucepan. Heat thoroughly. Divide evenly into 4 soup bowls. Makes 4 servings.

SEAFOOD SALAD

3 ounces cooked scallops, cut into ½-inch pieces
3 ounces flaked cooked crab meat or lobster
2 ounces peeled and deveined cooked baby shrimp
½ medium cucumber, pared, seeded, and diced
½ medium green pepper, seeded and diced
¼ cup finely diced celery
2 tablespoons chopped pimiento
1 tablespoon plus 1½ teaspoons lemon juice
1 tablespoon vegetable oil
Dash garlic powder
Salt and white pepper to taste
1 cup cooked green beans
10 cherry tomatoes

In medium bowl combine all ingredients except green beans and tomatoes; chill. Using a slotted spoon, remove seafood mixture from liquid and spoon onto serving platter. Add green beans and tomatoes to remaining liquid; toss to coat. Arrange green beans and tomatoes around seafood. Sprinkle with any remaining liquid. Makes 4 servings.

PARSLEY-RICE SALAD WITH MUSTARD DRESSING

2 cups cooked enriched rice
½ cup diced celery
¼ cup minced fresh parsley
¼ cup chopped scallions
Salt and white pepper to taste
Mustard Dressing (see following recipe)

Combine all ingredients except Mustard Dressing in medium bowl. Chill. Serve with Mustard Dressing. Makes 4 servings.

Mustard Dressing

1 tablespoon margarine
1 tablespoon flour
¾ cup evaporated skimmed milk
½ cup skim milk
1 tablespoon prepared mustard
¼ teaspoon paprika
Dash salt

Melt margarine in top of double boiler, over boiling water. Stir in flour; cook 5 minutes. Gradually add evaporated and skim milk, stirring constantly; continue to stir and cook until thickened. Add remaining ingredients; cook 4 minutes longer. Cool. Transfer to serving dish and refrigerate until chilled. Use as directed in recipe for Parsley-Rice Salad (see preceding recipe).

MINTED MELON BALLS OR GRAPEFRUIT CUP

In bowl combine 2 cups each cantaloupe and honeydew melon balls, or 1 cup each fresh pink and white grapefruit sections. Divide mixture evenly into 4 dessert cups. Garnish each portion with a fresh mint sprig. Serve chilled. Makes 4 servings.

RIJSTTAFEL, AN INDONESIAN BUFFET
FOR EIGHT

Gingered Chicken Bouillon

Pickled Mushrooms

Salmon-Stuffed Tomatoes

Chicken and Shrimp with Peppery Soy Sauce

Vegetable Platter with Nut-Flavored Sauce

White Rice

Spiced Bananas

Beverage

"What does *rijsttafel* mean?" your guests will eagerly ask. You can tell them that the Indonesian word translates into "rice table," and then steer them toward your figure-guarding adaptation. A *rijsttafel* is actually a reminder of Indonesia's past—a buffet that features some 30 or 40 dishes of both Dutch and Oriental origin, ranging from spicy ginger-flavored meat to bland tropical banana. Highly spiced chicken and shrimp are menu favorites in the Indonesian islands, and rice is a feature of every meal. Since fruit flourishes in abundance, colorful pyramids of fresh fruit grace their buffet tables.

At a *rijsttafel,* guests serve themselves. It is traditional to mound rice in the center of the plate, then surround it with helpings of other dishes. Each food is eaten in combination with the rice—but not with any other dish, since mixing flavors is not considered good "taste."

Create an exciting ambience for your *rijsttafel.* Use a batik cloth on your table, set it with your most interesting pottery, and enliven your party with lively Indonesian music.

SUGGESTED SHOPPING LIST

Staples and Miscellaneous

Artificial sweetener
Basil
Bay leaves
Cinnamon
Coarse salt
Crushed red pepper
Garlic powder
Instant chicken broth and seasoning
    mix or bouillon cube
Nut extract (any flavor)
Nutmeg
Peppercorns
Salt
Thyme

Cider vinegar
Soy sauce

Flour

Margarine

Additional Items

Chicken, 1 (3-pound)
    or chicken meat, cooked, 1 pound
Peeled and deveined shrimp, 1 pound
Salmon fillet, ¼ pound

Skim milk, 1 cup

Bananas, 4 medium
Lemons, 2 medium

Bean sprouts, ½ pound
Broccoli, 1 bunch
Carrots, 4 large
Cucumbers, 3 medium
Garlic clove, 1
Ginger root, 1
Green beans, 1 pound
Lettuce, 1 medium head

Mint, 1 bunch
Mushrooms, 1½ pounds
Onion, 1 medium
Parsley, 1 bunch
Radishes, 1 bag
Spinach, ½ pound
Tomatoes, 8 medium

Frozen pearl onions, 1 20-ounce bag

Canned pineapple chunks, no sugar
    added, 1 8-ounce can

Canned sliced bamboo shoots,
    1 8-ounce can

Hot chili peppers, 1 4-ounce jar

Enriched white rice, 1 16-ounce box

SUGGESTED EQUIPMENT LIST

Aluminum foil or plastic wrap
Baking dish
Bowls
Can opener
Chef's knife
Cutting board
Double boiler
Measuring cups
Measuring spoons

Metal spoon
Pepper mill
Pot holder·
Saucepans and covers
Scale
Soup ladle
Vegetable steamer or colander
    (heatproof)
Wooden spoon

GINGERED CHICKEN BOUILLON

1½ quarts chicken bouillon   Grated fresh ginger root to taste

Combine bouillon and ginger root in saucepan. Bring to a boil; reduce heat. Simmer 5 minutes. Makes 8 servings.

PICKLED MUSHROOMS

1 cup canned pineapple chunks,
  no sugar added, drained,
  reserve juice
½ cup water
½ cup cider vinegar
¼ cup finely diced onion
2 tablespoons chopped fresh
  parsley

1 garlic clove, crushed
1 teaspoon salt
½ teaspoon thyme
4 peppercorns
1 bay leaf
6 cups mushrooms

In saucepan combine pineapple juice with remaining ingredients except pineapple and mushrooms. Bring to a boil; reduce heat. Add pineapple and mushrooms. Cover; simmer 5 minutes. Remove from heat; transfer to bowl and allow to cool in cooking liquid. Refrigerate until chilled. Before serving remove peppercorns and bay leaf. Makes 8 servings.

SALMON-STUFFED TOMATOES

4 ounces salmon fillet, cut into
  ½-ounce slices
½ cup coarse salt
3 tablespoons lemon juice
8 medium tomatoes

1 teaspoon basil
1 teaspoon chopped fresh parsley
Salt to taste
Freshly ground pepper to taste
Parsley sprigs to garnish

In bowl combine salmon, coarse salt, and lemon juice. Cover; refrigerate overnight. Fish will become firm. Soak fish in cold water for 2 hours, changing water several times. Drain and set aside. Cut thin slice from top and bottom of each tomato. From stem end, scoop out seeds and pulp, leaving a shell about ¼-inch thick; discard seeds. Chop pulp; combine with basil, parsley, salt, and pepper. Spoon an equal amount of pulp mixture into each shell. Top pulp in each tomato shell with ½ ounce of salmon; garnish with parsley sprigs. Arrange on serving platter. Makes 8 servings.

CHICKEN AND SHRIMP WITH PEPPERY SOY SAUCE

3 tablespoons soy sauce
3 tablespoons water
1½ teaspoons crushed red
  pepper
Dash garlic powder
Dash artificial sweetener
3 cups shredded lettuce

1 pound cut-up cooked chicken,
  1½-inch pieces
12 ounces peeled and deveined
  cooked shrimp
1 cup sliced radishes
1 medium cucumber, pared and
  sliced

In bowl combine first 5 ingredients; set aside. Place lettuce on serving platter. Arrange chicken and shrimp on lettuce; top with reserved soy sauce mixture. Garnish with radishes and cucumber. Makes 8 servings.

VEGETABLE PLATTER WITH NUT-FLAVORED SAUCE

2 cups pearl onions
2 cups broccoli florets
2 cups julienne carrots
2 cups green beans
2 cups spinach leaves
2 cups bean sprouts

1 cup drained, canned sliced
  bamboo shoots
2 medium cucumbers, cut into
  ¼-inch slices
Nut-Flavored Sauce (see
  following recipe)

In vegetable steamer steam each vegetable separately until tender-crisp. Cooking times for various vegetables are as follows: onions—10 to 15 minutes; broccoli, carrots, and green beans—6 to 8 minutes; spinach, bean sprouts, bamboo shoots, and cucumbers—2 to 3 minutes. A steamer can be improvised by using a heatproof colander and any pot that has a tight-fitting cover. Place a small amount of water in the pot, keeping the water level below the bottom of the colander. Bring water to a boil; then place colander in pot. Cover and steam vegetables as directed above. Arrange steamed vegetables on serving platter. Serve with Nut-Flavored Sauce. Makes 8 servings.

Nut-Flavored Sauce

2 tablespoons plus 2 teaspoons
  margarine
2 canned hot chili peppers,
  seeded and chopped
¼ cup finely diced onion
⅛ teaspoon garlic powder
2 tablespoons plus 1 teaspoon
  flour

1 cup skim milk
¾ cup chicken bouillon
½ teaspoon nut extract, any
  desired flavor
¼ teaspoon salt

Melt margarine in top of double boiler, over boiling water. Add chili peppers, onion, and garlic powder; cook until onion is tender. Add flour; stir to combine. Slowly add milk and bouillon; cook, stirring constantly, until mixture thickens. Stir in extract and salt. Pour into serving bowl. Use as directed in recipe for Vegetable Platter (see preceding recipe).

WHITE RICE

Serve ½ cup cooked enriched rice per portion. For recipe, see page 32.

SPICED BANANAS

4 firm medium bananas, cut into
   halves lengthwise
2 teaspoons lemon juice
¾ teaspoon cinnamon

¼ teaspoon nutmeg
2 teaspoons margarine
Mint sprig to garnish

Arrange banana halves in baking dish, cut side down. Sprinkle each with ¼ teaspoon lemon juice. In small cup combine cinnamon and nutmeg. Sprinkle ⅛ teaspoon mixture over each banana half; dot each with ¼ teaspoon margarine. Bake at 375°F. for 15 minutes or until bananas begin to brown. Transfer to serving platter and garnish with mint. Serve immediately. Makes 8 servings.

FALL FOLIAGE FEAST FOR TWELVE

Curried Cocktail on the Rocks
Chicken in Mustard Sauce
Ketchup-Corn Bake
Parsnip Puffs
Cress 'n' Lettuce Salad with French Dressing
Sweet Spiced Peaches
Coffee Froth

A breezy autumn night . . . a gathering around the fireside . . . warmth and camaraderie . . . the perfect setting for an imaginative Fall Foliage Feast. Imbibe a "Curried Cocktail on the Rocks," then dine on festive foods that reflect the colorful tones of autumn. The corn harvest is transformed into an appetizing casserole, and parsnips, a pleasant vegetable that's too often neglected, appear shaped into interesting "Puffs." This is the season when the ancient Romans worshipped Pomona, the goddess of fruit—your guests can pay homage to an alluring peach dessert that combines the best of both sweet and spicy worlds. (They'll also pay tribute to a menu that lets them watch leaves instead of hidden calories!) Coffee Froth keeps the evening bubbling right to the finish.

Turn your home into a woodland retreat with arrangements of dried flowers, collages of brilliant leaves, and fragrant centerpieces made from pine cones, leaves, and pumpkins!

SUGGESTED SHOPPING LIST

Staples and Miscellaneous

Artificial sweetener
Cinnamon
Cinnamon sticks
Cloves
Curry powder
Dry mustard
Paprika
Pepper
Salt
Vanilla extract
White pepper

Cider vinegar
Dijon mustard
Hot sauce
Ketchup
Prepared mustard

Flour
Nonfat dry milk powder

Imitation (or diet) margarine
Vegetable oil

Additional Items

Skinned and boned chicken breasts,
  4½ pounds

Skim milk, 1 quart

Celery ribs with leaves, 12
Bibb lettuce, 2 large heads
Romaine lettuce, 2 medium heads
Onion, 1 large, ½ pound minimum
Parsley, 1 bunch
Parsnips, 1¼ pounds
Watercress, 2 bunches

Canned crushed pineapple, no sugar
  added, 1 20-ounce can

Canned peach halves, no sugar added,
  5 16-ounce cans

Canned whole-kernel corn, 4 12-ounce
  cans

Clam juice, 3 8-fluid-ounce bottles
Tomato juice, 2 46-fluid-ounce cans

Evaporated skimmed milk, 1 13-fluid-
  ounce can

Coffee-flavored dietetic soda, 2
  28-fluid-ounce bottles

SUGGESTED EQUIPMENT LIST

Blender
Bowls (medium, large)
Can opener
Casserole (2-quart)
Casserole (large)
Chef's knife
Colander
Cutting board
Double boiler
Jar with cover

Measuring cups
Measuring spoons
Nonstick baking sheets
Pitcher (large)
Potato masher
Pot holder
Saucepan with cover
Scale
Wire whisk
Wooden spoon

CURRIED COCKTAIL ON THE ROCKS

2¼ quarts tomato juice
3 cups clam juice
⅛ teaspoon curry powder

⅛ teaspoon hot sauce
Ice cubes
12 celery ribs with leaves

Combine all ingredients except ice cubes and celery in large pitcher. Chill.
Divide evenly into 12 tall glasses. Add enough ice cubes to each to fill
glass. Place a celery rib in each glass, leaf end up, to use as a stirrer.
Makes 12 servings.

CHICKEN IN MUSTARD SAUCE

¼ cup imitation (or diet)
  margarine
¼ cup flour
2¼ cups evaporated skimmed
  milk

¼ cup Dijon mustard
Salt and pepper to taste
4½ pounds skinned and boned
  chicken breasts
Chopped fresh parsley to garnish

[279]

Melt margarine in top of double boiler, over boiling water. Add flour; stir with wire whisk to combine. Continue to stir and add milk, mustard, salt, and pepper. Cook, stirring constantly, until thickened. Cut each chicken breast in half; place in large casserole. Pour sauce evenly over chicken. Bake at 350°F. for 35 to 45 minutes or until chicken is tender. Sprinkle with parsley. Makes 12 servings.

KETCHUP-CORN BAKE

6 cups drained canned whole-
  kernel corn
1 cup finely chopped onions
½ cup ketchup

1 tablespoon plus 1 teaspoon
  prepared mustard
½ teaspoon salt

Combine all ingredients in large bowl. Transfer to 2-quart casserole. Bake at 350°F. for 25 minutes or until piping hot. Makes 12 servings.

PARSNIP PUFFS

2 cups mashed cooked parsnips
1½ cups canned crushed
  pineapple, no sugar added
1 cup nonfat dry milk powder
Artificial sweetener to equal 12
  teaspoons sugar

1 tablespoon vanilla extract
¾ teaspoon cinnamon
Parsley sprigs to garnish

Combine all ingredients except parsley in medium bowl. Drop by tea-spoonsful onto 2 nonstick baking sheets. Bake at 350°F. for 40 minutes. Transfer to serving platter. Garnish with parsley sprigs. Makes 12 servings.

CRESS 'N' LETTUCE SALAD WITH FRENCH DRESSING

6 cups watercress leaves
6 cups torn Bibb lettuce, bite-
  size pieces
6 cups torn romaine lettuce,
  bite-size pieces

French Dressing (see following
  recipe)

Combine salad greens in large salad bowl. Add French Dressing; toss to combine. Makes 12 servings.

French Dressing

¼ cup vegetable oil
¼ cup cider vinegar
¼ cup water

¾ teaspoon paprika
½ teaspoon dry mustard
Salt and white pepper to taste

Combine all ingredients in jar with tight-fitting cover. Cover and shake well. Use as directed in recipe for Cress 'n' Lettuce Salad (see preceding recipe).

SWEET SPICED PEACHES

24 canned peach halves with
  1½ cups juice, no sugar
  added
Artificial sweetener to equal 24
  teaspoons sugar

12 cloves
3 cinnamon sticks

Combine all ingredients in saucepan. Cover and simmer 10 minutes. Remove and discard cloves and cinnamon sticks. Serve warm or chilled. Makes 12 servings.

COFFEE FROTH

Pour 1 cup coffee-flavored dietetic soda into blender container; add ¾ cup skim milk. Process to combine. With blender running, add 3 ice cubes, 1 at a time, processing until ice is crushed. Divide evenly into 2 tall glasses. Repeat procedure 5 more times. Serve with straws. Makes 12 servings.

BAGELS AND LOX BREAKFAST FOR EIGHT

Apricot-Glazed Grapefruit
Bagels and Lox with Creamy Cheese
Sliced Onion Salad
Beverage

What's the first thing you think of when you hear "bagels"? "Lox," of course! Along with cream cheese, this culinary combo is one of the most popular of all breakfast menus. Delight weekend guests with our interesting variation. Having citrus on the menu balances the saltiness of lox. You can turn ordinary grapefruit into a festive treat by broiling it with a glaze of apricot. Instead of calorie-laden cream cheese, blend a "creamy" substitute of cottage cheese and gelatin. Onions and tomatoes, also a traditional accompaniment, can be served in artistic-looking columns, interspersed with cucumber slices. (Cutting off the ends of the cucumber first will prevent a bitter taste.) Here's a breakfast that's an incredible combination of "diet" and "delicious"!

SUGGESTED SHOPPING LIST

Staples and Miscellaneous

Imitation butter flavoring
Vanilla extract

Unflavored gelatin

Enriched small bagels, 2 ounces each

Low-calorie apricot preserves

Additional Items

Lox (smoked salmon), ½ pound

Cottage cheese, 1 16-ounce container

Grapefruits, 4 medium

Cucumber, 1 medium
Onions, 2 medium
Tomatoes, 2 medium

[282]

Baking pan (9 x 13 x 2 inches, flameproof)
Blender
Chef's knife
Cutting board
Grapefruit knife
Measuring cups
Measuring spoons

Pan (3-cup)
Pot holder
Saucepans (small)
Scale
Rubber spatula
Spreading knife
Toaster
Vegetable peeler

APRICOT-GLAZED GRAPEFRUIT

4 medium grapefruits, cut into halves

2 tablespoons plus 2 teaspoons low-calorie apricot preserves

Using serrated grapefruit knife, remove seeds from each grapefruit half. Separate segments from membranes by carefully cutting around each segment. In small saucepan heat preserves until melted. Spread an equal amount of preserves over each grapefruit half. Place halves in flameproof, 9 × 13 × 2-inch baking pan. Broil 4 inches from source of heat for 2 minutes or until fruit is warm and preserves are bubbly. Makes 8 servings.

BAGELS AND LOX WITH CREAMY CHEESE

1 envelope unflavored gelatin
½ cup water
1⅓ cups cottage cheese
½ teaspoon vanilla extract
Dash imitation butter flavoring

8 enriched small bagels, 2 ounces each
8 ounces lox (smoked salmon), cut into ¼-inch-thick strips

In small saucepan sprinkle gelatin over water; let stand a few minutes to soften. Cook over low heat, stirring constantly, until gelatin is dissolved. Pour gelatin mixture into blender container. Add cheese, vanilla, and butter flavoring; process until smooth. Transfer to 3-cup pan and chill until set, about 2 hours. Unmold and slice into 16 equal portions. Cut each bagel in half; toast halves. Spread each half with 1 portion cheese and top with ½ ounce lox. Makes 8 servings.

SLICED ONION SALAD

4 cups onion rings
2 medium tomatoes, cut into ¼-inch slices

1 medium cucumber, cut into ¼-inch slices

Arrange onion rings, tomato, and cucumber slices in columns on serving platter. Makes 8 servings.

FAMILY WEDDING PARTY FOR EIGHT

Heart-Shaped Tomato Gelatin
Lemony Shrimp
Salmon in Creamy Sauce and Snow Peas
Stuffed Tomatoes
Pineapple Delight
Beverage

Feasting has been coupled with wedding festivities since ancient times. (The Romans used to break a cake over the bride's head for luck!) In time-honored tradition, serve an intimate dinner party "just for family and close friends." Mold gelatin imaginatively into a crimson heart (a feat you may wish to duplicate on Valentine's Day or for an anniversary dinner). The taste of ever-popular shrimp is enhanced by lemon—you can cheer the bridal couple on by informing them that the lemon was a symbol of plenty for the ancient Norse. Our entrée of canned salmon in a creamy sauce with Chinese snow peas is discreetly economical, a consideration since weddings tend to be expensive. Pineapple Delight makes a refreshing dessert—and an elegant one if you serve it in champagne glasses. (Equally refreshing is the fact that this celebration won't strain the seams of anyone's wedding finery!)

Set your table in the bride's favorite colors. For an unusual merrymaking centerpiece, combine toy-like symbols of the couple's favorite interests—along with a few good-luck items.

———————————•◆•———————————

SUGGESTED SHOPPING LIST

Staples and Miscellaneous

Chopped chives
Dill weed
Salt
Sherry extract
White pepper

Hot sauce
Worcestershire sauce

Flour
Unflavored gelatin

Margarine

Beef Stock, 3 cups (see page 31)

Additional Items

Canned salmon, 2 15¼-ounce cans

Peeled and deveined shrimp, 1½ pounds

Plain unflavored yogurt, 1 16-ounce container

Cantaloupe, 1 small

Lemons, 2

Chinese snow peas, 1 pound

Cucumbers, 4 medium

Mint, 1 bunch

Mushrooms, 1 pound

Onion, 1 small

Parsley, 1 bunch

Tomatoes, 8 medium, firm

Canned pineapple chunks, no sugar added , 3 16-ounce cans

Tomato juice, 1 18-fluid-ounce can

Evaporated skimmed milk, 1 13-fluid-ounce can

Raspberry-flavored dietetic soda, 1 28-fluid-ounce bottle

SUGGESTED EQUIPMENT LIST

Blender

Bowls (small)

Can opener

Chef's knife

Cutting board

Double boiler

Grater

Heart-shaped mold (6-cup)

Kitchen spoon

Measuring cups

Measuring spoons

Melon baller

Pot holder

Saucepans

Vegetable peeler

Wooden spoons

HEART-SHAPED TOMATO GELATIN

3 envelopes unflavored gelatin
3 cups Beef Stock (see page 31)
2 cups tomato juice
1 teaspoon Worcestershire sauce
1 teaspoon lemon juice
¼ teaspoon hot sauce
2 cups melon balls
Fresh mint leaves to garnish

In saucepan sprinkle gelatin over stock; let stand a few minutes to soften. Heat, stirring constantly, until gelatin is dissolved. Stir in tomato juice, Worcestershire, lemon juice, and hot sauce. Chill until consistency of unbeaten egg whites. If mixture is cloudy, stir until clear. Pour into 6-cup, heart-shaped mold; chill until set. Unmold onto serving platter; arrange melon balls on same platter and garnish with mint leaves. Makes 8 servings.

LEMONY SHRIMP

1 tablespoon plus 1 teaspoon margarine
1½ pounds peeled and deveined shrimp
2 tablespoons lemon juice
1 tablespoon chopped fresh parsley
2 teaspoons chopped chives
½ teaspoon grated lemon rind
Salt and white pepper to taste

Melt margarine in top of double boiler, over boiling water. Add shrimp; cook until shrimp are firm and pink. Stir in remaining ingredients. Transfer to serving dish. Makes 8 servings.

SALMON IN CREAMY SAUCE AND SNOW PEAS

2 tablespoons margarine
2 cups mushrooms, cut into quarters
1/4 cup finely diced onion
2 tablespoons flour
1 cup evaporated skimmed milk
1 pound drained canned salmon, flaked

2 teaspoons chopped fresh parsley
1/2 teaspoon Worcestershire sauce
1/4 teaspoon sherry extract
Chinese snow peas (see following recipe)

Melt margarine in top of double boiler, over boiling water. Add mushrooms and onion; cook until vegetables are tender. Sprinkle flour over vegetables; stir to combine. Cook 3 minutes, stirring frequently. Gradually add milk, stirring constantly; cook until thickened and smooth. Fold in remaining ingredients except Chinese snow peas; cook until heated throughout. Transfer mixture to serving platter; surround with Chinese snow peas. Makes 8 servings.

Chinese Snow Peas

Fresh Chinese snow peas from California and Mexico are generally available all year. Frozen pea pods are an acceptable substitute.

3¾ cups Chinese snow peas   Salt to taste

Rinse snow peas; snap off ends and remove string from each pea pod. Place in saucepan with boiling salted water to cover. Return water to boil; reduce heat. Cook 2 minutes; drain. Season. Serve as directed in recipe for Salmon in Creamy Sauce (see preceding recipe).

STUFFED TOMATOES

8 firm medium tomatoes
Salt and white pepper to taste
4 medium cucumbers, pared, seeded, and sliced
1 cup plain unflavored yogurt

2 tablespoons chopped fresh parsley
2 teaspoons chopped chives
1/4 teaspoon dill weed

Cut thin slice from stem end of each tomato. Scoop out pulp and seeds from each, leaving a 1/4-inch-thick shell; discard seeds and reserve pulp. Sprinkle inside of each shell with salt and pepper. Invert on platter; set aside for 20 minutes to drain. In bowl sprinkle cucumbers with salt and set aside for 15 minutes. Rinse cucumbers; combine in bowl with yogurt, parsley, chives, and dill weed. Spoon an equal amount of cucumber mixture into each tomato shell. Place each stuffed tomato in an individual serving dish. Chop reserved tomato pulp. Place in small bowl; season with salt and pepper. Spoon an equal amount of pulp over each stuffed tomato. Chill until ready to serve. Makes 8 servings.

PINEAPPLE DELIGHT

4 cups canned pineapple chunks,   12 ice cubes
    no sugar added, divided
2 cups raspberry-flavored
    dietetic soda, divided

In blender container combine 2 cups pineapple with 1 cup soda; process until smooth. Add 6 ice cubes, 1 at a time, processing after each addition, until all ice is crushed. Pour into freezer tray. Repeat process with remaining ingredients. Freeze until slushy. Divide evenly into 8 champagne glasses. Makes 8 servings.

HALLOWEEN SUPPER FOR TWELVE

Herbed Tomato Juice Cocktail
Tossed Salad with Garlic-Yogurt Dressing
Festive Chicken Salad
Curried Macaroni Salad
Jack O'Lantern Fruit Salad
Pumpkin in "Crème"
Hot Coffee

A banquet table to placate *ghostly* guests!—that was the hosting style on All Hallows Eve in pagan times. So what could be more appropriate for your trick-or-treating youngsters and their friends than a buffet-style party? Or treat your *own* friends to this fun fete! "Trick" is a euphemism for mischief, but our menu won't do mischief to any figures! Nor will it haunt your busy schedule, because it's all do-ahead fare (which frees you to accompany the children on their rounds). Let the Pumpkin in "Crème" chill for several hours during that time. The foods take care of themselves once they're set out, so you can relax and enjoy the party. Guests of all ages will be enchanted by the imaginative "Jack O' Lantern" Fruit Salad. A wondrous tale for you to spin is that the name comes from a man named Jack, who—so legend has it—because of his evil ways, was condemned to roam the world eternally, lighting his path by a pumpkin with a candle in it.

Decorate in bewitching Halloween style—black cats, a pumpkin centerpiece, and all—for an in-the-spirit party to remember!

SUGGESTED SHOPPING LIST

Staples and Miscellaneous

Artificial sweetener
Celery salt
Curry powder
Dried mint
Green peppercorns
Instant chicken broth and seasoning mix
Oregano
Salt
Vanilla extract
White pepper

Capers
Hot sauce
Worcestershire sauce

Coffee
Cornstarch
Unflavored gelatin

Margarine
Imitation mayonnaise

Additional Items

Chickens, 3 (3 pounds each)

Plain unflavored yogurt, 2 16-ounce containers
Skim milk, 1½ quarts

Lemons, 5

Celery, 5 ribs
Cucumbers, 3 medium
Garlic cloves, 3
Green peppers, 3 medium
Lettuce, 1 medium head
Mushrooms, ¾ pound
Onion, 1 small
Parsley, 1 bunch

Canned sliced peaches, no sugar added, 2 16-ounce cans

Canned pumpkin, 1 16-ounce can
Pimientos, 1 4-ounce jar

Tomato juice, 3 1-quart bottles

Enriched elbow macaroni, 1 16-ounce box
Prunes, large, 1 12-ounce box

Dietetic ginger ale, 1 16-fluid-ounce bottle

SUGGESTED EQUIPMENT LIST

Aluminum foil or plastic wrap
Bowls (large, 1½-quart, 2-quart)
Can opener
Chef's knife
Cutting board
Double boiler
Measuring cups
Measuring spoons

Paring knife
Pot holder
Saucepans (medium, large)
Scale
Slotted spoon
Vegetable peeler
Wooden spoon

HERBED TOMATO JUICE COCKTAIL

3 quarts tomato juice
2 cups diced celery
¼ cup lemon juice
1 tablespoon Worcestershire
sauce, or to taste
Artificial sweetener to equal 3
teaspoons sugar (optional)

2 packets instant chicken broth
and seasoning mix
1½ teaspoons celery salt
1 teaspoon oregano
½ teaspoon hot sauce, or to taste
12 lemon slices

Combine all ingredients except lemon slices in large saucepan. Bring to a boil; reduce heat and simmer for 10 minutes. Serve hot or refrigerate until chilled. Garnish with lemon slices. Makes 12 servings.

TOSSED SALAD WITH GARLIC-YOGURT DRESSING

3 cups plain unflavored yogurt
3 garlic cloves, minced
1 tablespoon dried mint
1 teaspoon salt, or to taste
¼ teaspoon white pepper, or to
taste

6 cups torn lettuce, bite-size
pieces
3 medium cucumbers, pared,
scored, and sliced
2½ medium green peppers,
seeded and diced

In large bowl combine yogurt, garlic, mint, salt, and pepper. Add remaining ingredients; toss and serve. Makes 12 servings.

FESTIVE CHICKEN SALAD

2 cups sliced mushrooms
½ cup water
3 pounds cut-up, cooked
chicken, bite-size pieces
½ cup plus 2 tablespoons
imitation mayonnaise
¼ cup chopped fresh parsley

2 tablespoons lemon juice
2 teaspoons drained capers
½ teaspoon drained green
peppercorns
½ medium green pepper, seeded
and cut into rings

In saucepan combine mushrooms and water. Bring to a boil; reduce heat and simmer for 7 minutes or until mushrooms are tender. Remove mushrooms with slotted spoon and place in large serving bowl; discard liquid. Add remaining ingredients except green pepper; mix well. Cut each pepper ring in half. Garnish salad with pepper slices. Cover and refrigerate until chilled. Makes 12 servings.

CURRIED MACARONI SALAD

8 cups cooked enriched elbow
  macaroni
½ cup finely chopped onion
¼ cup chopped pimientos,
  reserve 1 tablespoon for
  garnish

¼ cup imitation mayonnaise
1 tablespoon curry powder
Artificial sweetener to equal 2
  teaspoons sugar (optional)

In large serving bowl combine all ingredients except garnish. Cover and refrigerate until chilled. Just before serving, garnish with reserved pimientos. Makes 12 servings.

JACK O'LANTERN FRUIT SALAD

2½ cups canned sliced peaches,
  no sugar added
2 cups dietetic ginger ale

2 envelopes unflavored gelatin
2 large prunes, pitted
1 cup finely chopped celery

Drain liquid from peach slices into saucepan; set fruit aside. Add ginger ale and gelatin to liquid; allow gelatin to soften. Place over low heat and cook, stirring constantly, until gelatin dissolves. Pour ½-inch layer of gelatin mixture in bottom of mold and chill. Using a sharp paring knife, cut prunes into shapes that resemble a Jack O'Lantern's eyes, nose, and mouth. Before gelatin becomes fully set, arrange "face" over gelatin layer. Spoon small amounts of remaining gelatin mixture over and around prunes. Chill again. Gently arrange peach slices over second gelatin layer. Carefully pour remaining liquid over peaches. Chill until almost set. Sprinkle celery around center of mold. Chill until firm. Unmold onto serving platter. Makes 12 servings.

PUMPKIN IN "CRÈME"

1½ quarts skim milk
2 tablespoons vanilla extract
Dash salt
½ cup plus 2 tablespoons
  cornstarch, dissolved in ½
  cup water

1½ cups canned pumpkin
Artificial sweetener to equal 24
  teaspoons sugar
2 tablespoons margarine

In top of a double boiler, over boiling water, combine milk, vanilla, and salt; heat. Stir in dissolved cornstarch; continue to stir and cook until thickened. Remove from heat. Add pumpkin, sweetener, and margarine; stir until smooth. Transfer to 2-quart bowl; cover and refrigerate for at least 3 hours. Makes 12 servings.

November

Join our pilgrimage through November
in traditional holiday style, or start your
own tradition with a meal minus the
customary big bird! And you'll truly
have reason to give thanks this month,
for our additional menu selections offer
ease and economy. In this beautiful season
of retrospect, you can also look ahead to
a beautiful new you!

A CHINESE REPAST FOR FOUR

Gingered Chicken Broth
Lemon Chicken on Rice
Spinach and Tangerine Salad
Sesame Salad Dressing
Pineapple-Yogurt Freeze
Chinese Tea

In China, eating is thought of as more than just a physical necessity, and the ability to prepare food correctly is a greatly respected art. You too can enjoy great respect for your excellent hosting with our easy-to-prepare Chinese Repast. Gingered Chicken Broth lends an authentic touch, for chicken bouillon appears in a preponderance of Chinese recipes, and fresh ginger root is almost invariably used with beef and chicken. (Use it *gingerly*, however, for its strong flavor can easily overwhelm a dish.) When preparing the Lemon Chicken, dice the vegetables carefully into uniform pieces to conform to the Chinese emphasis on visual appeal. The green and orange salad adds vibrant colors to a November meal—colors well worth duplicating in your table decor. The wise Chinese are not fond of sweets, preferring to end a meal with fruit. We offer Pineapple-Yogurt Freeze. Of course, you'll serve rice, which has been called the Asian "staff of life," and provide refreshing cups of Chinese tea, charmingly served from a tea set Centuries ago, a famous Chinese emperor lauded tea as "that precious beverage which drives away the five causes of sorrow." Certainly one of the causes of *happiness* is being able to enjoy succulent flavors in honorable weight-saving style!

------- ◆•◆ -------

SUGGESTED SHOPPING LIST

Staples and Miscellaneous

Artificial sweetener
Crushed red pepper
Instant chicken broth and seasoning
   mix
Vanilla extract

Chinese mustard
Soy sauce

Chinese tea
Cornstarch

Sesame oil
Vegetable oil

Chicken Stock, 1 quart plus ½ cup
   (see page 31)

Additional Items

Skinned and boned chicken breasts,
  1½ pounds

Plain unflavored yogurt, 1 16-ounce
  container

Lemon, 1
Tangerines, 4 large

Celery, 2 ribs
Chinese pea pods, ¼ pound
Garlic clove, 1
Ginger root, 1

Mint, 1 small bunch
Mushrooms, ½ pound
Onion, 1 medium
Red onion, 1
Scallions, 2 bunches
Spinach. 1½ pounds

Frozen orange juice concentrate,
  1 6-fluid-ounce can

Canned crushed pineapple, no sugar
  added, 1 16-ounce can

Enriched white rice, 1 16-ounce box

SUGGESTED EQUIPMENT LIST

Bowls (small)
Chef's knife
Cutting board
Jar with cover
Measuring cups
Measuring spoons

Paper towels
Pot holder
Saucepans (small, wide/shallow)
Scale
Wooden spoon

GINGERED CHICKEN BROTH

> 3 cups Chicken Stock (see page
>   31)
> 2 packets instant chicken broth
>   and seasoning mix

> 1 teaspoon sliced fresh ginger
>   root
> ½ cup Scallion Brushes (see page
>   18)

Combine stock, broth mix, and ginger root in medium saucepan; cover and simmer for 15 minutes. Remove and discard ginger root. Divide broth evenly into 4 small soup bowls. Garnish each portion with ¼ of the Scallion Brushes. Makes 4 servings.

LEMON CHICKEN ON RICE

Serve with soy sauce and Chinese mustard.

> 1½ pounds skinned and boned
>   chicken breasts
> 1½ cups Chicken Stock (see
>   page 31)
> 1 cup sliced mushrooms
> 1 cup diced celery
> ¼ cup diced onion

> 2 teaspoons cornstarch,
>   dissolved in 2 teaspoons water
> 1 tablespoon lemon juice
> 2 cups hot Fluffy White Rice (see
>   page 32)
> ¾ cup cooked Chinese pea pods

In wide, shallow saucepan bring to a boil enough water to cover chicken. Reduce heat. Add chicken in 1 layer; cover and simmer about 20 to 30 minutes or until chicken is done. Remove chicken from liquid and dice.

Combine stock, mushrooms, celery, and onion in saucepan. Cover and cook until vegetables are tender. Stirring constantly, add cornstarch and cook until thickened. Stir in lemon juice. Add diced chicken and stir to combine. Reduce heat and simmer 7 minutes or until chicken is thoroughly heated. Serve over rice and surround with Chinese pea pods. Makes 4 servings.

Note: To use poaching liquid as stock, chill liquid until fat congeals on top. Remove and discard congealed fat. Liquid may be measured and frozen for use at another time.

SPINACH AND TANGERINE SALAD

Serve with Sesame Salad Dressing (see recipe below).

4 cups spinach leaves
½ cup red onion rings

4 large tangerines, peeled and sectioned

Chill 4 salad plates. Wash spinach leaves well in cold water and shake to remove excess moisture. Tear into bite-size pieces; wrap in paper towels. Refrigerate until needed. When ready to serve, arrange 1 cup spinach leaves on each chilled salad plate. Top each portion with ¼ of the onion rings. Arrange an equal amount of tangerine sections in a spiral pattern over each serving. Makes 4 servings.

SESAME SALAD DRESSING

Serve with Spinach and Tangerine Salad (see recipe above).

1 garlic clove, minced
Artificial sweetener to equal 1 teaspoon sugar
½ teaspoon crushed red pepper, or to taste
¼ cup water

3 tablespoons lemon juice
2 tablespoons frozen orange juice concentrate
1 tablespoon soy sauce
2 teaspoons sesame oil
2 teaspoons vegetable oil

Combine garlic, sweetener, and pepper in jar with tight-fitting cover; add remaining ingredients. Cover and set aside for at least 1 hour. Before serving, shake well to combine. Makes 4 servings.

PINEAPPLE-YOGURT FREEZE

1 cup canned crushed pineapple, no sugar added
1 cup plain unflavored yogurt
Artificial sweetener to equal 2 teaspoons sugar (optional)

1 teaspoon vanilla extract
Mint leaves to garnish

Chill 4 dessert glasses. Combine all ingredients except mint leaves in shallow 2½-cup container. Freeze, stirring occasionally, until mixture is frozen to firm but not solid consistency. Divide evenly into chilled glasses. Garnish with mint leaves. Makes 4 servings.

SPECIAL SUNDAY BREAKFAST FOR FOUR

Citrus Sections with Rose Water
Toad in a Hole
Cinnamon Coffee or Mint Tea

Too cold to go swimming . . . too warm to go skiing? Don't let dreary November weekends make life drab. Treat your family to another kind of experience—imbibing new taste sensations. Rose water, a delicate Eastern touch, adds extraordinary flavor to ordinary breakfast fruit. (Buy rose water in a specialty shop or in the specialty department of your local supermarket.) Then let your family play a guessing game by announcing that you're serving "Toad in a Hole"! The secret is a baked egg imaginatively tucked into a custard cup lined with dark bread triangles. Such an innovation could hardly be followed by an ordinary potful of coffee. Flavor it with a cinnamon stick for a Sunday special. Never mind November—you'll get year-round demands for this menu! And dare to be experimental by trying rose water in other dishes as well.

SUGGESTED SHOPPING LIST

Staples and Miscellaneous

Artificial sweetener
Cinnamon stick
Pepper
Salt

Rose water

Coffee
Mint tea

Margarine

Whole wheat bread

Additional Items

Eggs, 4

Skim milk, ½ cup

Grapefruit, 1 medium
Oranges, 2 small

SUGGESTED EQUIPMENT LIST

Blender or food processor
Bowls (small, medium)
Chef's knife
Custard cups (4 ¾-cup)
Measuring cups

Measuring spoons
Paring knife
Pot holder
Saucepan (medium)
Wooden spoon

CITRUS SECTIONS WITH ROSE WATER

1 medium grapefruit, peeled,   ½ teaspoon rose water
  pitted, and sectioned
2 small oranges, peeled, pitted,
  and sectioned

In bowl combine all ingredients. Chill at least 30 minutes. Makes 4 servings.

TOAD IN A HOLE

4 slices whole wheat bread   Salt and pepper to taste
2 teaspoons margarine   4 eggs

Preheat oven to 350°F. Cut 3 slices of bread into quarters, from corner to corner, to make 12 triangles. Stand 3 bread triangles, points up, in a 6-ounce custard cup, leaving a well in center. Repeat with remaining triangles and 3 more custard cups. Make remaining slice of bread into crumbs. In small bowl combine crumbs, margarine, salt, and pepper; mix until crumbly. Crack 1 egg into well in each custard cup; bake for 8 minutes. Spoon an equal amount of crumb mixture over each egg and bake 2 minutes longer. Makes 4 servings.

CINNAMON COFFEE

3 cups coffee   Artificial sweetener to equal 2
½ cup skim milk   teaspoons sugar
1 cinnamon stick

In medium saucepan combine all ingredients. Simmer for 5 minutes. Remove cinnamon stick. Makes 4 servings.

FOOTBALL WATCH—EASY AND ECONOMICAL LUNCHEON FOR FOUR

Hot Chicken and Tomato Bisque
Stuffed Eggplant
Casserole of Mixed Vegetables au Gratin
Pineapple-Filled Baked Apples
Beverage

Getting together with family or friends to watch the game? Score points on the board with a luncheon that cooks itself while you join in the excitement! Prepare the ingredients before game time, then allow an hour for the total cooking. Since all three oven dishes bake at the same temperature, they can be cooked simultaneously. "Kick off" by starting the Baked Apples, which need the longest time: one hour. You can pop the Vegetable Casserole and Stuffed Eggplant into the oven together during the final twenty minutes. What a thrifty fuel saver this is! Meanwhile, the Bisque is simmering on the stove to warm those who come in shivering from the cold November weather. In case a larger crowd shows up, the recipes are easy to multiply. They still add up to economical serving, especially when you make use of a year-round vegetable like eggplant. Cheer everyone on by reminding them that your dishes team well with a weight-loss plan. Bet you score a touchdown with this one!

———— ••• ————

SUGGESTED SHOPPING LIST

Staples and Miscellaneous

Bay leaves	Worcestershire sauce
Cloves	
Dry mustard	Imitation (or diet) margarine
Garlic powder	
Instant chicken broth and seasoning mix	Flour
Pepper	Enriched white bread
Salt	
Thyme	
White pepper	

Additional Items

Chicken, 1 2½-pound
Swiss cheese, ¼ pound

Skim milk, 1 cup

Apples, 4 small

Carrots, 6 medium
Celery, 4 medium ribs
Eggplants, 2 (1 pound each)
Onion, 1 large
Parsley, 1 bunch
Tomatoes, 2 medium
Zucchini, 1 medium

Frozen pearl onions, 1 20-ounce bag
Frozen peas, 1 10-ounce package

Canned tomatoes, 1 16-ounce can

Canned crushed pineapple, no sugar
   added, 1 8-ounce can

Evaporated skimmed milk, 1 13-fluid-
   ounce can

Prunes, large, 1 12-ounce box

Orange-flavored dietetic soda,
   1 12-fluid-ounce can

SUGGESTED EQUIPMENT LIST

Baking pan
Baking sheet
Blender
Bowls (small)
Can opener
Casserole (1-quart)
Chef's knife
Corer
Cutting board
Double boiler

Grater
Measuring cups
Measuring spoons
Metal spoon
Paring knife
Pot holder
Scale
Saucepans and covers (medium)
Vegetable peeler
Wooden spoon

HOT CHICKEN AND TOMATO BISQUE

1 cup diced celery
1 cup diced carrots
½ cup diced onion
2 packets instant chicken broth
   and seasoning mix
2 cups canned tomatoes, chopped
1½ cups water

½ teaspoon chopped fresh
   parsley
4 cloves
1 small bay leaf
⅛ teaspoon thyme
Salt and pepper to taste
½ cup evaporated skimmed milk

Combine celery, carrots, onion, and broth mix in medium saucepan. Cook 5 minutes, stirring frequently. Add tomatoes, water, parsley, cloves, bay leaf, thyme, salt, and pepper; bring to a boil. Reduce heat; cover and simmer 40 minutes. Remove and discard cloves and bay leaf. In batches, puree mixture in blender container. Return to saucepan; cook 3 minutes. Add milk; heat 5 minutes longer, but *do not boil*. Divide evenly into 4 large mugs. Makes 4 servings.

STUFFED EGGPLANT

2 medium eggplants, about 1
  pound each
1 cup diced zucchini
2 medium tomatoes, diced
½ cup diced onion
1 tablespoon chopped fresh
  parsley
2 packets instant chicken broth
  and seasoning mix

⅛ teaspoon garlic powder
Salt and pepper to taste
8 ounces diced cooked chicken
2 slices enriched white bread,
  made into crumbs
2 tablespoons imitation (or diet)
  margarine, melted

Cut each eggplant in half lengthwise. Scoop out pulp, leaving 4 shells, each about ½ inch thick. Dice pulp; place in medium saucepan. Add zucchini, tomatoes, onion, parsley, broth mix, garlic powder, salt, and pepper. Cook, stirring occasionally, 20 minutes or until vegetables are tender. Add chicken; cook 10 minutes longer. Spoon an equal amount of mixture into each eggplant shell. In small bowl combine bread crumbs and margarine; sprinkle an equal amount over each portion of chicken mixture. Place stuffed shells on baking sheet. Bake at 350°F. for 20 minutes or until topping is golden. Makes 4 servings.

CASSEROLE OF MIXED VEGETABLES AU GRATIN

2 slices enriched white bread,
  made into crumbs
2 tablespoons imitation (or diet)
  margarine
1 tablespoon plus 1 teaspoon
  flour
1 cup skim milk
4 ounces Swiss cheese, grated

½ teaspoon Worcestershire sauce
¼ teaspoon salt
⅛ teaspoon white pepper
⅛ teaspoon dry mustard
1 cup cooked diced carrots
½ cup cooked peas
½ cup cooked small white onions

Place bread crumbs in small bowl. Melt margarine in top of double boiler, over boiling water. Combine 1 tablespoon melted margarine with bread crumbs; set aside. Blend flour into remaining margarine; cook, stirring frequently, about 5 minutes. Stirring constantly, gradually add milk and cook until mixture thickens. Add cheese, Worcestershire, salt, pepper, and dry mustard. Continue to stir and cook until cheese melts. Combine carrots, peas, and onions in 1-quart casserole. Pour cheese mixture over vegetables; sprinkle with bread crumb mixture. Bake at 350°F. for 20 minutes or until topping is golden. Makes 4 servings.

PINEAPPLE-FILLED BAKED APPLES

4 small apples, cored
½ cup canned crushed pineapple,
  no sugar added, drain and
  reserve juice

½ cup orange-flavored dietetic
  soda
4 large prunes, pitted and
  finely diced

Pare apples from stem end, about ⅓ of the way down; place in baking pan. Fill each cavity with ¼ of the pineapple. In small bowl combine reserved pineapple juice, soda, and prunes; pour over apples. Bake at 350°F. for 40 minutes, basting frequently with pan juices. Makes 4 servings.

TRADITIONAL THANKSGIVING DINNER
FOR SIX

Spiced Mixed Fruit
Leek and Cauliflower Soup
Roast Turkey with Vegetable-Sage Dressing
Spinach-Topped Tomatoes
Lettuce Wedges with Chili-Russian Dressing
Pumpkin-Pineapple Pie with Whipped Topping
Beverage

Thanksgiving trimmings in trimming ways! That's our welcome menu motif. Serve old-fashioned roast turkey—a Thanksgiving tradition—but add a very modern touch. Today's nutrition-conscious chefs cook stuffing separately rather than inside the bird. Pumpkin has been a standby of the Thanksgiving table ever since that well-recorded first American banquet. But did you know the Pilgrims served pumpkins fresh from harvest, rather than as rich desserts? (Proving the proper Pilgrim folk knew a thing or two about proper eating!) Our version gives you the best of both worlds—a memorable pumpkin pie you won't have to pay for on the scale.

Why not grace your holiday table with other harvest treasures? A bowl or woven basket of dried leaves, pines, acorns, and berries adds a fragrant rustic centerpiece.

———————— •▪•— ————————

SUGGESTED SHOPPING LIST

Staples and Miscellaneous

Artificial sweetener
Chili powder
Cinnamon
Cinnamon sticks
Cloves
Dehydrated bell pepper flakes
Dehydrated onion flakes
Garlic salt
Instant chicken broth and seasoning
  mix
Nutmeg
Peppercorns
Pumpkin pie spice
Rosemary
Sage
Salt
Vanilla extract
White pepper

Nonfat dry milk powder
Nonstick cooking spray
Unflavored gelatin

Mayonnaise

Enriched white bread

Additional Items

Turkey, 1

Apples, 2 small
Lemon, 1
Oranges, 2 small

Carrot, 1 small
Celery, 1 stalk
Green beans, fresh or frozen French-
  style, 1 pound
Iceberg lettuce, 1 medium head
Leeks, ¾ pound
Mushrooms, 1 pound
Parsley, 1 bunch
Spinach, 2 pounds
Tomatoes, 3 medium

Frozen apricot halves, no sugar added,
  1 16-ounce bag
Frozen cauliflower, 3 10-ounce
  packages

Canned pineapple chunks, no sugar
  added, 1 20-ounce can

Canned pumpkin, 1 16-ounce can
Tomato puree, 1 16-ounce can

Evaporated skimmed milk, 2 13-fluid
  ounce cans

SUGGESTED EQUIPMENT LIST

Baking sheet
Blender
Bowls
Can opener
Casserole (1½-quart)
Chef's knife
Colander
Corer
Cutting board
Measuring cups

Measuring spoons
Meat thermometer
Pepper mill
Pot holder
Pie plate (9-inch)
Saucepans (small, medium, large)
Shallow roasting pan and rack
Slotted spoon
Vegetable peeler
Wooden spoon

SPICED MIXED FRUIT

8 frozen apricot halves, no sugar
added
½ cup water
Artificial sweetener to equal 6
teaspoons sugar
1 tablespoon lemon juice

2 cinnamon sticks
¼ teaspoon whole cloves
¼ teaspoon rosemary
2 small apples, cored and sliced
2 small oranges, peeled and
sectioned

Place apricots in bowl; allow to thaw. Drain juice from apricots into small saucepan; add water, sweetener, lemon juice, cinnamon sticks, cloves, and rosemary. Bring to a boil; reduce heat and simmer 10 minutes or until syrupy. Remove from heat and cool. Strain syrup into bowl over apricots, and discard spices. Add apples and oranges; mix well. Cover and chill. To serve, divide fruit and syrup evenly into 6 sherbet glasses. Makes 6 servings.

LEEK AND CAULIFLOWER SOUP

3 cups frozen cauliflower
2 cups thinly sliced leeks, white
portion only
½ cup chopped fresh parsley
6 packets instant chicken broth
and seasoning mix, dissolved
in 1½ quarts hot water

1 tablespoon dehydrated onion
flakes
1½ cups evaporated skimmed
milk
Salt and white pepper to taste
Dash nutmeg
Parsley sprigs to garnish

Combine first 5 ingredients in large saucepan; bring to a boil. Reduce heat and simmer about 10 minutes or until vegetables are tender. Using a slotted spoon, transfer vegetables to blender container; add 1 cup cooking liquid. Process until smooth. Return to saucepan containing remaining liquid. Add milk and seasonings; reheat but *do not boil*. Divide evenly into 6 soup bowls. Garnish each portion with parsley. Makes 6 servings.

ROAST TURKEY

Place turkey, breast side up, on rack in shallow roasting pan. Roast uncovered at 325°F. Allow about 20 minutes per pound for a turkey under 12 pounds and about 15 minutes per pound if over 12 pounds. If meat thermometer is used, insert in center of inner thigh muscle. Baste every ½ hour with mixture of dehydrated onion flakes, dehydrated bell pepper flakes, and chopped celery, cooked in 1½ cups chicken bouillon. When thermometer registers 180° to 185°F., turkey is done. Transfer to serving platter and garnish with parsley sprigs and 2 carrot curls (see page 13). When ready to serve, remove and discard skin; carve and weigh portions. Serve each guest 4 ounces sliced turkey.

VEGETABLE-SAGE DRESSING

3 cups sliced mushrooms
3 cups frozen French-style green
   beans, thawed and finely
   chopped
1½ cups diced celery
2 tablespoons dehydrated onion
   flakes

2 packets instant chicken broth
   and seasoning mix, dissolved
   in 2 cups hot water
1 teaspoon sage
Freshly ground pepper to taste
6 slices day-old enriched white
   bread,* cut into ½-inch cubes

In medium saucepan combine mushrooms, green beans, celery, onion flakes, and dissolved broth mix; cook until vegetables are tender and liquid has been reduced in volume to ½ cup. Add sage and pepper. Gently fold in bread and transfer to 1½-quart casserole that has been sprayed with nonstick cooking spray. Cover and bake at 325°F. for 25 to 30 minutes or until thoroughly heated. For drier stuffing, remove cover for last 5 to 7 minutes. Makes 6 servings.

* If using fresh bread, place on baking sheet and bake at 250°F. for 15 to 20 minutes or until dry.

SPINACH-TOPPED TOMATOES

1½ cups well-drained cooked
   chopped spinach
½ packet instant chicken broth
   and seasoning mix
¼ teaspoon nutmeg

Salt to taste
3 medium tomatoes, cut into
   halves crosswise
Freshly ground pepper to taste

Place spinach in medium bowl. Season with broth mix, nutmeg, and salt. Arrange tomato halves, cut side up, on baking sheet. Season with salt and pepper. Top each tomato half with ⅙ of the spinach mixture. Bake at 325°F. for 25 to 30 minutes or until tomatoes are tender but retain their snape. Arrange on platter or around Roast Turkey. Makes 6 servings.

LETTUCE WEDGES WITH CHILI-RUSSIAN DRESSING

¾ teaspoon chili powder
½ teaspoon water
3 tablespoons mayonnaise
3 tablespoons tomato puree

¼ teaspoon garlic salt
1 medium head iceberg lettuce,
   cut into 6 wedges, chilled

In small bowl or cup combine chili powder and water. In separate bowl blend mayonnaise, tomato puree, and garlic salt. Stir in chili powder mixture; mix until smooth. Let stand at least 30 minutes. Place 1 lettuce wedge on each of 6 salad plates. Just before serving pour ⅙ of dressing over each lettuce wedge. Makes 6 servings.

PUMPKIN-PINEAPPLE PIE
WITH WHIPPED TOPPING

*1½ cups canned pineapple
chunks, no sugar added,
drain and reserve juice*
1 envelope unflavored gelatin
2 tablespoons water
1 cup canned pumpkin
1 cup nonfat dry milk powder

*Artificial sweetener to equal 4
teaspoons sugar, or to taste*
½ teaspoon cinnamon
¼ teaspoon pumpkin pie spice
*3 recipes Whipped Topping (see
page 30)*

Pour ½ of reserved pineapple juice into blender container. Sprinkle gelatin over juice and allow to soften. Combine remaining pineapple juice and water in saucepan; heat until liquid begins to boil. Pour into blender container; process 30 seconds or until gelatin dissolves. Add remaining ingredients except Whipped Topping; process until smooth. Transfer to 9-inch pie pan that has been sprayed with nonstick cooking spray. Tap pan on counter several times to level top and release air bubbles. Refrigerate until set. Top evenly with Whipped Topping. Makes 6 servings.

THANKSGIVING SANS TURKEY FOR SIX

Mixed Vegetable Juice
Roast Cornish Hens with Spiced Apricot Sauce
Crisp-Baked Potatoes with Lemon "Butter"
Creamed Onions
Eggplant Provençal
Bananas in Orange Sauce
Beverage

The Pilgrims' famed Thanksgiving feast lasted for three days, but turkeys never appeared on the menu! There's no rule that says you have to serve them either—so for an off-the-beaten "course," substitute one of America's favorite poultry dishes: Rock Cornish hen. You can enlighten your guests with the fascinating food fact that Cornish hens are actually most appropriate for the holiday, since the breed originated as a cross between Plymouth Rock hens and various other small game! In your sophisticated menu, the hens are spiced with a sauce flavored with an ancient Eastern fruit: apricot. Baked potatoes are a filling Western accompaniment and, as an energy saver, can be cooked in the oven at the same time as your entrée. Eggplant Provençal brings the flavor of the Old World to an American table. Thanksgiving became a national holiday via President Lincoln's proclamation to "observe the blessings of fruitful fields." Bananas in Orange Sauce is an appropriately fruitful dish to top off this festive feast served in ample (but not too ample!) style.

———◆•◆———

SUGGESTED SHOPPING LIST

Staples and Miscellaneous

Artificial sweetener	Marjoram
Basil	Nutmeg
Cinnamon sticks	Oregano
Cloves	Paprika
Garlic powder	Pepper
Instant chicken broth and seasoning	Salt
mix or bouillon cubes	Thyme
	Cornstarch
	Flour
	Margarine

Cornish hens, 3, 1½ pounds each

Skim milk, 1 cup

Bananas, 3 medium
Lemon, 1

Garlic cloves, 3
Eggplants, 3 medium (about 1 pound each)
Parsley, 1 bunch
Potatoes, 6, 4 ounces each

Frozen orange juice concentrate, 1 6-fluid-ounce can

Frozen pearl onions, 2 16-ounce bags

Canned apricot halves, no sugar added, 1 16-ounce can

Canned crushed tomatoes, 1 16-ounce can

Mixed vegetable juice, 2 32-fluid-ounce cans

Dietetic ginger ale, 1 12-fluid-ounce can

SUGGESTED EQUIPMENT LIST

Baking dish (shallow)
Baster
Bowl (small)
Can opener
Chef's knife
Cutting board
Double boiler
Kitchen spoon
Measuring cups

Measuring spoons
Nonstick baking sheet
Pot holder
Roasting pan and rack
Saucepans (medium)
Scale
Wire whisk
Wooden spoons

MIXED VEGETABLE JUICE

Serve ½ cup chilled mixed vegetable juice to each person. Garnish each with a lemon wedge.

ROAST CORNISH HENS WITH SPICED APRICOT SAUCE

3 Cornish hens, 1½ pounds each
Salt, white pepper, garlic powder, and paprika to taste
¾ cup chicken bouillon
6 canned apricot halves with 3 tablespoons juice, no sugar added
½ cup dietetic ginger ale

Artificial sweetener to equal 1 teaspoon sugar
¼ cinnamon stick
¼ teaspoon lemon juice
1 clove
2 teaspoons cornstarch, dissolved in 1 tablespoon water

Rub hens with salt, pepper, garlic powder, and paprika. Place on rack in roasting pan; roast at 350°F. for 45 minutes or until done. Baste occasionally with bouillon. While hens are roasting, slice each apricot half into 3 strips; set aside. Combine juice from apricots, ginger ale, sweetener, cinnamon stick, lemon juice, and clove in small saucepan. Cook 10 minutes. Add dissolved cornstarch and cook, stirring often, until mixture thickens. Add sliced apricots; continue to stir and cook until apricots are heated and thoroughly coated with sauce. To serve, cut each hen in half; remove and discard skin. Place each half on a plate and top with ⅙ of the apricot sauce. Makes 6 servings.

CRISP-BAKED POTATOES WITH LEMON "BUTTER"

These can be baked at the same time as Cornish hens.

2 tablespoons margarine
½ teaspoon chopped fresh
  parsley
½ teaspoon lemon juice
6 potatoes, 4 ounces each

In small bowl combine first 3 ingredients; refrigerate. Scrub potatoes. Bake at 350°F. for 30 to 40 minutes or until tender. Cut slit in top of each potato. Divide Lemon "Butter" into 6 equal portions. Place 1 portion in each hot potato. Makes 6 servings.

CREAMED ONIONS

2 tablespoons margarine
2 tablespoons flour
1 cup skim milk
3 cups cooked frozen pearl
  onions
¼ teaspoon paprika
¼ teaspoon thyme
Dash nutmeg
Salt and pepper to taste

In top of double boiler, over boiling water, melt margarine. Stir in flour; cook for 2 minutes. Stirring with wire whisk, gradually add milk. Cook, stirring often, until thickened. Add remaining ingredients; cook for 15 minutes, stirring often. Makes 6 servings.

EGGPLANT PROVENÇAL

3 medium eggplants, about 1
  pound each
3 garlic cloves, minced
1 cup canned crushed tomatoes
1½ teaspoons basil
1 teaspoon oregano
¼ teaspoon marjoram
3 tablespoons chopped fresh
  parsley

Cut each eggplant in half lengthwise. Scoop out pulp; reserve shells. Cut pulp into ½-inch dice. In medium saucepan cook garlic for 2 minutes, stirring constantly. Add diced eggplant, crushed tomatoes, basil, oregano, and marjoram. Cook for 15 minutes, stirring often. Divide eggplant mixture evenly into eggplant shells. Place in nonstick baking pan; bake at 350°F. for 30 minutes. Garnish each half with 1½ teaspoons parsley. Makes 6 servings.

BANANAS IN ORANGE SAUCE

¾ cup orange juice
2 teaspoons cornstarch,
   dissolved in 3 tablespoons
   freshly squeezed lemon juice

2 tablespoons margarine
3 medium bananas
Dash nutmeg

Pour orange juice into saucepan and bring to a boil. Stir in cornstarch mixture. Cook, stirring constantly, until thickened. Remove from heat. Stir in margarine. Cut each banana in half lengthwise, then in half again, crosswise. Arrange banana quarters in a shallow baking dish. Spoon sauce over bananas. Bake at 350°F. for 20 minutes or until bananas are tender. Makes 6 servings.

THANKS AGAIN—TURKEY ANOTHER WAY FOR SIX

Turkey Broth
"Waldorf" Salad
Turkey Salad
Pumpkin Pie with Whipped Topping
Beverage

Exhausted from holiday hosting? Make life easier for yourself by serving leftovers in rewardingly un-leftover style. The turkey carcass won't go to waste (or to waist!) in this hearty broth. You can make the meat go a long way, too, economically stretched with eggs, bread, and vegetables into a nourishing salad. The original Waldorf Salad gained fame during the 1890s at Manhattan's elite Waldorf Hotel; you can create a welcome duplicate of that long-popular treat with harvest fruits. Except for the Whipped Topping, the Pumpkin Pie—a lingering reminder of Thanksgiving—can actually be prepared in advance of the holiday. On the other hand, if you're turkeyed-out, convert leftovers into "plan-overs" by freezing the bird and planning to have this luncheon in the near future when the memory of your Thanksgiving table isn't quite so vivid. Either way, this adds up to an easygoing menu your family will be thankful for.

———————— •••• ————————

SUGGESTED SHOPPING LIST

Staples and Miscellaneous

Artificial sweetener
Bay leaves
Cinnamon
Peppercorns
Pumpkin pie spice
Salt
Sesame seeds
Thyme
Vanilla extract

Chili sauce

Flour
Unflavored gelatin

Imitation mayonnaise
Margarine

Enriched white bread
Raisin bread

Additional Items

Eggs, 6
Cooked boneless turkey, ¾ pound
Turkey carcass, 1

Plain unflavored yogurt, 1 8-ounce
    container

Apples, 4 small
Lemon, 1

Cabbage, 1 small head
Celery, 5 ribs
Cherry tomatoes, 1 pint
Green pepper, 1 medium
Lettuce, 1 head

Onion, 1
Parsley, 1 bunch

Canned grapefruit sections, no sugar
    added, 2 16-ounce cans

Canned pumpkin, 1 16-ounce can
Canned water chestnuts, 1 8-ounce
    can

Evaporated skimmed milk, 2 13-fluid-
    ounce cans

Prunes, large, 1 12-ounce box

SUGGESTED EQUIPMENT LIST

Bowls (large)
Chef's knife
Cutting board
Fork
Measuring cups
Measuring spoons

Large pot with cover
Pot holder
Saucepan (medium)
Strainer
Wire whisk
Wooden spoon

TURKEY BROTH

1 turkey carcass, cut up
3 quarts water
2 celery ribs with leaves, sliced
9 peppercorns

5 parsley sprigs
1½ bay leaves
¼ teaspoon thyme, or to taste
Salt to taste

Combine all ingredients in large pot. Bring to a boil; reduce heat. Simmer
for 1¾ hours. Strain to remove solids. Refrigerate liquid until fat congeals
on top; remove and discard congealed fat. Measure 1 quart plus ½ cup
broth;* pour into saucepan and heat. Makes 6 servings.

* Any remaining broth can be measured and frozen for use at another time.

"WALDORF" SALAD

*4 small apples, pared, cored, and
    diced*
2 teaspoons lemon juice
¾ cup diced celery
*¼ cup plus 2 tablespoons
    imitation mayonnaise*
*6 large prunes, pitted and
    diced*

*⅓ cup drained canned water
    chestnuts, sliced*
¼ teaspoon cinnamon
Dash salt
*1½ teaspoons sesame seeds,
    toasted*
*3 cups grapefruit sections, no
    sugar added*

Chill 6 salad plates. Place apples in large salad bowl. Sprinkle with lemon juice and toss to coat apples. Add remaining ingredients except sesame seeds and grapefruit; toss to combine. Sprinkle with sesame seeds. Divide evenly onto chilled plates. Surround each serving of salad with ½ cup grapefruit sections. Makes 6 servings.

TURKEY SALAD

12 ounces sliced cooked turkey,
    cut into thin strips
4 eggs, hard-cooked and chopped
½ cup shredded cabbage
¼ cup plus 2 tablespoons plain
    unflavored yogurt
⅓ cup finely diced onion
½ medium green pepper, seeded
    and finely chopped

2 tablespoons chili sauce
1 teaspoon lemon juice
Salt to taste
Lettuce leaves
15 cherry tomatoes, cut into
    halves
3 slices enriched white bread,
    toasted and diced

In bowl combine first 9 ingredients; chill. When ready to serve, place bed of lettuce leaves on serving platter; mound salad on lettuce leaves. Garnish with cherry tomatoes and bread cubes. Makes 6 servings.

PUMPKIN PIE WITH WHIPPED TOPPING

Filling:

1⅓ cups canned pumpkin
2 eggs, slightly beaten
Artificial sweetener to equal 4
    teaspoons sugar

1½ teaspoons pumpkin pie spice
1 teaspoon vanilla extract
Dash cinnamon
¾ cup evaporated skimmed milk

Crust:

3 slices raisin bread, toasted and
    made into crumbs
1 tablespoon flour

¼ teaspoon each pumpkin pie
    spice and vanilla extract
2 tablespoons margarine

Topping:

3 recipes Whipped Topping (see page 30)

To Prepare Filling: In bowl, stirring with wire whisk, combine first 6 ingredients. Add milk, stirring constantly.

To Prepare Crust: In another bowl combine next 3 ingredients. Add margarine; stir with fork until mixture forms little balls about the size of small peas. Mound mixture in center of 8-inch pie pan. Using the back of a teaspoon, which has been moistened with water, spread mixture outward to cover bottom and sides of pan.

To Prepare Pie: Pour filling into crust. Bake at 400°F. for 40 minutes or until a knife, when inserted in center, comes out clean. Cool.

To Serve: Divide pie evenly onto 6 serving plates. Top each portion with ⅙ of the Whipped Topping. Makes 6 servings.

December

When Jack Frost starts nipping at your nose, come in from the cold to one of our festive holiday meals. Our December menus are filled with holiday cheer—and you'll cheer when you step on the scale. Then bid the year adieu in guilt-free contentment with a Bon Voyage Dinner.

PURSE-STRING LUNCHEON WITH PANACHE FOR FOUR

Vegetable Garden Salad with Tangy Dressing
Baked Ziti and Eggplant Sicilian Style
Cherry-Pear Chiffon
Percolator Espresso

Easy on your budget and possible on a hectic pre-holiday schedule, this simple vegetarian-style luncheon economically avoids costly meat yet can be served with culinary style. Pasta shows nutritional know-how, and eggplant provides a highly satisfying vegetable filling. Combined, they thriftily stretch your meal—without stretching your figure. As a time saver, the dish can be prepared in advance and warmed up in the oven before serving. Accompany your entrée with an aromatic salad, kept inexpensive by taking advantage of vegetables in season all year and made interesting by the addition of blanched broccoli. Your meal *looks* expensive without *being* so. The mouth-watering dessert is just as deceptive, for who would believe this chiffon treat isn't fattening? It saves last-minute rushing, too, since it can be prepared earlier in the day with easily available canned fruits. As you'll discover, this low-budget menu supplies appealing aromas and appearance as well as tastiness. Top it off with a Continental touch—espresso. No one need ever know it was brewed in your everyday percolator! A most enjoyable luncheon that trims pennies as well as pounds.

———————— ••• ————————

SUGGESTED SHOPPING LIST

Staples and Miscellaneous

Almond extract
Artificial sweetener (optional)
Basil
Cinnamon
Garlic powder
Oregano

Pepper
Salt
Tarragon

Cider vinegar

Ground espresso coffee
Nonfat dry milk powder
Unflavored gelatin

Imitation mayonnaise

Additional Items

Grated Parmesan or Romano cheese, 1 6-ounce container

Part skim ricotta cheese, 1 16-ounce container

Plain unflavored yogurt, 1 16-ounce container

Lemon, 1 medium

Broccoli, 1 medium bunch
Cucumber, 1 medium
Eggplant, 1 medium
Mushrooms, 1 pound

Parsley, 1 bunch
Radishes, 1 bag
Scallions, 6
Tomato, 1 medium

Canned pear halves, no sugar added, 1 16-ounce can
Canned pitted cherries, no sugar added, 1 16-ounce can

Tomato sauce, 1 28-ounce can

Enriched ziti, 1 16-ounce box

SUGGESTED EQUIPMENT LIST

Blender
Bowls (small, medium)
Broiler pan
Can opener
Casserole with cover (2½-quart)
Chef's knife
Colander
Cutting board
Measuring cups
Measuring spoons

Paper towels
Paring knife
Percolator
Pot holder
Saucepans (medium)
Scale
Shallow container (1-quart)
Spatula
Wooden spoon

VEGETABLE GARDEN SALAD WITH TANGY DRESSING

2¼ cups broccoli florets
1½ cups sliced mushrooms
1 medium cucumber, pared and sliced
1 medium tomato, cut into wedges

¾ cup scallions
¼ cup sliced radishes
Tangy Dressing (see recipe, page 321)

In medium saucepan blanch broccoli in boiling salted water for 2 minutes or until bright green. Drain immediately; place in cold water to cool. Drain. Arrange broccoli and remaining vegetables on serving platter. Serve with Tangy Dressing. Makes 4 servings.

Tangy Dressing

1 cup plain unflavored yogurt
¼ cup imitation mayonnaise
1 tablespoon cider vinegar
2 teaspoons chopped fresh
  parsley

¾ teaspoon tarragon
Dash salt

Combine all ingredients in small bowl. Chill. Serve as directed in recipe for Vegetable Garden Salad (see recipe, page 320).

BAKED ZITI AND EGGPLANT SICILIAN STYLE

4 cups thinly sliced, pared
  eggplant, about 1 pound
Salt, pepper, and garlic powder
  to taste
1⅓ cups part skim ricotta cheese
4 ounces grated Romano or
  Parmesan cheese, divided

1 teaspoon chopped fresh
  parsley
½ teaspoon basil
½ teaspoon oregano
2⅔ cups cooked enriched ziti
2 cups tomato sauce

Sprinkle eggplant slices with salt; let drain 30 minutes. Rinse and pat dry with paper towels. Season with salt, pepper, and garlic powder. Place slices in one layer in broiler pan; broil 4 inches from source of heat until golden, turning once. In medium bowl combine ricotta cheese, 2 ounces grated cheese, parsley, basil, oregano, salt, pepper, and garlic powder; fold in ziti. Spread thin layer of tomato sauce over bottom of 2½-quart casserole. Add a layer of ½ the ziti mixture; top with ½ the eggplant slices, ½ the remaining sauce, and 1 ounce grated cheese; repeat layers. Cover and bake at 400°F. for 30 minutes; uncover. Bake 15 minutes longer or until cheese is lightly browned. Makes 4 servings.

CHERRY-PEAR CHIFFON

½ cup canned pitted cherries, no
  sugar added
4 canned pear halves with ¼ cup
  juice, no sugar added
1 envelope unflavored gelatin
1 cup boiling water

⅓ cup nonfat dry milk powder
Artificial sweetener to equal 4
  teaspoons sugar
⅛ teaspoon almond extract
Dash cinnamon
4 ice cubes

Drain juice from cherries into blender container; add pear juice and 2 pear halves; reserve cherries and remaining pear halves. Process until smooth. Sprinkle gelatin over fruit juice mixture; allow to soften. Add boiling water; process until gelatin is dissolved. Add remaining ingredients except ice cubes and reserved fruit; process until smooth. Add ice cubes, 1 at a time, processing after each addition until smooth. Pour into shallow container; chill until slightly thickened. Dice reserved pear halves; fold cherries and diced pears into gelatin mixture. Chill until firm. Divide evenly into 4 dessert dishes. Makes 4 servings.

PERCOLATOR ESPRESSO

No special equipment is needed, but if you do have the little silver pot called a macchinetta, by all means use it. In our recipe, espresso is made in a standard percolator.

> ¼ cup plus 2 tablespoons ground   4 twists lemon rind
>   espresso coffee   Artificial sweetener to taste
> 3 cups cold water   (optional)

Place ground espresso coffee in percolator basket; set aside. Pour water into percolator. Bring to a boil; remove from heat. Insert basket in percolator. Cover; return to heat. Allow to percolate 6 to 8 minutes. Remove from heat. Discard coffee grounds and serve. Garnish each portion with a lemon twist and serve with sweetener if desired. Makes 4 servings.

HANNUKAH LUNCHEON FOR FOUR

Tossed Salad with Lemon Dressing
Cabbage Soup with Garlic Sticks
Potato Latkes with "Sour Cream" and Apple-Peach Topping
Coffee or Tea

Hanukkah . . . beloved festival of lights, laughter—and latkes! The holiday's meals are traditionally dairy dishes, and this festive menu enables you to serve up the old customs with new embellishments. Both the Potato Latkes and the equally ritual Cabbage Soup are made with a clever buttermilk adaptation of sour cream, and Garlic Sticks provide a novel accompaniment. Lemon juice adds a pleasant aroma to the salad and the Apple-Peach Topping on the latkes is a most appealing bonus. At Hanukkah, children whirl dreidels in lively games of chance. Isn't it winning to be able to enjoy a festival without having to take chances with your good resolutions?

SUGGESTED SHOPPING LIST

Staples and Miscellaneous

Caraway seeds
Chopped chives
Cinnamon stick
Garlic salt
Instant chicken broth and seasoning
   mix
Salt
White pepper

Coffee or tea
Matzo meal

Imitation mayonnaise
Imitation (or diet) margarine
Vegetable oil

Enriched white bread

Additional Items

Buttermilk, ¼ cup
Cottage cheese, 1 16-ounce container
Eggs, 4

Apples, Delicious, 2 small
Lemon, 1

Cabbage, 1 head
Iceberg lettuce, 1 medium head

Onion, 1 medium
Potatoes, 1 pound
Radishes, 1 bag
Watercress, 1 bunch

Canned sliced peaches, no sugar
   added, 1 16-ounce can

Pimientos, 1 4-ounce jar

[323]

Baking sheet
Blender
Bowls (large salad, medium)
Chef's knife
Colander
Cutting board
Grater
Measuring cups
Measuring spoons

Paper towels
Pot holder
Saucepans (small, medium)
Scale
Spatula
Spreading knife
Strainer
Wooden spoons

TOSSED SALAD WITH LEMON DRESSING

Salad:

1 medium head iceberg lettuce
1 bunch watercress

½ cup sliced radishes
1 tablespoon chopped chives

Dressing:

1 tablespoon plus 1½ teaspoons
    vegetable oil
1 tablespoon imitation
    mayonnaise

1 teaspoon lemon juice
1 teaspoon water
1 teaspoon diced pimiento
Salt to taste

To Prepare Salad: Remove base from lettuce; break off leaves. Wash well and drain. Wash watercress and pat dry with paper towel. Tear lettuce and watercress into bite-size pieces. Combine in large salad bowl; add radishes and chives. Chill.

To Prepare Dressing: Combine all ingredients except pimiento and salt in blender container; process until smooth. Add pimiento and season to taste.

To Serve: Pour dressing over salad; toss to combine. Makes 4 servings.

CABBAGE SOUP

Serve with Garlic Sticks (see recipe, page 325).

4 cups shredded cabbage
1 cup sliced onion
4 packets instant chicken broth
    and seasoning mix

½ teaspoon caraway seeds
1 quart water
½ cup "Sour Cream" (see recipe,
    page 325)

Combine cabbage, onion, broth mix, and caraway seeds in medium saucepan. Cook, stirring often, until vegetables are tender. Add water. Bring to a boil; reduce heat and simmer for 20 minutes, stirring occasionally. Divide cabbage soup evenly into 4 soup bowls. Top each portion of soup with 2 tablespoons "Sour Cream." Makes 4 servings.

GARLIC STICKS

Serve with Cabbage Soup (see recipe, page 324).

> 2 slices enriched white bread, cut in half horizontally to make 4 thin slices
>
> 1 tablespoon plus 1 teaspoon imitation (or diet) margarine
> Garlic salt to taste

Spread each thin slice of bread with 1 teaspoon margarine. Sprinkle each with garlic salt. Cut each slice into 4 equal sticks. Place on baking sheet, margarine side up; bake at 250°F. until crisp. Makes 4 servings.

POTATO LATKES WITH "SOUR CREAM" AND APPLE-PEACH TOPPING

> 2 slices enriched white bread, torn into pieces
> 4 eggs
> 1 pound pared potatoes, coarsely grated
> 1/3 cup minced onion
> 2 tablespoons matzo meal
>
> 1 tablespoon plus 1 teaspoon vegetable oil
> Salt and white pepper to taste
> 1 cup "Sour Cream" (see following recipe)
> Apple-Peach Topping (see recipe, page 326)

Preheat oven to 450°F. In blender container combine bread and eggs; process until smooth. Pour into medium bowl. Set aside. Place grated potatoes into strainer. Squeeze out excess moisture with back of spoon. Add potatoes, onion, matzo meal, oil, salt, and pepper to egg mixture; stir to combine. Drop rounded 1/4 cup of mixture onto nonstick baking sheet that has been sprayed with nonstick cooking spray. Flatten to form a round pancake. Repeat with remaining mixture. Bake latkes for 5 to 8 minutes or until browned on bottom. Remove from oven and carefully turn with spatula. Return to oven and bake for 5 minutes longer or until other side browns. Divide latkes into 4 equal servings. Top each serving with 1/4 cup "Sour Cream" and 1 portion Apple-Peach Topping. Makes 4 servings.

"Sour Cream"

Serve with Cabbage Soup and Potato Latkes (see recipes, page 324 and above).

> 1 1/3 cups cottage cheese
> 1/4 cup buttermilk
>
> 2 teaspoons lemon juice

Combine all ingredients in blender container. Process until smooth. Chill at least 1 hour. Serve as directed in recipes for Cabbage Soup and Potato Latkes.

Apple-Peach Topping

Serve with Potato Latkes (see recipe, page 325).

2 small Delicious apples, pared, cored, and diced	¼ cup water
1 cup canned sliced peaches, no sugar added	1 cinnamon stick
	Dash salt

Combine all ingredients in small saucepan. Bring to a boil; reduce heat and simmer for 15 minutes, stirring often. Remove cinnamon stick. Chill at least 1 hour. Divide into 4 equal portions. Serve as directed in recipe for Potato Latkes.

A CHRISTMAS EVE BUFFET FOR TWELVE

Mushrooms in Soy Sauce Vinaigrette
Roasted Fresh Ham
Artichoke Hearts and Wild Rice Casserole
Puree of Carrots in Orange Cups
Apple "Crème"
Beverage

> "So well doth the weather
> And our stomachs agree . . ."

. . . So exults a seventeenth-century Christmas melody that jubilantly sings of holiday dishes! Your guests will go home singing, too, when they feast on your elaborate (but conveniently easy) buffet. Ham is a holiday tradition and a popular buffet item since it is so easy to serve. As an unexpected addition, artichokes appear on your party table. They're *not* traditional, but perhaps they should be, for they add an elegant note. Buffet foods should be selected with thought as to how easily they can be handled. Orange Cups are a clever touch, since any food served in cup form is easier for guests to maneuver. It is also easier for you, since you can pre-measure the amounts. And special presentations like these attractive cups say to your guests: "I went to extra effort for you." Just make sure those extra efforts are completed well in advance to avoid party-day panic! Since apples harmonize with ham (as well as with pork and lamb), our Apple "Crème" parfait is a perfect finish.

Staples and Miscellaneous

Artificial sweetener	Red wine vinegar
Basil	Soy sauce
Cinnamon	
Garlic powder	Nonfat dry milk powder
Ginger	Unflavored gelatin
Instant chicken broth and seasoning	
mix	Imitation (or diet) margarine
Pepper	Vegetable oil
Peppercorns	
Salt	
Thyme	
Vanilla extract	

Additional Items

Fresh ham, cut from the shank portion, 7½ to 8 pounds	Frozen artichoke hearts, 3 10-ounce packages
Lemons, 3	Applesauce, no sugar added, 1 15-ounce jar
Oranges, 6 small	
Red apple, 1 small	
	Enriched white rice, 1 16-ounce box
Carrots, 16 medium	Wild rice, 1 16-ounce box
Garlic cloves, 4	
Mushrooms, 2¼ pounds	

SUGGESTED EQUIPMENT LIST

Blender or food processor	Metal spoon
Bowls (medium)	Pepper mill
Can opener	Pot holder
Casserole (2-quart)	Saucepans (medium)
Chef's knife	Scale
Cutting board	Shallow baking pans, 2 (9 x 12 inches)
Kitchen fork	and 1 rack
Measuring cups	Wooden spoon
Measuring spoons	

MUSHROOMS IN SOY SAUCE VINAIGRETTE

½ cup red wine vinegar
3 tablespoons vegetable oil
2 tablespoons soy sauce
⅛ teaspoon basil
⅛ teaspoon garlic powder
⅛ teaspoon pepper
6 cups sliced mushrooms

In salad bowl combine vinegar, oil, soy sauce, basil, garlic powder, and pepper. Add mushrooms; toss to coat. Marinate mushrooms in refrigerator for at least 3 hours. Makes 12 servings.

ROASTED FRESH HAM

1 fresh ham, cut from the shank
    portion, 7½ to 8 pounds
4 garlic cloves, minced
2 teaspoons salt

1 teaspoon freshly ground
    pepper, medium grind
½ teaspoon ginger

Score ham. In a cup or using a mortar and pestle, combine garlic and salt to make a paste; mix in pepper and ginger. With tip of sharp pointed knife make slits in ham and fill with garlic mixture. Spread remaining mixture over scored ham. Insert meat thermometer in center of largest lean muscle, not touching bone. Place ham on rack in roasting pan and roast at 325°F. for 35 to 40 minutes per pound or until thermometer registers 170°F. Slice and serve each guest 4 ounces ham. Makes 12 servings.

ARTICHOKE HEARTS AND WILD RICE CASSEROLE

6 cups frozen artichoke hearts,
    thawed
3 cups cooked enriched rice
3 cups cooked wild rice
4 packets instant chicken broth
    and seasoning mix

3 cups boiling water
1 teaspoon thyme
¼ cup imitation (or diet)
    margarine

Combine artichokes and rice in 2-quart casserole. In medium bowl dissolve broth mix in water; stir in thyme. Pour over rice mixture. Bake at 325°F. for 30 minutes. Dot evenly with margarine. Bake 10 minutes longer. Makes 12 servings.

PUREE OF CARROTS IN ORANGE CUPS

8 cups cooked sliced carrots
¼ cup imitation (or diet)
    margarine, melted
Artificial sweetener to equal 1
    teaspoon sugar

1 teaspoon lemon juice
¼ teaspoon cinnamon
Salt and pepper to taste
12 orange cups (see Note)
12 lemon slices

Puree carrots in food mill, food processor, or blender container. Place in bowl. Stir in margarine, sweetener, lemon juice, cinnamon, salt, and pepper. Spoon an equal amount of mixture into each Orange Cup. Fluff tops with fork. Place in shallow baking pan. Bake at 325°F. for 15 minutes. Garnish each Orange Cup with a lemon slice. Makes 12 servings.

Note: To make 12 Orange Cups, 6 small oranges are needed. Several weeks before Christmas, as you use oranges, start collecting orange shells. Cut oranges in half crosswise. Remove fruit from skin with a grapefruit knife, leaving skin intact; scrape insides of shells clean. Store in freezer in plastic bags.

APPLE "CRÈME"

2 envelopes unflavored gelatin
½ cup cold water, divided
½ cup boiling water, divided
1 cup applesauce, no sugar
  added, divided
1⅓ cups nonfat dry milk
  powder, divided

Artificial sweetener to equal 12
  teaspoons sugar, divided
2 teaspoons vanilla extract,
  divided
¼ teaspoon cinnamon, divided
12 ice cubes
1 small red apple

In blender container sprinkle 1 envelope gelatin over ¼ cup cold water; allow gelatin to soften. Add ¼ cup boiling water; process until gelatin is dissolved. Add ½ cup applesauce; process to combine. Add ⅔ cup dry milk, sweetener to equal 6 teaspoons sugar, 1 teaspoon vanilla, and ⅛ teaspoon cinnamon; process until smooth. Add 6 ice cubes, 1 at a time, processing after each addition until all ice is crushed; pour into large serving bowl. Repeat procedure; chill. When ready to serve, core and dice apple. Garnish chilled mixture with diced apple. Makes 12 servings.

CHRISTMAS DAY BREAKFAST FOR EIGHT

Shampaign Punch
Christmas Scramble
Garlicky Potato Slices
Peach Sherbet with Strawberry Sauce
Hot Coffee or Tea

Play Santa by hosting a Christmas Day Breakfast that's a gift in itself. Invite figure-conscious friends to drink to the occasion with a sparkling substitute for champagne served in elegant wine glasses. "Scramble" for compliments by adding Christmas colorings of red (tomatoes) and green (parsley) to dress up morning eggs. Garlicky Potato Slices—ruddy with paprika—make a festive alternative to toast. Delight children of all ages by serving sherbet for breakfast. This one takes Strawberry Sauce—also a vivid Christmas red! Don't miss the chance to carry out your color game in the tablecloth and napkins . . . and how about leaving a fun memento beside each person's plate? What a rosy beginning to a memorable day!

——————◆•◆——————

SUGGESTED SHOPPING LIST

Staples and Miscellaneous

Artificial sweetener
Garlic powder
Paprika
Vanilla extract

Coffee or tea

Imitation (or diet) margarine

Additional Items

Eggs, 8

Lemon, 1

Onion, 1 small
Parsley, 1 bunch
Tomatoes, 2 medium

Frozen strawberries, no sugar added,
1 16-ounce package

Black-cherry-flavored dietetic soda,
1 28-fluid-ounce bottle

Dietetic ginger ale, 1 28-fluid-ounce
bottle
Sparkling mineral water, 1 23-fluid-
ounce bottle

Canned sliced peaches, no sugar
added, 2 16-ounce cans

Canned potatoes, 2 28-ounce cans

Evaporated skimmed milk, 1 13-fluid-
ounce can

Aluminum foil
Blender
Bowls (medium, large)
Can opener
Casserole (shallow, 2½-quart)
Chef's knife
Cutting board
Double boiler

Electric mixer
Freezer container (shallow)
Measuring cups
Measuring spoons
Pot holder
Punch bowl
Scale
Wooden spoons

SHAMPAIGN PUNCH

3 cups chilled black-cherry-
    flavored dietetic soda
3 cups chilled dietetic ginger ale

2 cups chilled sparkling mineral
    water

In punch bowl combine all ingredients. Serve immediately. Makes 8 servings.

CHRISTMAS SCRAMBLE

¼ cup imitation (or diet)
    margarine
⅓ cup minced onion
1 tablespoon chopped fresh
    parsley

8 eggs
⅛ teaspoon garlic powder
2 medium tomatoes, diced

In top of double boiler, over boiling water, melt margarine. Add onion and parsley. Cook until onion is tender. Combine eggs and garlic powder in medium bowl and beat. Add to onion mixture and cook, stirring constantly, until done to taste. Transfer to serving dish and top with diced tomatoes. Makes 8 servings.

GARLICKY POTATO SLICES

2 pounds drained canned
    potatoes, cut into ¼-inch
    slices
¼ cup imitation (or diet)
    margarine

¼ teaspoon paprika
¼ teaspoon garlic powder

Combine all ingredients in a shallow 2½-quart casserole. Bake at 425°F. for 30 minutes. Makes 8 servings.

PEACH SHERBET WITH STRAWBERRY SAUCE

Sherbet:

3 cups canned sliced peaches, no
    sugar added
1 cup evaporated skimmed milk

1 tablespoon lemon juice
3 cups ice cubes, divided

Sauce:

2 cups frozen strawberries, no
    sugar added, thawed
Artificial sweetener to equal 12
    teaspoons sugar

1 teaspoon vanilla extract

To Prepare Sherbet: Combine peaches, milk, and lemon juice in medium bowl. Pour ½ of mixture into blender container; process until pureed. Continue to process and add 1½ cups ice cubes, 1 ice cube at a time. Process until ice is crushed. Pour into shallow freezer container. Repeat with remaining peach mixture. Cover container with aluminum foil and place in freezer. Stir every ½ hour, until mixture is completely frozen. Scrape into large bowl. Beat with electric mixer for about 1 minute. Divide evenly into 8 balls. Freeze 1 hour longer.

To Prepare Sauce: Combine strawberries, sweetener, and vanilla in blender container; process until smooth. Chill.

To Serve: Place each sherbet ball in a dessert dish. Top each with ⅛ of the Strawberry Sauce. Makes 8 servings.

CHRISTMAS DINNER FOR SIX

Hot Tomato Bouillon
Parsley Roast Leg of Lamb
Caper Sauce
Creamy Baked Potatoes
Tasty Green Beans
Season's Greetings Salad with Mushroom Dressing
Pineapple-Berry Parfait with "Crème" Fluff
Beverage

Here's a holiday feast guaranteed to brighten Yule spirits. First warm up shivering arrivals with spicily flavored hot bouillon. Tomato juice goes well with almost anything—especially the holiday, since it's appropriately Christmas red. Lamb is a festive roast and makes a most attractive entrée when well garnished. The delicate flavor should never be overwhelmed by elaborate sauces. Instead, we suggest our version of Caper Sauce, the traditional accompaniment. Gift your guests with Season's Greetings Salad, a whimsical mixture of Yuletide reds and greens! The Christmas colors hold fast in our selection of green beans. After such a hearty repast, fluffy parfait is a welcome present for figures as well as palates.

For all four of our Christmas menus, we suggest a decor that carries out the holiday theme in brilliant Yuletide tones.

———— •◆• ————

SUGGESTED SHOPPING LIST

Staples and Miscellaneous

Artificial sweetener
Bay leaves
Chervil
Chili powder
Chopped chives
Cloves
Imitation butter flavoring
Instant beef broth and seasoning mix
Onion powder
Paprika
Peppercorns
Pineapple extract
Raspberry or cherry extract
Rosemary
Salt
Vanilla extract
White pepper

Browning sauce
Capers
Hot sauce
Prepared mustard
Wine vinegar
Worcestershire sauce

Nonfat dry milk powder
Unflavored gelatin

Vegetable oil

Additional Items

Leg of lamb, 1 (5 pounds)

Plain unflavored yogurt, 1 16-ounce container

Lemons, 4

Celery, 10 ribs
Garlic clove, 1
Green beans, 1 pound
Green pepper, 1 medium
Iceberg lettuce, 1 head
Mint, 1 bunch
Mushrooms, 1 pound
Onions, 2 medium

Parsley, 1 bunch
Potatoes, 6 (4 ounces each)
Romaine lettuce, 1 head

Frozen raspberries, no sugar added, 1 16-ounce bag

Canned crushed pineapple, no sugar added, 1 20-ounce can

Canned crushed tomatoes, 1 16-ounce can
Pimientos, 1 4-ounce jar
Tomato puree, 1 16-ounce can

Tomato juice, 1 46-fluid-ounce can

SUGGESTED EQUIPMENT LIST

Baking sheet
Blender
Bowl (small)
Can opener
Carving knife
Cheesecloth and tie
Chef's knife
Cutting board
Jar with cover
Measuring cups

Measuring spoons
Meat thermometer
Pastry bag
Pepper mill
Pot holder
Roasting pan and rack
Salad bowl (1 large)
Saucepans with covers (large)
Scale
Wooden spoons

HOT TOMATO BOUILLON

1 quart plus ½ cup tomato juice
3 cups water
3 packets instant beef broth and
  seasoning mix

1 tablespoon Worcestershire
  sauce
Few drops hot sauce
6 mint sprigs

Combine all ingredients except mint in large saucepan. Bring to a boil.
Reduce heat and simmer 5 minutes. Divide evenly into 6 soup bowls.
Garnish each serving with a mint sprig. Makes 6 servings.

PARSLEY ROAST LEG OF LAMB
Serve with Caper Sauce (see recipe below).

1 leg of lamb, about 5 pounds
½ cup lemon juice
¼ cup chopped fresh parsley
2 tablespoons prepared mustard

¾ teaspoon rosemary
Salt and pepper to taste
Parsley sprigs or celery leaves to
  garnish

Place lamb on rack in roasting pan. Insert meat thermometer in center
of largest lean muscle, not touching bone. Roast at 325°F. for 1 hour. In
small bowl combine lemon juice, chopped parsley, mustard, and rosemary;
mix well and pour over lamb. Sprinkle with salt and pepper. Roast about
10 to 12 minutes longer per pound, or until thermometer registers 140°F.
for rare; about 12 to 15 minutes per pound, or until thermometer registers
160°F. for medium; about 15 to 20 minutes per pound, or until thermometer registers 170° to 180°F. for well done. Carve and weigh portions.
Serve each guest 4 ounces lamb. Garnish each serving with parsley or
celery leaves. Makes 6 servings.

CAPER SAUCE

Serve with Parsley Roast Leg of Lamb (see recipe above).

4 cups thinly sliced celery
1 quart water
4 packets instant beef broth and
  seasoning mix

½ cup drained capers
¼ cup caper liquid
1½ teaspoons browning sauce

Combine celery, water, and broth mix in large saucepan; cook about 15
minutes or until celery is soft. Transfer to blender container; process until
smooth. Return to saucepan; stir in remaining ingredients; heat. Makes 6
servings.

CREAMY BAKED POTATOES

6 baked potatoes, 4 ounces each
1 cup plain unflavored yogurt
2 tablespoons chopped chives
½ teaspoon imitation butter
  flavoring

½ teaspoon salt, or to taste
Dash white pepper
Paprika to garnish

Cut each baked potato in half lengthwise. Scoop out enough pulp from 6 potato halves so as to leave firm shells. Place pulp in mixing bowl and reserve shells. Scoop out all the potato from remaining halves; add to mixing bowl. Combine remaining ingredients, except paprika, with potatoes; mix well. Divide into 6 equal portions. Using a pastry bag, pipe each portion into a reserved shell. Sprinkle lightly with paprika. Place on baking sheet; bake at 325°F. for about 30 minutes or until hot. Serve immediately. Makes 6 servings.

TASTY GREEN BEANS

3 cups green beans
3 cups thinly sliced onions
1 cup chopped celery
¼ cup plus 2 tablespoons
  canned crushed tomatoes
¾ medium green pepper, seeded
  and finely chopped
¼ cup water

½ teaspoon salt, or to taste
¼ teaspoon freshly ground
  pepper
6 parsley sprigs
2 cloves
1 bay leaf
½ teaspoon chervil

In saucepan cook green beans in small amount of water for 10 to 15 minutes or until tender. Combine next 7 ingredients in large saucepan. Tie parsley, cloves, bay leaf, and chervil in cheesecloth and add to vegetable mixture. Cover and simmer 10 to 15 minutes or until vegetables are tender. Add green beans; continue simmering, uncovered, until beans are hot. Remove spice bag. Makes 6 servings.

SEASON'S GREETINGS SALAD WITH MUSHROOM DRESSING

Salad:

3 cups torn romaine lettuce, bite-
  size pieces
3 cups torn iceberg lettuce, bite-
  size pieces

2⅔ cups sliced mushrooms
3 tablespoons sliced pimiento

Dressing:

¼ cup plus 2 tablespoons
vegetable oil
⅓ cup sliced mushrooms
3 tablespoons tomato puree
3 tablespoons wine vinegar
1 small garlic clove
¾ teaspoon chili powder

½ teaspoon onion powder
½ teaspoon Worcestershire
sauce
Dash salt, or to taste
Dash each artificial sweetener and
hot sauce

To Prepare Salad: Combine salad ingredients in large salad bowl; toss. Chill.

To Prepare Dressing: Combine dressing ingredients in blender container. Process until smooth. Transfer to small jar with tight-fitting cover.

To Serve: Cover and shake dressing well. Pour over chilled salad; toss lightly. Makes 6 servings.

PINEAPPLE-BERRY PARFAIT WITH "CRÈME" FLUFF

2 cups canned crushed pineapple,
no sugar added, divided
1 cup frozen raspberries, no sugar
added, thawed
Artificial sweetener to equal 4
teaspoons sugar

½ teaspoon raspberry or cherry
extract
½ teaspoon pineapple extract
"Crème" Fluff (see following
recipe)

Place 1½ cups pineapple in blender container; process until smooth. Transfer to 1½-quart bowl. Reserve 6 raspberries. Add remaining berries and pineapple to pureed pineapple. Stir in sweetener and extracts. Divide evenly into 6 parfait glasses. Top each serving with an equal amount of "Crème" Fluff and 1 reserved raspberry. Refrigerate or serve immediately. Makes 6 servings.

"Crème" Fluff

1 envelope unflavored gelatin
¼ cup cold water
½ cup boiling water
⅔ cup nonfat dry milk powder

Artificial sweetener to equal 4
teaspoons sugar
1 teaspoon vanilla extract
6 to 8 ice cubes

In blender container sprinkle gelatin over cold water; let stand a few minutes to soften. Add boiling water; process until dissolved. Add remaining ingredients except ice cubes; process until smooth. Add ice cubes, 1 at a time, processing after each addition, until smooth. Use as directed in recipe for Pineapple-Berry Parfait (see preceding recipe).

CHRISTMAS AT HOME FOR SIX

Holiday Fruit Wreaths
Spinach Crêpes with Velvet Sauce
Red and Green Rice
Lemony Mushroom Caps
Salad Crunch with Creamy Bleu Cheese Dressing
Heavenly Lemon Pie
Hot Spiced Christmas Punch ☐ Iced Christmas Punch

The magic ingredient in this Christmas menu is imagination—and it flavors every dish, especially the fruit charmingly transformed into Holiday Wreaths. All it takes is some food, some trimmings, and a huge helping of inventiveness. It's not as complicated as it may appear to admiring guests either, for our easy directions guide you every fun step of the way. It's imagination, too, that gives Spinach Crêpes a snowy covering of Velvet Sauce. Still on a color spree, decorate standard white rice with touches of red and green! Mushrooms—one of the most useful vegetables in the world—dress up for the holiday in Lemony Caps. Most people think it would be heavenly to have dessert on a weight-loss program, so our Heavenly Lemon Pie with Meringue Topping lets you play Santa to those wishes! Generously offer not one but two kinds of punch: Hot Spiced (like a mull) or refreshingly iced. If you expansively decide to host an open house, these recipes will expand to meet the occasion. Just keep additional Wreaths in the refrigerator, and be prepared to whip up extra batches of the swift-cooking crêpes. A joyous feast like this is cause for celebration— and your guests can carry the recipes home as very special "trimmings"!

SUGGESTED SHOPPING LIST

Staples and Miscellaneous

Artificial sweetener
Brandy extract
Cinnamon sticks
Cloves
Cream of tartar
Dry mustard
Garlic powder
Instant chicken broth and seasoning
  mix
Lemon extract
Nutmeg
Peppercorns
Salt
Vanilla extract

Worcestershire sauce

Cornstarch
Flour
Nonstick cooking spray
Tea

Imitation (or diet) margarine

Enriched white bread
Raisin bread

Additional Items

Bleu cheese, 6 ounces
Eggs, 6
Plain unflavored yogurt, 1 16-ounce
  container

Apples, 3 small
Lemons, 3
Pineapple, 1 small

Cauliflower, 1 head
Celery, 2 ribs
Cucumber, 1 medium
Green pepper, 1 medium
Iceberg lettuce, 1 head
Mushrooms, 1 pound
Spinach, 1 pound

Frozen orange juice concentrate,
  1 6-fluid-ounce can

Canned mandarin orange sections, no
  sugar added, 1 10½-ounce can

Pimientos, 1 4-ounce jar

Evaporated skimmed milk, 2 13-fluid-
  ounce cans

Dietetic soda, any flavor, 1 28-fluid-
  ounce bottle
Black-cherry-flavored dietetic soda,
  1 16-fluid-ounce bottle
Club soda, 1 16-fluid-ounce bottle
Grape-flavored dietetic soda,
  1 16-fluid-ounce bottle

Enriched white rice, 1 16-ounce box

SUGGESTED EQUIPMENT LIST

Aluminum foil
Baking dish (shallow, 2-quart)
Blender
Bowls (small, medium, large salad)
6 small bows or tiny Christmas
  corsages
Can opener
Chef's knife
Corer
Cutting board
Double boiler
Electric mixer
Food processor (optional)
Measuring cups

Measuring spoons
Nonstick skillet (7-inch)
Pepper mill
Pie pan (9-inch)
Pitcher (large)
Pot holder
Saucepans (medium)
Scale
Spatula
Strainer
Vegetable peeler
Wire whisk
Wooden spoon

HOLIDAY FRUIT WREATHS

To create this attractive dish, you will need 6 small bows or tiny Christmas corsages and a roll of aluminum foil.

1 small pineapple
1 small apple, cored and diced

½ cup canned mandarin orange sections, no sugar added

Trim off ends of pineapple and cut fruit into 6 slices. With a sharp knife, cut pulp from each slice, leaving 6 firm, round shells. Cut out and discard core from each pineapple slice. Dice fruit and place in small bowl. Add diced apple and orange sections; refrigerate. Tie a bow or corsage onto each pineapple shell; place each on a serving plate. Shape 6 aluminum foil cups to fit shells; place 1 cup in each shell. Divide fruit evenly into cups. Makes 6 servings.

SPINACH CRÊPES WITH VELVET SAUCE

Velvet Sauce:

2 tablespoons imitation (or diet) margarine
1 tablespoon plus 1 teaspoon flour

2 packets instant chicken broth and seasoning mix
1 cup water
½ cup evaporated skimmed milk

Filling:

2 cups cooked chopped spinach, well drained of all excess moisture
½ cup Velvet Sauce

⅛ teaspoon nutmeg
Salt and freshly ground pepper to taste

Crêpes:

3 eggs
1½ slices enriched white bread
3 tablespoons water

1 tablespoon plus 1 teaspoon flour

To Prepare Sauce: Melt margarine in top of double boiler, over boiling water. Add flour and broth mix, stirring with wire whisk to combine. Add water, stirring until smooth. Add milk; cook, stirring occasionally, until sauce thickens.

To Prepare Filling: Place spinach, ½ cup Velvet Sauce, the nutmeg, salt, and pepper in bowl; stir to combine.

To Prepare Crêpes: Combine crêpe ingredients in blender container; process until smooth. Let stand 5 minutes. Heat 7-inch nonstick skillet that has been sprayed with nonstick cooking spray. Pour ⅙ of batter into skillet, quickly tilting skillet to spread batter evenly over surface of pan. Cook until underside is done and bubbles form on surface. Turn and cook until other side is done, about 15 seconds. Remove from heat. Repeat procedure 5 more times, to make 6 crêpes.

To Serve: Divide spinach filling into 6 equal portions. Place 1 portion on each crêpe; roll crêpes. Place in shallow 2-quart baking pan. Top with remaining Velvet Sauce. Bake at 350°F. for 15 minutes or until piping hot. Makes 6 servings.

RED AND GREEN RICE

> 1 medium green pepper, seeded and finely diced
> 2 packets instant chicken broth and seasoning mix
>
> 1 teaspoon Worcestershire sauce
> 3 cups hot, cooked enriched rice
> 3 tablespoons diced pimiento

In medium saucepan combine green pepper, broth mix, and Worcestershire sauce. Cook, stirring occasionally, until green pepper is tender. Add rice and pimiento; stir to combine. Remove from heat and serve. Makes 6 servings.

LEMONY MUSHROOM CAPS

> 3 cups mushroom caps
> ½ cup water
> 2 tablespoons lemon juice
>
> ½ teaspoon garlic powder
> Salt and freshly ground pepper to taste

In saucepan combine mushrooms, water, lemon juice, and garlic powder. Bring to a boil; reduce heat and simmer for 15 minutes. Drain; season with salt and pepper. Makes 6 servings.

SALAD CRUNCH WITH CREAMY BLEU CHEESE DRESSING

Salad:

> 3 cups torn, crisp iceberg lettuce, bite-size pieces
> 1½ cups cauliflower florets
> 1 cup diced celery
>
> 1 medium cucumber, pared, scored, and sliced
> 1½ small apples, cored and diced
> 1 tablespoon lemon juice

Dressing:

> 6 ounces Bleu cheese, divided
> 1 cup plain unflavored yogurt
>
> ⅛ teaspoon each garlic powder and dry mustard

To Prepare Salad: Combine lettuce, cauliflower, celery, and cucumber in large salad bowl. In small bowl toss apples with lemon juice. Add apples to salad; toss to combine. Chill.

To Prepare Dressing: Combine 3 ounces Bleu cheese, the yogurt, and seasonings in blender container or food processor; process until smooth. Transfer to small bowl. Crumble remaining cheese and add to yogurt mixture; stir to combine. Cover and chill.

To Serve: Pour dressing over salad and toss to combine. Makes 6 servings.

HEAVENLY LEMON PIE

Pie Crust:

4½ slices raisin bread
¼ cup plus 2 tablespoons water

½ teaspoon vanilla extract

Pie Filling:

2 cups evaporated skimmed milk
3 egg yolks
Artificial sweetener to equal 12
   teaspoons sugar
1 tablespoon lemon juice

1 tablespoon vanilla extract
2 teaspoons grated lemon rind
1½ teaspoons lemon extract
1 tablespoon cornstarch,
   dissolved in 1 tablespoon water

Meringue Topping:

3 egg whites
¼ teaspoon cream of tartar
Artificial sweetener to equal 12
   teaspoons sugar

1 teaspoon vanilla extract

To Prepare Pie Crust: Make bread into crumbs. Combine water and vanilla in mixing bowl. Add bread crumbs and stir with fork until crumbs are evenly moistened. Press mixture into 9-inch pie pan that has been sprayed with nonstick cooking spray. Bake at 400°F. for 10 to 12 minutes. Cool.

To Prepare Pie Filling: In top of double boiler, over boiling water, combine milk, egg yolks, sweetener, lemon juice, vanilla, lemon rind, and lemon extract. Cook for 10 minutes, stirring frequently. Stirring constantly, add cornstarch and cook until mixture thickens. Pour into prepared crust. Let stand 15 minutes.

To Prepare Meringue Topping: In medium bowl beat egg whites with electric mixer until frothy. Add cream of tartar; beat until stiff peaks form. Beat in sweetener and vanilla.

To Serve: Top filling evenly with Meringue Topping. Bake at 425°F. for 8 to 10 minutes or until top is lightly browned. Serve warm or chilled. Makes 6 servings.

HOT SPICED CHRISTMAS PUNCH

    1 quart hot tea   *2 cloves*
    1½ cups orange juice   *6 thin lemon slices*
    1 cinnamon stick

In medium saucepan combine tea, orange juice, cinnamon stick, and cloves. Bring to a boil; reduce heat and simmer for 5 minutes. Remove from heat. Discard cinnamon stick and cloves. Divide evenly into 6 coffee cups. Garnish each with a lemon slice. Makes 6 servings.

ICED CHRISTMAS PUNCH

    3 cups dietetic soda, any flavor   *2 cups club soda*
    2 cups black-cherry-flavored   *2 tablespoons lemon juice*
      dietetic soda   *¼ teaspoon brandy extract*
    2 cups grape-flavored dietetic   *Ice cubes*
      soda

Combine all ingredients except ice in large pitcher. Serve over ice in tall glasses. Makes 6 servings.

BON VOYAGE DINNER FOR SIX

Tossed Salad with Lemon-Vinaigrette Dressing
Broccoli Soup
Baked Chicken Breasts with Hominy Stuffing
Turnip Medley
Baked Apple with Crumble Topping
"Cold Duck"

Say good-bye so deliciously your guests will be eager to say hello again! Here's a menu that has it all—tastiness, economy, eye-appeal, and the do-it-ahead ease that puts *you* into the party, too. Launch your dinner with a salad that isn't just "tossed" together but displays an interesting international combination: Boston lettuce, Chinese cabbage, and the watercress so typical of Britain, served in first-class style with French Lemon-Vinaigrette Dressing. Baked Chicken Breast travels easily with a stuffing based on that Southern favorite: hominy grits. Our menu thriftily helps you save for *your* vacation by taking advantage of produce in season all year. Turnip Medley skillfully combines colors and textures, and Broccoli Soup has a distinctive flavor from the added nutmeg, a holiday spice that blends well with "creamed" vegetables. (As an interesting substitute, you might try mace—which is actually the outer coating of nutmeg—but use it in smaller quantities, since the flavor is stronger.) "Top" off your dinner with a Crumble Topping that expertly contrasts with your hometown hit: Baked Apples. As a farewell drink, our wine-extract version of Cold Duck will send everyone off in high spirits. And aren't you proud to help your guests travel *light*???

SUGGESTED SHOPPING LIST

Staples and Miscellaneous

Artificial sweetener
Cayenne pepper
Cinnamon
Garlic powder
Instant chicken broth and seasoning
  mix
Nutmeg
Paprika
Pepper
Peppercorns
Poultry seasoning
Salt
White pepper
Wine extract

Browning sauce
Rice vinegar
Worcestershire sauce

Nonfat dry milk powder
Nonstick cooking spray

Imitation (or diet) margarine
Vegetable oil

Whole wheat bread

Additional Items

Skinned and boned chicken breasts,
  6 (6 ounces each)

Lemons, 2
MacIntosh apples, 6 small

Boston lettuce, 1 head
Broccoli, 2 bunches
Celery, 3 ribs
Chinese cabbage, 1 head
Garlic cloves, 2
Green peppers, 2 medium
Onions, 2 medium

Parsley, 1 bunch
Radishes, 1 bag
Turnips, 9 medium
Watercress, 1 bunch

Black-cherry-flavored dietetic soda,
  1 12-fluid-ounce can
Club soda, 2 28-fluid-ounce bottles

Evaporated skimmed milk, 1 13-fluid-
  ounce can

Hominy grits, 1 16-ounce container

SUGGESTED EQUIPMENT LIST

Baking pan
Baking pan (8 x 8 x 2 inches)
Blender
Bowls (salad, large)
Can opener
Casserole (shallow, 2½-quart)
Chef's knife
Colander
Corer
Cutting board
Jar with tight-fitting cover

Measuring cups
Measuring spoons
Pepper mill
Pitcher
Pot holder
Rack
Saucepans (large)
Scale
Small container
Vegetable peeler
Wooden spoon

TOSSED SALAD WITH LEMON-VINAIGRETTE DRESSING

1 head Boston lettuce, torn into
  bite-size pieces
1 head Chinese cabbage, cut into
  1-inch-thick slices
1 bunch watercress, stems
  removed

4 radishes, thinly sliced
Lemon-Vinaigrette Dressing (see
  following recipe)

Combine first 4 ingredients in salad bowl; chill. When ready to serve, add Lemon-Vinaigrette Dressing; toss to coat. Makes 6 servings.

Lemon-Vinaigrette Dressing

2 tablespoons vegetable oil
1 tablespoon plus 2 teaspoons
  rice vinegar
1 tablespoon chopped fresh
  parsley

1 teaspoon lemon juice
1/4 teaspoon salt, or to taste
1/8 teaspoon minced fresh garlic
Freshly ground pepper to taste

Combine all ingredients in jar with tight-fitting cover. Cover and shake well before using. Serve as directed in recipe for Tossed Salad (see preceding recipe).

BROCCOLI SOUP

4 cups chopped broccoli
1 quart water
2 packets instant chicken broth
  and seasoning mix

1/2 teaspoon salt
1/2 cup evaporated skimmed milk
1/8 teaspoon nutmeg
Dash cayenne pepper

In large saucepan combine broccoli, water, broth mix, and salt; bring to a boil. Reduce heat and simmer for 15 minutes. Transfer 1/2 of mixture to blender container; process until smooth. Pour into large bowl and repeat with remaining mixture. Add remaining ingredients and return mixture to saucepan. Cook, stirring often, until thoroughly heated. *Do not boil*. Makes 6 servings.

BAKED CHICKEN BREASTS WITH HOMINY STUFFING

6 skinned and boned chicken
  breasts, 6 ounces each, reserve
  skin
Salt, pepper, garlic powder, and
  paprika to taste

Hominy Stuffing (see recipe, page
  348)

Season both sides of chicken with salt, pepper, garlic powder, and paprika. Tuck in ends of each chicken breast to form rounded mound. Replace skin over each breast. Place on baking sheet and bake at 400°F. for

15 to 20 minutes or until tender. Remove and discard skin. Divide stuffing into 6 equal portions. Top each portion with 1 chicken breast. Makes 6 servings.

Hominy Stuffing

1½ cups finely diced celery
1 cup finely diced onions
¼ medium green pepper, finely diced
¼ cup imitation (or diet) margarine
1½ packets instant chicken broth and seasoning mix
4½ cups cooked enriched hominy grits

3 slices whole wheat bread, cut into cubes
½ cup water
¾ teaspoon each poultry seasoning and browning sauce
½ teaspoon salt
¼ teaspoon garlic powder
⅛ teaspoon white pepper

Preheat oven to 450°F. Combine celery, onions, green pepper, margarine, and broth mix in shallow 2½-quart casserole that has been sprayed with nonstick cooking spray. Bake 8 to 10 minutes or until onions are transparent. Remove casserole from oven. Reduce oven temperature to 400°F. Add remaining ingredients; stir to combine. Return to oven and bake for approximately 30 minutes or until heated throughout and top is golden brown. Serve as directed in recipe for Baked Chicken Breasts (see recipe, page 347).

TURNIP MEDLEY

6 cups julienne, pared turnips
1 cup diced onions
¾ cup julienne green peppers
Salt to taste
1 tablespoon imitation (or diet) margarine

2 packets instant chicken broth and seasoning mix
½ teaspoon Worcestershire sauce
⅛ teaspoon garlic powder
Freshly ground pepper to taste

In saucepan combine turnips, onions, and green peppers. Add enough boiling water to cover; add salt and cook until vegetables are tender. Drain; place vegetables in serving bowl. Add next 4 ingredients. Season to taste with salt and pepper; toss to combine. Makes 6 servings.

BAKED APPLE WITH CRUMBLE TOPPING

Serve warm or chilled.

6 small MacIntosh apples
1½ cups black-cherry-flavored
   dietetic soda
Artificial sweetener to equal 10
   teaspoons sugar, divided
½ teaspoon cinnamon, divided

3 slices whole wheat bread, made
   into crumbs
⅓ cup nonfat dry milk powder
⅛ teaspoon nutmeg
1 tablespoon imitation (or diet)
   margarine, melted

Pare apples halfway down. Remove core from each apple to ½ inch from bottom. Arrange apples in 8 × 8 × 2-inch baking pan. Pour soda over fruit. In small container combine artificial sweetener to equal 4 teaspoons sugar and ¼ teaspoon cinnamon; sprinkle over apples. In bowl combine remaining sweetener and cinnamon with bread crumbs, milk, and nutmeg; mix well. Add margarine; mix until crumbly. Divide crumb mixture into 6 equal portions. Place 1 portion in palm of hand and press top of apple into mixture. Press together to form a mound. Repeat procedure with remaining crumbs and apples. Return apples to pan. Bake, covered, at 350°F. for 30 minutes or until apples are tender. Makes 6 servings.

"COLD DUCK"

1½ quarts club soda
2 tablespoons lemon juice
Artificial sweetener to equal 6
   teaspoons sugar

1½ teaspoons wine extract
Crushed ice
6 twists lemon rind

In pitcher combine club soda, lemon juice, sweetener, and extract; stir well. Fill each of six 12-ounce glasses ½ full with crushed ice. Pour an equal amount of "Cold Duck" into each glass. Garnish each portion with lemon rind. Makes 6 servings.

Appendix

Menu Equivalents for Each Serving

January

1. *New Year's Day Breakfast for Four*
   2 ounces Fish; 1 serving Bread; 1½ servings Vegetables; ¼ cup Limited Vegetable; 2 servings Fat; 1 serving Fruit; ⅛ serving Milk (1 tablespoon yogurt); ⅛ serving Bonus (2 tablespoons clam juice); 2 servings Extras (1 packet broth mix, 1 teaspoon cornstarch)

2. *Scandinavian Koldt Bord for Eight*
   ⅜ ounce Smoked Fish; 2½ ounces Fish; 1 ounce Poultry; 1 serving Bread Substitute; 8⅔ servings Vegetables; ½ cup Limited Vegetable; 2 servings Fat; 1¼ servings Fruit; 1¼ servings Milk (½ cup plus 3¾ teaspoons yogurt, 2¼ teaspoons evaporated skimmed milk); ¼ serving Bonus (¼ cup tomato juice); 2 servings Extras (¼ envelope gelatin, 1½ teaspoons chili sauce, ¾ teaspoon ketchup, ⅜ teaspoon cornstarch)

3. *Après Skating or Skiing for Four*
   4 ounces Meat Group; 1 serving Bread; 4¼ servings Vegetables; ¼ cup plus 1 tablespoon Limited Vegetable; ¾ serving Fat; 1½ servings Fruit; 1⅛ servings Milk (½ cup plus 1 tablespoon evaporated skimmed milk); 1/16 serving Bonus (1½ teaspoons tomato puree); 2¾ servings Extras (½ packet broth mix, ⅜ teaspoon gelatin, 3/16 teaspoon sesame seeds, 1½ teaspoons cocoa)

4. *Slumber Party for Eight*
   2 ounces Meat Group; 3 ounces Legumes; 1 serving Bread Substitute; 1 serving Bread; 4¼ servings Vegetables; 1 tablespoon Limited Vegetable; 1¾ servings Fat; 1¾ servings Fruit; 1 serving Milk (1 tablespoon yogurt, 3 tablespoons evaporated skimmed milk, 3 ounces frozen dessert); 1 serving Bonus (½ cup tomato sauce); 2¾ servings Extras (¼ teaspoon sesame seeds, ¾ teaspoon cocoa, ½ teaspoon cornstarch, ½ envelope gelatin)

5. *Teen Scene Breakfast for Eight*
   ¾ ounce Cereal; 1 serving Bread; ½ serving Vegetables; ½ serving Fat; 1¼ servings Fruit; ¾ serving Milk (½ cup skim milk, 4 tea-

spoons nonfat dry milk); ¾ serving Bonus (¾ cup tomato juice); 3 servings Extras (½ teaspoon sesame seeds, ½ envelope gelatin, 1 teaspoon cocoa); 4 calories Specialty Foods (2 teaspoons preserves)

6. *Hearty Winter Luncheon for Four*
⅓ cup Soft Cheese; 2 ounces Fish; 1 serving Bread Substitute; 2¼ servings Vegetables; ¾ serving Fat; 1 serving Fruit; ¼ serving Milk (¼ cup skim milk); 1¾ servings Extras (¾ teaspoon flour, ¾ cup bouillon)

February

1. *A Midday Meal for Winter Weekend Guests for Four*
1 Egg; 1½ ounces Meat Group (cured); 1 serving Bread; 4 servings Vegetables; ½ cup Limited Vegetable; 1 serving Fat; 1½ servings Fruit; 2 servings Milk (1 cup skim milk, ½ cup yogurt); 3 servings Extras (1½ teaspoons flour, ¼ envelope gelatin, 1 teaspoon cocoa); 4 calories Specialty Foods (1½ teaspoons preserves, ¼ cup soda)

2. *Hearty New Orleans Breakfast for Eight*
1 ounce Poultry; 2 servings Bread; ¼ serving Vegetables; ¼ serving Fat; 1 serving Fruit; ¼ serving Milk (2 tablespoons evaporated skimmed milk); 2 servings Extras (¾ cup bouillon, ½ teaspoon flour, ½ teaspoon cornstarch)

3. *Campus Party for Six*
4 ounces Liver; 1 serving Bread Substitute; 4⅓ servings Vegetables; ⅓ cup Limited Vegetable; 2 servings Fat; ⅓ serving Fruit; ⅔ serving Milk (⅓ cup evaporated skimmed milk); ⅔ serving Bonus (⅓ cup tomato sauce); 1⅓ servings Extras (¾ cup stock, ⅓ packet broth mix)

4. *An Elegant Winter Luncheon for Four*
4 ounces Meat Group (once-a-week selection); 1 serving Bread Substitute; 1½ servings Vegetables; ½ cup Limited Vegetable; 2 servings Fat; ¾ serving Fruit; ½ serving Milk (2 tablespoons evaporated skimmed milk, 2 tablespoons yogurt); 2¼ servings Extras (¾ cup bouillon, ¾ teaspoon cornstarch, ¼ envelope gelatin); 8 calories Specialty Foods (1½ teaspoons marmalade)

5. *A Frankly Delicious Washington's Birthday Menu for Six*
3 ounces Meat Group (cured; once-a-week selection); 1 serving Bread Substitute; 2¼ servings Vegetables; ½ cup Limited Vegetable; 1½ servings Fruit; ¾ serving Milk (2 tablespoons evaporated skimmed milk, ¼ cup yogurt); ½ serving Bonus (½ cup mixed vegetable juice); 3 servings Extras (1½ teaspoons cornstarch, ¼ cup bouillon, ½ teaspoon poppy seeds, ⅙ packet broth mix)

6. *The Chinese Fire Pot for Four*
4 ounces Fish; 1 serving Bread Substitute; 3⅛ servings Vegetables; 1¾ servings Fruit; ¼ serving Bonus (2 tablespoons tomato puree);

2¾ servings Extras (1¼ packets broth mix, ½ teaspoon cornstarch, 2 teaspoons ketchup)

March

1. *Simple Soiree for Six*
   4 ounces Veal; 1 serving Bread Substitute; 2½ servings Vegetables; ½ cup Limited Vegetable; 1 serving Fat; 1 serving Fruit; $\frac{1}{24}$ serving Milk (1 teaspoon yogurt); ⅓ serving Extras (⅓ packet broth mix); 6 calories Specialty Foods (⅓ cup low-calorie gelatin, ½ cup soda)
2. *Anniversary Party for Eight*
   4 ounces Liver; 1 serving Bread Substitute; 7 servings Vegetables; ¼ cup plus 2 tablespoons Limited Vegetable; 2 servings Fat; ½ serving Fruit; ½ serving Milk (2 tablespoons evaporated skimmed milk, 4 teaspoons nonfat dry milk); ¼ serving Bonus (2 tablespoons tomato puree); 3 servings Extras (1½ packets broth mix, 1 teaspoon cornstarch, ½ teaspoon gelatin)
3. *Birthday Fare for Eight*
   4 ounces Meat Group; 1 serving Bread Substitute; 7¼ servings Vegetables; ½ cup Limited Vegetable; 1½ servings Fat; 1½ servings Fruit; ¼ serving Milk (2 tablespoons yogurt); 1¼ servings Extras (¼ packet broth mix, ½ teaspoon flour, ¼ envelope gelatin); ½ calorie Specialty Foods (3 tablespoons soda)
4. *Erin Go Bragh for Four*
   4 ounces Fish; 1 serving Bread Substitute; 3½ servings Vegetables; ¼ cup plus 1 tablespoon Limited Vegetable; ¾ serving Fat; ¾ serving Milk (6 tablespoons evaporated skimmed milk); ¼ serving Bonus (2 tablespoons tomato puree); 1 serving Extras (1 packet broth mix); 12 calories Specialty Foods (1½ tablespoons low-calorie whipped topping)
5. *A Continental Dinner for Eight*
   4 ounces Meat Group; 1 serving Bread Substitute; 2½ servings Vegetables; ¼ cup plus 2 tablespoons Limited Vegetable; 3 servings Fat; 1 serving Fruit; ¼ serving Milk (2 tablespoons yogurt); ¼ serving Bonus (2 tablespoons tomato sauce); ⅜ serving Extras (⅜ packet broth mix)
6. *Cocktail Supper Party for Six*
   2 ounces Fish; 2 ounces Veal; 7 servings Vegetables; ½ cup Limited Vegetable; 2 servings Fat; ⅓ serving Fruit; ½ serving Milk (4 teaspoons yogurt, 8 teaspoons evaporated skimmed milk); ¼ serving Bonus (2 tablespoons tomato sauce); 1½ servings Extras (2 teaspoons ketchup); 5⅓ calories Specialty Foods (⅙ envelope low-calorie gelatin)

April

1. *Swing into Spring Luncheon for Four*
   1 Egg; ⅓ cup Soft Cheese; 1 serving Bread; 5⅔ servings Vegetables; 3 servings Fat; 2 servings Fruit; ¾ serving Milk (6 tablespoons evaporated skimmed milk)
2. *Passover Seder for Eight*
   4 ounces Poultry; 1 serving Bread; 6 servings Vegetables; ½ cup Limited Vegetable; 1½ servings Fat; 1 serving Fruit; 2 servings Extras (1½ cups broth)
3. *Easter Breakfast for Six*
   1 Egg; 2 servings Bread; 4½ servings Vegetables; 2 tablespoons Limited Vegetable; 2 servings Fat; 1½ servings Fruit; ⅔ serving Milk (8 teaspoons skim milk, 3 ounces frozen dessert); ½ serving Bonus (½ cup mixed vegetable juice); 1¼ servings Extras (1 teaspoon flour, ¼ teaspoon cornstarch); ⅛ calorie Specialty Foods (4 teaspoons root beer)
4. *An Elegant Easter Dinner for Twelve*
   4 ounces Meat Group; 1 serving Bread Substitute; 4⅓ servings Vegetables (add ¼ serving if variation is used); 2 teaspoons Limited Vegetable; 1½ servings Fat; 1 serving Fruit; ⅔ serving Milk (¼ cup evaporated skimmed milk, 4 teaspoons yogurt); ⅓ serving Bonus (⅓ cup mixed vegetable juice); 1⅙ servings Extras (½ cup stock, ³⁄₁₂ envelope gelatin)
5. *From Russia with Taste—for Eight*
   4 ounces Meat Group; 1 serving Bread; 1 serving Bread Substitute; 6 servings Vegetables; ½ cup Limited Vegetable; 1½ servings Fat; 1¼ servings Fruit; ¼ serving Milk (2 tablespoons yogurt); 3 servings Extras (⅜ packet broth mix, ⅛ teaspoon caraway seeds, 3 tablespoons stock, 2⅛ teaspoons cornstarch)
6. *Confirmation Party for Twelve*
   4 ounces Veal; 1 serving Bread Substitute; 3⅔ servings Vegetables; ¼ cup Limited Vegetable; 2¾ servings Fat; 1¼ servings Fruit; ⅓ serving Milk (8 teaspoons evaporated skimmed milk); ⅚ serving Bonus (½ cup tomato juice, 8 teaspoons tomato puree); 1⅔ servings Extras (⅔ packet broth mix, ⅔ teaspoon cornstarch, ⅙ envelope gelatin)

May

1. *A Simple Spring Buffet for Eight*
   4 ounces Meat Group; 1 serving Bread Substitute; 4¾ servings Vegetables; ½ cup Limited Vegetable; 2 servings Fat; 1 serving Fruit; 1 serving Extras (3 tablespoons bouillon, ½ teaspoon cornstarch, ⅛ packet broth mix)

2. *Bridge Club Buffet for Eight*
   1 Egg; ⅓ cup Soft Cheese; 1 serving Bread Substitute; 7 servings Vegetables; ¾ serving Fat; 1½ servings Fruit; ¾ serving Milk (10½ teaspoons yogurt, 4½ teaspoons evaporated skimmed milk, 4½ teaspoons buttermilk); 2 servings Extras (1⅛ teaspoons ketchup, 1¼ teaspoons cornstarch)
3. *Let's Tour Turkey for Six*
   4 ounces Meat Group; 1 serving Bread Substitute; 4⅙ servings Vegetables; ¼ cup plus 2 tablespoons Limited Vegetable; ½ serving Fruit; 1¼ servings Milk (10 teaspoons evaporated skimmed milk, 8 teaspoons yogurt, ½ cup skim milk); 1 serving Bonus (½ cup tomato puree); ⅓ serving Extras (⅓ packet broth mix)
4. *Mother's Day Tray for One*
   ⅓ cup Soft Cheese; 1 serving Bread Substitute; ½ serving Fat; 1½ servings Fruit; 12 calories Specialty Foods (1½ tablespoons low-calorie whipped topping)
5. *A Taste of the Orient for Six*
   4 ounces Fish; 1 serving Bread Substitute; 5⅓ servings Vegetables; ½ cup Limited Vegetable; 1½ servings Fruit; ⅙ serving Milk (2 tablespoons buttermilk); ½ serving Extras (½ packet broth mix)
6. *Memorial Day on the Patio for Four*
   1 Egg; 1 ounce Hard Cheese; 1 serving Bread; 4¾ servings Vegetables; 1 tablespoon Limited Vegetable; 1¾ servings Fat; 1 serving Fruit; 1 serving Milk (¼ cup skim milk, 6 tablespoons yogurt); ½ serving Extras (¼ envelope gelatin)

June

1. *No-Cooking Supper for Two*
   3 ounces Meat Group (cured); 1 serving Bread; 4½ servings Vegetables; 2 tablespoons Limited Vegetable; 2¼ servings Fat; 2 servings Fruit; ½ serving Milk (¼ cup yogurt); ¾ serving Bonus (½ cup tomato juice, ¼ cup clam juice)
2. *Country French Dinner for Four*
   4 ounces Poultry; 1 serving Bread Substitute; 2½ servings Vegetables; ¼ cup plus 2 tablespoons Limited Vegetable; 1 serving Fat; 2 servings Fruit; ¼ serving Bonus (2 tablespoons tomato sauce); 2 servings Extras (1 packet broth mix, 1 teaspoon cornstarch)
3. *Wedding Reception for Twelve*
   3 ounces Meat Group (cured); 1 serving Bread Substitute; 2⅔ servings Vegetables; ½ cup Limited Vegetable; 3 servings Fat; 1½ servings Fruit; 1 serving Milk (¼ cup evaporated skimmed milk, 3 ounces frozen dessert); 2½ servings Extras (⅔ teaspoon chili sauce, 1⅓ packets broth mix, ⅔ teaspoon cornstarch, ³⁄₁₆ teaspoon gelatin); 3⅓ calories Specialty Foods (1½ teaspoons jelly, ¼ cup ginger ale)

4. *The Chic of Greek Dining for Six*
   4 ounces Meat Group; 1 serving Bread Substitute; 7⅓ servings Vegetables; ½ cup Limited Vegetable; 1 serving Fruit; ⅜ serving Milk (3 tablespoons yogurt); ⅙ serving Bonus (2 teaspoons tomato paste); ⅓ serving Extras (⅓ packet broth mix)
5. *Graduation Party for Eight*
   1 Egg; 1½ ounces Meat Group (cured; once-a-week selection); 1 serving Bread; ⅓ serving Vegetables; 1¾ servings Fat; 1¾ servings Fruit; ¼ serving Milk (4 teaspoons nonfat dry milk); ½ serving Extras (¼ envelope gelatin); ⅔ calorie Specialty Foods (½ cup soda)
6. *High Tea in the Garden for Six*
   1 Egg; ⅓ cup Soft Cheese; 1 serving Bread; 5⅔ servings Vegetables; 1 tablespoon plus 1 teaspoon Limited Vegetable; 1 serving Fat; ⅔ serving Milk (⅓ cup yogurt); 1½ servings Extras (1½ teaspoons cornstarch)

July

1. *For the Fourth of July—Red, White, and Blueberry for Six*
   1 Egg; 2 ounces Fish; 1 serving Bread; 1 serving Bread Substitute; 3 servings Vegetables; ⅓ cup Limited Vegetable; ½ serving Fat; ½ serving Fruit; ⅔ serving Milk (2 teaspoons evaporated skimmed milk, ½ cup plus 4 teaspoons skim milk); ⅔ serving Bonus (½ cup tomato juice, 2 teaspoons tomato puree); 1⅔ servings Extras (1 teaspoon flour, ⅓ packet broth mix, ¼ teaspoon cornstarch)
2. *Japanese Feast for Two*
   2 ounces Meat Group; 4 ounces Legumes (soybean curd); 1 serving Bread Substitute; 6½ servings Vegetables; ½ cup Limited Vegetable; 1 serving Fruit; ⅜ serving Bonus (6 tablespoons clam juice); 2⅓ servings Extras (⅝ cup bouillon, ½ teaspoon sesame seeds, ¼ envelope gelatin)
3. *A Shore Dinner for Six*
   4 ounces Fish; 1 serving Bread Substitute; 4 servings Vegetables; 1 tablespoon plus 1 teaspoon Limited Vegetable; 2 servings Fat; 1 serving Fruit; ⅔ serving Milk (8 teaspoons yogurt, 8 teaspoons evaporated skimmed milk); ⅔ serving Bonus (⅓ cup clam juice, 8 teaspoons tomato puree); ½ serving Extras (⅓ packet broth mix, ¼ teaspoon gelatin)
4. *Summer Luncheon Supreme for Four*
   4 ounces Poultry; 1 serving Bread; 3½ servings Vegetables; 2 tablespoons Limited Vegetable; 2½ servings Fat; 2 servings Fruit; ¼ serving Milk (2 tablespoons yogurt); 1½ servings Extras (¼ envelope gelatin, ½ packet broth mix, ½ teaspoon cornstarch)

5. *Tote-a-Lunch for One*
   1½ ounces Smoked Fish; 2 ounces Meat Group; 1 serving Bread; 4 servings Vegetables; 1 serving Fat; 2 servings Fruit; 1 serving Milk (½ cup yogurt); 1 serving Bonus (1 cup tomato juice)
6. *Hoolaulea—a Midsummer Party for Eight*
   1 ounce Fish; 3 ounces Meat Group; 1 serving Bread Substitute; 1½ servings Vegetables; ¼ cup plus 2 tablespoons Limited Vegetable; 1¼ servings Fat; 2 servings Fruit; ⅛ serving Milk (1 tablespoon evaporated skimmed milk); ⅛ serving Bonus (1 tablespoon tomato puree); ⅔ serving Extras (¼ teaspoon sesame seeds, 1½ teaspoons bouillon)

August

1. *A Taste of Italy for Four*
   4 ounces Fish; 1 serving Bread Substitute; 7½ servings Vegetables; ½ cup Limited Vegetable; 2 servings Fat; 1½ servings Fruit
2. *Poolside Splash—a Hamburger Party for Eight*
   4 ounces Meat Group; 2 servings Bread; 9⅓ servings Vegetables; ½ cup Limited Vegetable; 3 servings Fat; 1¾ servings Fruit; ¼ serving Milk (2 tablespoons yogurt); 3 servings Extras (½ teaspoon seeds, 2 teaspoons ketchup, 2 teaspoons chili sauce)
3. *Continental Breakfast for Four*
   1 Egg; 1 serving Bread; 1½ servings Fat; 2 servings Fruit; ¾ serving Milk (¼ cup skim milk, 8 teaspoons nonfat dry milk); 3 servings Extras (1 tablespoon flour)
4. *Barbecue with a Mideast Flavor for Four*
   4 ounces Liver; 1 serving Bread Substitute; 6½ servings Vegetables; ½ cup Limited Vegetable; 2 servings Fat; 1¼ servings Fruit; 1¼ servings Milk (½ cup plus 1½ teaspoons yogurt, 2 tablespoons skim milk, 1½ teaspoons evaporated skimmed milk); ⅛ serving Bonus (1 tablespoon tomato puree); 2¼ servings Extras (1 tablespoon ketchup, 6 tablespoons stock, ³⁄₁₆ teaspoon gelatin)
5. *A Very Chic Summer Buffet for Eight*
   4 ounces Fish; 1 serving Bread; 3⅓ servings Vegetables; ¼ cup plus 1 tablespoon Limited Vegetable; 3 servings Fat; 1 serving Fruit; ¾ serving Milk (2 tablespoons yogurt, ¼ cup evaporated skimmed milk); 2 servings Extras (½ envelope gelatin, ¾ cup stock)
6. *A Summer Sunday Picnic for Four*
   4 ounces Poultry; 1 serving Bread Substitute; 5 servings Vegetables; 2½ tablespoons Limited Vegetable; 1½ servings Fat; 1¼ servings Fruit; ¾ serving Milk (2 tablespoons evaporated skimmed milk, ¼ cup yogurt); 1 serving Extras (¾ cup stock)

September

1. *Labor Day Menu without Much Labor for Four*
   4 ounces Fish; 1 serving Bread; 1 serving Bread Substitute; 5 servings Vegetables; ½ cup Limited Vegetable; 3 servings Fat; 1¼ servings Fruit; ½ serving Milk (2 tablespoons evaporated skimmed milk, 4 teaspoons nonfat dry milk); 1¼ servings Extras (¾ cup bouillon, ¼ teaspoon cornstarch)

2. *Frugal and Fun Chili Party for Twelve*
   2 ounces Meat Group; 3 ounces Legumes; 2 servings Bread; 3 servings Vegetables; ½ cup Limited Vegetable; 1 serving Fat; 1¼ servings Fruit; ⅛ serving Milk (1 tablespoon evaporated skimmed milk); 1 serving Bonus (½ cup tomato juice, 8 teaspoons tomato puree); ⅜ serving Extras (⅜ teaspoon cocoa); 2⅔ calories Specialty Foods (1 cup soda)

3. *La Comida Mexicana for Six (a Mexican Main Meal)*
   4 ounces Poultry; 1 serving Bread Substitute; 2⅔ servings Vegetables; ½ cup Limited Vegetable; 2 servings Fat; 2 servings Fruit; 1 serving Milk (½ cup evaporated skimmed milk); 1 serving Bonus (½ cup tomato juice, ¼ cup tomato puree); 1⅙ servings Extras (⅙ packet broth mix, ½ teaspoon cocoa, 1 teaspoon ketchup)

4. *Scandinavian Wedding Breakfast for Eight*
   2 ounces Fish; 1 serving Bread; 1 serving Vegetables; 1½ servings Fat; 1 serving Fruit

5. *Oktoberfest for Eight*
   1 ounce Poultry; 1 ounce Meat Group; ¾ ounce Meat Group (cured; once-a-week selection); ¾ ounce Meat Group (cured); 1 serving Bread Substitute; 1 serving Bread; 3½ servings Vegetables; ½ cup Limited Vegetable; 2½ servings Fat; 1 serving Fruit; ⅛ serving Milk (1 tablespoon yogurt); 2¾ servings Extras (2 teaspoons ketchup, 2 teaspoons chili sauce, ¼ teaspoon caraway seeds, ¼ packet broth mix); 2½ calories Specialty Foods (¼ teaspoon jelly, 1½ cups root beer)

6. *Thali—a Tray Buffet Indian Style for Six*
   2 ounces Meat Group; 3 ounces Legumes; 1 serving Bread Substitute; 3⅓ servings Vegetables; ⅓ cup Limited Vegetable; 1½ servings Fat; 1½ servings Fruit; 1¾ servings Milk (2 teaspoons yogurt, 8 teaspoons skim milk, ¼ cup evaporated skimmed milk, ½ cup yogurt or ¾ cup buttermilk); 2¾ servings Extras (9 tablespoons stock, 2 teaspoons flour)

October

1. *Ciao on Columbus Day for Four*
   4 ounces Fish; 1 serving Bread Substitute; 3½ servings Vegetables; 3 tablespoons Limited Vegetable; 1½ servings Fat; 1 serving Fruit; ½

serving Milk (3 tablespoons evaporated skimmed milk, 2 tablespoons skim milk); ¾ serving Extras (¾ teaspoon flour)

2. *Rijsttafel—an Indonesian Buffet for Eight*
   2 ounces Poultry; 2 ounces Fish; 1 serving Bread Substitute; 8⅛ servings Vegetables; ¼ cup plus 1 tablespoon Limited Vegetable; 1¼ servings Fat; 1¼ servings Fruit; ⅛ serving Milk (2 tablespoons skim milk); 2 servings Extras (¾ cup plus 1½ tablespoons bouillon, ⅞ teaspoon flour)

3. *Fall Foliage Feast for Twelve*
   4 ounces Poultry; 1 serving Bread Substitute; 3½ servings Vegetables; ¼ cup Limited Vegetable; 1½ servings Fat; 1¼ servings Fruit; 1 serving Milk (6 tablespoons skim milk, 4 teaspoons nonfat dry milk, 3 tablespoons evaporated skimmed milk); 1 serving Bonus (¾ cup tomato juice, ¼ cup clam juice); 2 servings Extras (1 teaspoon flour, 2 teaspoons ketchup); ⅔ calorie Specialty Foods (½ cup soda)

4. *Bagels and Lox Breakfast for Eight*
   ⅙ cup Soft Cheese; 1 ounce Fish; 2 servings Bread; ¾ serving Vegetables; ½ cup Limited Vegetable; 1 serving Fruit; ¼ serving Extras (⅛ envelope gelatin); 2 calories Specialty Foods (1 teaspoon preserves)

5. *Family Wedding Party for Eight*
   4 ounces Fish; 3½ servings Vegetables; ½ cup Limited Vegetable; 1¼ servings Fat; 1¼ servings Fruit; ½ serving Milk (2 tablespoons evaporated skimmed milk, 2 tablespoons yogurt); ¼ serving Bonus (¼ cup tomato juice); 2 servings Extras (⅜ envelope gelatin, 6 tablespoons stock, ¾ teaspoon flour); ¼ calorie Specialty Foods (¼ cup soda)

6. *Halloween Supper for Twelve*
   4 ounces Poultry; 1 serving Bread Substitute; 3 servings Vegetables; 2 tablespoons plus 2 teaspoons Limited Vegetable; 2¼ servings Fat; ½ serving Fruit; 1 serving Milk (¼ cup yogurt, ½ cup skim milk); 1 serving Bonus (1 cup tomato juice); 3 servings Extras (⅙ packet broth mix, ⅙ envelope gelatin, 2½ teaspoons cornstarch); ¼ calorie Specialty Foods (8 teaspoons ginger ale)

November

1. *A Chinese Repast for Four*
   4 ounces Poultry; 1 serving Bread Substitute; 3 servings Vegetables; ½ cup Limited Vegetable; 1 serving Fat; 1¾ servings Fruit; ½ serving Milk (¼ cup yogurt); 2½ servings Extras (1⅛ cups stock, ½ packet broth mix, ½ teaspoon cornstarch)

2. *Special Sunday Breakfast for Four*
   1 Egg; 1 serving Bread; ½ serving Fat; 1 serving Fruit; ⅛ serving Milk (2 tablespoons skim milk)

3. *Football Watch—Easy and Economical Luncheon for Four*
1 ounce Hard Cheese; 2 ounces Poultry; 1 serving Bread; 8 servings Vegetables; ½ cup Limited Vegetable; 1½ servings Fat; 1¾ servings Fruit; ½ serving Milk (2 tablespoons evaporated skimmed milk, ¼ cup skim milk); 2 servings Extras (1 packet broth mix, 1 teaspoon flour); ⅙ calorie Specialty Foods (2 tablespoons soda)

4. *Traditional Thanksgiving Dinner for Six*
4 ounces Poultry; 1 serving Bread; 7½ servings Vegetables; ½ cup Limited Vegetable; 1½ servings Fat; 1½ servings Fruit; 1⅛ servings Milk (5 tablespoons evaporated skimmed milk, 8 teaspoons nonfat dry milk); ⅟₁₆ serving Bonus (1½ teaspoons tomato puree); 2⅛ servings Extras (1⅚ packets broth mix, 4½ teaspoons bouillon, ⅞ teaspoon gelatin)

5. *Thanksgiving Sans Turkey for Six*
4 ounces Poultry; 1 serving Bread Substitute; 4⅓ servings Vegetables; ½ cup Limited Vegetable; 3 servings Fat; 1½ servings Fruit; ⅙ serving Milk (8 teaspoons skim milk); ½ serving Bonus (½ cup mixed vegetable juice); 2 servings Extras (2 tablespoons bouillon, ⅔ teaspoon cornstarch, 1 teaspoon flour); ⅛ calorie Specialty Foods (4 teaspoons ginger ale)

6. *Thanks Again—Turkey Another Way for Six*
1 Egg; 2 ounces Poultry; 1 serving Bread; 1 serving Vegetables; ⅓ cup Limited Vegetable; 2½ servings Fat; 2 servings Fruit; ½ serving Milk (1 tablespoon yogurt, 3 tablespoons evaporated skimmed milk); 2¾ servings Extras (¾ cup broth, ¼ teaspoon sesame seeds, 1 teaspoon chili sauce, ½ teaspoon flour, ⅜ teaspoon gelatin)

December

1. *Purse-String Luncheon with Panache for Four*
⅓ cup Soft Cheese; 1 ounce Hard Cheese; 1 serving Bread Substitute; 4¾ servings Vegetables; 3 tablespoons Limited Vegetable; 1½ servings Fat; ¾ serving Fruit; ¾ serving Milk (¼ cup yogurt, 4 teaspoons nonfat dry milk); 1 serving Bonus (½ cup tomato sauce); ½ serving Extras (¼ envelope gelatin)

2. *Hannukah Luncheon for Four*
1 Egg; ⅓ cup Soft Cheese; 1 serving Bread; 1 serving Bread Substitute; 7¼ servings Vegetables; ⅓ cup Limited Vegetable; 3 servings Fat; 1 serving Fruit; ⅟₁₂ serving Milk (1 tablespoon buttermilk); 2¾ servings Extras (1 packet broth mix, ⅛ teaspoon caraway seeds, 1½ teaspoons matzo meal)

3. *Christmas Eve Buffet for Twelve*
4 ounces Meat Group; 1 serving Bread Substitute; 2⅓ servings Vegetables; ½ cup Limited Vegetable; 1¾ servings Fat; ¼ serving Fruit;

⅓ serving Milk (5⅓ teaspoons nonfat dry milk); ⅔ serving Extras (⅓ packet broth mix, ⅓ envelope gelatin)

4. *Christmas Day Breakfast for Eight*
1 Egg; 1 serving Bread Substitute; ½ serving Vegetables; 2 teaspoons Limited Vegetable; 1½ servings Fat; 1 serving Fruit; ¼ serving Milk (2 tablespoons evaporated skimmed milk); 1 calorie Specialty Foods (¾ cup soda)

5. *Christmas Dinner for Six*
4 ounces Meat Group; 1 serving Bread Substitute; 6 servings Vegetables; ½ cup Limited Vegetable; 3 servings Fat; 1 serving Fruit; ⅔ serving Milk (8 teaspoons yogurt, 5⅓ teaspoons nonfat dry milk); 1 serving Bonus (¾ cup tomato juice, 1½ teaspoons tomato puree); 1½ servings Extras (1⅙ packets broth mix, ⅙ envelope gelatin)

6. *Christmas at Home for Six*
1 Egg; 1 ounce Hard Cheese; 1 serving Bread; 1 serving Bread Substitute; 4⅛ servings Vegetables; ½ serving Fat; 1¾ servings Fruit; 1⅙ servings Milk (⅓ cup plus 4 teaspoons evaporated skimmed milk, 8 teaspoons yogurt); 2½ servings Extras (1⅓ teaspoons flour, ⅔ packet broth mix, ½ teaspoon cornstarch); 1½ calories Specialty Foods (1⅙ cups soda)

7. *Bon Voyage Dinner for Six*
4 ounces Poultry; 1 serving Bread; 1 serving Bread Substitute; 6⅔ servings Vegetables; ⅓ cup Limited Vegetable; 2½ servings Fat; 1 serving Fruit; ⅓ serving Milk (4 teaspoons evaporated skimmed milk, 2⅔ teaspoons nonfat dry milk); 1 serving Extras (1 packet broth mix); ⅓ calorie Specialty Foods (¼ cup soda)

Weight Watchers Metric Conversion Table

WEIGHT

To Change	To	Multiply by
Ounces	Grams	30.0
Pounds	Kilograms	.48

VOLUME

To Change	To	Multiply by
Teaspoons	Milliliters	5.0
Tablespoons	Milliliters	15.0
Cups	Milliliters	250.0
Cups	Liters	.25
Pints	Liters	.5
Quarts	Liters	1.0
Gallons	Liters	4.0

LENGTH

To Change	To	Multiply by
Inches	Millimeters	25.0
Inches	Centimeters	2.5
Feet	Centimeters	30.0
Yards	Meters	0.9

TEMPERATURE

To change degrees Fahrenheit to degrees Celsius subtract 32° and multiply by $5/9$.

Oven Temperatures

Degrees Fahrenheit =	Degrees Celsius		Degrees Fahrenheit =	Degrees Celsius
250	120		400	200
275	140		425	220
300	150		450	230
325	160		475	250
350	180		500	260
375	190		525	270

METRIC SYMBOLS

Symbol	=	Metric Unit		Symbol	=	Metric Unit
g		gram		°C		degrees Celsius
kg		kilogram		mm		millimeter
ml		milliliter		cm		centimeter
l		liter		m		meter

Index

[371]

[372]